Pore Folks, Potlucks, and Parables
Remembering Life in the Upper Cumberland

Smith County Court House – Carthage, Tennessee

Memories and Musings of Life in Middle Tennessee
By: Robert Rogers Chaffin

Published by Westview, Nashville, Tennessee

- Robert Rogers Chaffin -

PUBLISHED BY WESTVIEW, INC.
P.O. Box 210183
Nashville, Tennessee 37221
www.publishedbywestview.com

ISBN 978-1-935271-56-7

First edition, May 2010

Printed in the United States of America on acid free paper.

This book is dedicated to The Brown Eyed Girl
And the other women in my life
all of whom have loved me beyond what I deserved,
taught me beyond my capability,
and corrected me when the need was apparent.

My sincere thanks to Cousin Barney Smith, Sister Marie Tinsley, and friend John Waggoner Jr. who made significant and unique contributions to this book.

Pore Folks, Potlucks, and Parables

The Upper Cumberland
History and Geography

The best I am able to tell, the term "Upper Cumberland" was born in steamboat times when the area from the mouth of the Cumberland at the Ohio River, to Carthage was considered the Lower Cumberland, and the Area from Carthage to Burnside, Ky. was considered the Upper Cumberland. Most steamboats and their pilots were not licensed to operate the length of the Cumberland, that is all the way to Burnside, beyond which the river was no longer navigable, but cargos were unloaded from steamboat packets at Carthage, the reloaded onto Upper Cumberland packets which plied the river stopping at places like Grandville and Anderson's Landing in Jackson County, Butler's Landing in Clay County, and up the river through Overton County to Burnside. The term became expanded to include those rivers navigable from the Cumberland such as the Caney Fork and the Obey and thus counties like Dekalb and White were included along with Counties like Putnam which were sandwiched between.

It is generally hill country from Carthage east, although it includes many rich river and creek bottom lands also. From Carthage eastward the roads rise quickly, ascending from the low land of the Central Basin of Middle Tennessee, to the Highland Rim which can be easily seen as one goes up Highway 70 N from Elmwood to Chestnut Mound, once an important stage stop on the old Walton Road. Or can be easily witnessed as one ascends form the basin floor at Buffalo Valley to the edge of the rim at Silver Point, TN where highway 56 heads south toward Smithville. Although the local newscasters and TV weathermen tend to refer to the area around Cookeville as "The Plateau," that is strictly speaking, incorrect, since there is a second ascension from Cookeville up the side of the Cumberland Plateau, passing through Monterey and leveling out just west of Crossville which in fact puts one on top of the Cumberland Plateau.

The area along the river became pretty heavily settled early in the white settler history of the region since it was serviced by both the Avery Trace and Walton Road, which brought settlers over the mountains in the decade just prior to the turn of the nineteenth century, and the river itself which made the area accessible by flatboat from the region of the upper Ohio as well as Up the Mississippi from New Orleans. A sub-culture developed in the area, mostly influenced by the predominantly Scotch-Irish settlers, but rather different from the more isolated regions of Appalachia, since interchange with others from outside the region was more frequent and therefore seems to have had more impact on the area.

The Cumberland was the cradle of settlement in the area and a rich, but primarily undocumented history and culture, developed which was distinctly different from the highlander mountain culture to the east toward the Smoky Mountains and the plantation culture to the west toward Nashville. The Upper Cumberland is its own land and its people and stories are unique.

If you would seek a more scholarly view of the area I would encourage you to start with Seedtime on the Cumberland, and Flowering of the Cumberland, each of which are works by Harriette Arnow, or Don't Go Up Kettle Creek for a view of Steamboat times in the Upper Cumberland.

My intent is to give one a feel for the region in the stories and happenings that come to my mind when I hear WHUB in Cookeville intone, "the hub city of the Upper Cumberland."

⊶⇒ **Prologue** ⇐⊶

This Evolving World We Live In-----

Once upon a time, in a land far, far away, things were very different than they are in this land in which you and I live, even if perchance your address has remained static. No one I knew could even pronounce Vietnam, nor did they know or care where it was, or who was in charge of it. Harry, Ike, and Jack were our presidents in these times and, unlike the land we now live in, we all wanted to believe that they were true, capable and cared about each of us.

We watched June Clever on TV and did not even question why she wore pearls around her neck, high heels on her feet, and an apron around her waist when Ward came home for dinner – we wanted to believe that world and wanted to be part of it. We watched Uncle Milty perform on the Texaco Hour, dressed in drag every week and did not question his *sexual orientation*; in fact we would have likely not known what that meant. Watching Red Skelton turn his hat upside down and be a little boy, or get dragged under the curtain every Sunday night never ceased to be funny. Some moms worked outside the home but most stayed home and took care of the kids.

We took our cars to *filling stations* with big porches for us to drive under and the man who ran it came out in a uniform and filled the tank, checked the oil and water, put air in the tires, and tore off some green stamps which you mother could trade for toasters, and electric skillets. Lots of mothers could not drive and no self respecting man would ride in a car

1

with a woman driving – it was un-manly. A good sized house was 2000 square feet and often less, and a farm could be bought for 7 thousand dollars.

Rock and Roll was just hitting the radio, but Your Hit Parade was what everyone was watching on TV. No one thought Rock and Roll was here to stay, except the teenagers – Frank, Perry, Rosemary, and Dean were where it was at on the music scene, and the other was just a passing fad.

Words were used differently and a *hoe* was what you used to chop the garden, if you were *gay* you were only lively and happy, no one thought regular people would ever become *dope eaters*. *Alternate lifestyles, live-ins, and Johnny has Two Mommies* were meaningless phrases and most of us were without a clue concerning those things and wished to stay that way. People could be *pro-choice* and *pro-life* both then, they were not mutually exclusive term.

When I was growing up in Carthage we went to *Prayer Meeting* on Wednesday night. Bread came in two distinct groups, that which you made at home which included Corn *Pone* and *Hoe Cakes* or Biscuits and yeast rolls or you could eat *Loaf bread* from the store. We had *Arsh* (Irish)_ potatoes and sweet potatoes with *dried beans* – never white beans or great northerns. Adie made *teacakes* (cookies) every Saturday and we kept the milk cold in the *frigidare*. When we went to the store we had thing put in a *poke*, never a bag like now or a sack like up north. Old men wore shoes through the week, but *slippers* on Sunday. Everyone went to the grocery store to get food, and no one went to a *Supermarket*. On Halloween we had a *punkin* and pumpkin seemed pretentious. We got *dog tired* and my grandmother said you were *bilious* when your stomach hurt. The few cars that had turn signals we said to have *blinkers* and I suspect my grandchildren will never know what *fender skirts* were. Our fathers took a *turn of corn* to mill and our grandmothers kept flour in the *flour barrel*. When we were sick we went to the drug store and bought *patent medicine*.

In those days no one had ever heard of NASA, and the moon just might still be made of green cheese. Cars and homes didn't have air conditioning and businesses that did advertized "*Come inside it's Cool*" Pantyhose was not know as a single word, and women going into public barelegged was as unthinkable as a preacher wearing a Speedo in the pulpit. Church houses in the country did not have pews, they had benches, and a Sanctuary was a place birds were kept. No one had ministers, or pastors, but everyone had *preachers* and that was their main job description. Businesses had calculators and comptometers and Dell was a valley, Gateway was something you walked through, and Apple was something you ate. People dressed up to go to church and wore ties to go shopping downtown. Women wore white gloves on their hands and girdles on the rest of them.

Everyone read the comic strip every day, and almost everyone could tell you what Mutt and Jeff, Beetle Bailey, Snuffy Smith, and Dick Tracy were doing the day before. Sitting in the shade was a favorite pastime and no one ate Cantaloupe but everyone had *Mush Mellon*. You went down to the *cellar* to bring up a can of green beans you mother had canned last summer and out to the smokehouse to cut off a slice of *middlin* for breakfast. No one had bathrooms but everyone had a *toilet* and people burned their trash in the *burn barrel* in back of the house or threw it on the trash pile at the end of some country road.

3

Cokes were 6 cents and came out of a red and white box with water and ice inside and giant Baby Ruth Bars were a dime. If you picked up bottles from *Co colas*, you could get a penny for them from the store. Milk came in glass bottles, and freezers on the *ice box* were roughly the size of two shoe boxes, which was ok because not many frozen items were available at the store. People we knew didn't eat in restaurants except when there was no other choice and they were called Cafes – unless of course it was an automat.

My mama and daddy were masters at finding lessons in everything in life and helping you understand why some things were a bad idea without ever forbidding you to take part in them, and understanding why others were wholesome and good, without ordering you to take them up. They taught in parables, I think it was not expressly to be like Jesus, I think it just happened. Perhaps that is why I have chosen this format for the book; it is Christ-like by virtue of personal leaning rather than by intention.

Yep, lots of things have changed, since that land long ago and far away, but a few things remain the same. God still loves us and expects us to show our love for Him by the way we treat other people. We still have but one life to live, and only one shot at getting it right and living to the praise of his glory. (Eph. 1) While the world around evolves, almost daily, He remains a constant rock in a raging sea. I sincerely hope you enjoy these parables from daily life.

Bob

⤖ Chapter I ⤕
Sunday-Go-to-Meeting Memories

Daddy, Donnieta, me on the arm of the chair, and Mama

1. Is the only Constant Change?

When I can first remember, my family went to church in a car. It was 1947, the war had ended and, the reemergence of new cars out of Detroit, made used cars relatively cheap. One of my cousins, James Gentry, remembers that his family came in a wagon. In fact, he and I were walking around the old church grounds (the old hip roof building that once was Morrison's Creek Church of Christ, is now gone, replaced by a nice little brick building.); anyway, we were walking around the grounds, when he pointed to a tree near the once graveled road. There, he said, is where my daddy always tied the mules when we got to church. He had picked a spot that kept them in the shade for the duration of the service and allowed them to pick a little grass while the preacher "waxed elephants," as the saying went. You know;

> Now I sit me down to sleep.
> The preacher's boring the subjects deep,
> If he should quit before I wake,
> Please give me a little shake!

The building was both church and school and the trappings of a school room were evident in the one room building. Blackboards, and banners showing both cursive (we called it writing) and printing (we called it printing) were on the walls together with the obligatory picture of George Washington, "Father of Our Country" with his wooden false teeth obviously killing him.

My great granddaddy, "Little Billy Gentry" was the head man since his daddy had given the land that the church sat upon, and he did most of the work around the building. Now no one had appointed him an elder, but he surly was the chief shepherd, and shepherds are born not appointed.

The Lord's Supper was spread on a table, where the fancy container holding the grape juice was flanked by the two ornate goblets into which it would be poured, and the bread had been home baked (without yeast, of course.)

There would be no sermon, since no young "preacher boy" from David Lipscomb College was available more than two Sundays each month and even the meager sum they received was beyond the means of this country congregation. When my great uncle, Winters Gentry, started the first song there were not over three grown men inside the whole meeting house. The balance of the male population, including my daddy, were standing around in the church yard, smoking and talking crops and weather.

Little Billy Gentry (Pappy) celebrates his 90th birthday with an assorted collection of Great Grandchildren. I am the tall kid on the left in the back and Donnieta is just to the right of me. Mark, Cheryl, Phillip, Teresa, Evelyn, and Edward David (?) Gentry are the little ones in front.

If a person responded to the invitation and came forward desired to be baptized that day, they would be taken down to the creek and Pappy Gentry, or Uncle Winters, or more likely a visiting preacher would immerse them in the deeper pool scooped out of the creek bed gravel using a pond scoop and a team of mules. It was kept that way so the usually shallow creek would be deep enough for a full body immersion.

Our song selections tended to be the same from week to week with On Jordan's (pronounced Jer den's) Stormy Banks, Above the Bright Blue, Just As I Am, Standing On the Promises, Let the Lower Lights Be Burning, and other such old reliable standbys. There was generally a "main" prayer after the third song, in which the prayer leader invariably prayed for "missionaries in foreign fields everywhere," "a ready recollection" for the preacher, and the "sick and afflicted." *Thanks* was invariably given that we lived in a free country where we could meet together "without fear of molestation."

It was a rare occasion that we sang any new songs, but if we were to sing a new song that day, Uncle Winters and the critical core of good singers would sing it through a few times, just using the do re mi shape notes, and then add the words later. I suspect that anyone in the crowd would have been scandalized by a song leader using any songbook that did not contain *Sacred Harp* type shape notes.

At the end of the assembly, it might be announced that so and so from such and such community was there today and he was hoping to buy a young mule if anyone had one to sell. Everyone would dutifully look around the crowd to try and spot a likely seller. Then, the song leader might announce that

Gospel Meetings were being held at Forks of the Creek, and Center Grover Congregation and let the group know that Brother J. B. Gaither and Brother Reader Oldham would be doing the speaking. With that, the song leader would look around the room, and spot some male member whom he would ask to lead the closing prayer. Generally everyone knew who led public prayer and who did not, so confusion was avoided, but occasionally a visiting preacher or song leader would call on some male who did not consider leading public prayer within his ability, and the called upon would in turn call upon someone else.

It was a far different assembly worship experience than that which most of us took part in this week – and was perhaps no less appropriate for the day and time.

When we set our minds on never allowing things to change – not matters of faith and doctrine, but matters of the mechanics of "doing church," the tone and tenor of the assembly – we delude ourselves. Change will come, and it will be too fast for some and too slow for others, so we simply need to manage change within the bounds of the New Testament examples, and the Apostle Paul's charge of assemblies which are decent and orderly.

By the way, not all things that I don't personally like are indecent and disorderly.

2. A Trip to Cookeville

When I was a boy, there were few things my family did on Sunday afternoons other than sit in the shade of the trees which fronted our house, visit with relatives, or go for a ride.

Of course, for a 12 year old boy, there were plenty of things needing to be taken care of down at the creek, out on my bike, or on the top of Battery Hill.

I remember especially one very hot Sunday afternoon when everyone was sitting around in the shade fanning when my dad said, "Well, its pretty lazy around here, anyone want to ride up to Cookeville and back?"

Now going to Cookeville from Carthage then, was much different than in 1956. Now one can simply hop on interstate 40 and, zoom, you are there. In those days you had to wind your way up old highway 70N, past Elmwood, up Chestnut Mound hill, and out the crooked road that followed the old stagecoach route along the backbone of the ridges from Chestnut Mound to Cookeville. It was the same route that the old Walton Road had taken into the wilderness and the route had scarcely been improved upon in 100 years.

I said, "OK", even though what I really wanted to do was hang out with a couple of the other neighborhood boys down at the creek. I didn't say so though, because my mother was convinced that Polio probably came as a result of hanging around that creek and there had been several new cases lately. My mother, always compliant, simply got up, took off the apron she was still wearing from dinner (never lunch in Carthage) and Aunt Ada, as always, simply said, "Well, I'm just with the bunch."

All five of us loaded into the old 54 green and white Buick and away we went. My sister and I always wanted to make sure that of all things we did not stop at some relative's house, as we so often did, and spend an hour with the grown-ups droning on endlessly about weather, relatives, and old times; so we immediately said, "Let's don't stop at anybody's house, Ok?"

It was sweltering hot, the old Buick was, of course, not air-conditioned, and with five people in the car, it was more than a little uncomfortable. The trip seemed endless. A logging truck pulling up Chestnut Mound hill slowed us to a crawl, then cars were lined up for miles following a slow moving farm truck, which it seemed was also headed for Cookeville. Passing was hardly and option on the curvy road which had nearly unbroken double yellow lines.

Four hours later, we finally had made the circle and got home – hot, clothes sticking to our bodies, short tempered, red faced, and weary. As we were getting out of the car Daddy said, "Well, when I offered to go, I was hoping that no one would want to go – but all of you did, so I went on."

Mama gave him that look – you know the one – and said, "Well I was sure happy resting in the shade, but you mentioned going and I didn't want to be the one to say, no."

Donnieta announced that she had had homework to do, but just went because she didn't want to be "fussed on." Aunt Ada said, "I was just with the bunch." I wisely kept my own council concerning the creek.

I did learn something from that afternoon, however. I learned that people often take a trip they do not really want to take because they are afraid of upsetting someone else. They have not learned, as the Apostle Paul said to, "speak the truth in love." Over the years I have seen many people "on a trip to Cookeville" in a proverbial sense as they were led along into things and into places they did not want to go. It is important that somehow we learn as a community to be able to express our desire not to take a particular "trip" without being unpleasant about it. To learn to disagree, without being disagreeable is a rare gift indeed.

3. <u>Crossing the Road at Midnight</u>

Sometime after Daddy bought the Studebaker Champion, my Great Granddaddy Maberry died. His name was Monroe Maberry, named after President Monroe, I guess. There were a lot of Monroe namesakes in those days, but it would be a real shock if a twenty something mom showed off her new baby body and said, "This is Monroe, everybody." Just not a name you hear a lot today. Today they tend to be named Poem, or Apple, or Plumb; thankfully I have not run into one named after Cousin It.

Pappy Maberry was what some people called "a religious fanatic" in that he loved to read and argue the bible. He had no use for discussing or listening, just arguing the thing. He had four sons, Earnest, Claude, Charlie, and Edgar, my Pa Maberry. There were also several girls in the family, although for the most part the only one I even marginally knew was Aunt Annie Hawkins. The other girls didn't visit much and one of the girls had gone to California years before and never returned in my lifetime, that I am aware. Despite being a strict member of the Church of Christ, most of Pappy Maberry's children did not remain faithful to the way, although one or two of them, as in Pa Maberry's case were brought back to faith through the good and faithful efforts of a Christian wife. My mother lived with them during her teen age years and thus was able to go to high school, but would often tell of trying to study by the only coal oil lamp Pappy would have burning, he reading the bible and her studying. According to her, she could hardly get any school work done for him interrupting to have her listen to long passages from the bible. When she would object, he would remind her that "Thy word is a lamp unto my feet" and go on reading, much to her frustration.

Although I was as afraid of Pappy Maberry as I would have been a haint in the night, Mammy Maberry made up for it. She had been an Anderson before they married and was a woman of good humor, boundless energy, and cooking skills that were second to no one. She could make a blackberry cobbler that would melt in you mouth.

Anyway, when Pappy Maberry (Monroe) died they lived out on Burgess Falls Road in the eighth district of Putnam County. We went to the house to "set up all night with the body" as folks did in those days. Pappy Maberry had spent most of his life there on Burgess Falls Road, and no one thought that there was any reason to change his location at this late date. As the night wore on and the crowd grew thinner, several of the cousins were put to bed crossways in one of the other rooms, but Donnieta really didn't want us to be the seventh or eighth cousins in that bed, so she made a plea for her and I to sleep in the car, which was sitting in Pappy's front yard. The house sat a long way back from Burgess Falls Road and it did not seem like there was any danger, so Mama relented and we crawled into the Studebaker, me in the front and her in the back since she was still taller than I in those, long since past days. Now she is shorter than I, but still older..

When we woke up the next morning, the emergency brake had failed and the Studebaker had rolled backward, down through the yard, across the road, and into the yard of a little house across the road. Neither Donnieta nor I ever woke up through the ride and I suppose there was not as much danger in the whole affair as you might think, since the traffic on Burgess Falls Road after 11:00 p.m. in the early fifties was pretty minimal.

Nevertheless, we were still sleeping when Daddy came out early, just at dawn, to check on us and found we, like Elvis, had left the area. He was more than a little excited and soon after traded the Studebaker for a big Grey 1952 Buick. I tell you, there was enough metal in that Buick to make a dozen of the little pieces of fluff they call a car today.

It was only slightly lighter than a Sherman Tank and had a DynaFlow Transmission, a straight eight engine, two tone paint (grey and grey?), and a bumper that would put a one ton truck brush guard to shame. When you got on the highway with that car, you could rock and roll. In fact the suspension was of the marshmallow variety and it smoothed out every bump in the road. Given the roads in the fifties, "the feel of the road" was not a highly sought after commodity. When we loaded into that baby there was plenty of room for all five of us to stretch out. Buick called them Roadmasters, but the rest of the world called them Road Monsters. Besides all of the other clever things, it had a radio "aerial" (commonly pronounced earl) that stuck right out of the top of the car and could be rotated down using a ball on the inside just above the windshield.. We had arrived, were in the lap of luxury – never mind the fact the car was probably 3 or 4 years old when we acquired it. It was a Buick and it had three holes in the

side to prove it – a styling Q that remains to this day. Besides, the parking brake worked and would not let your children end up in some other part of the county when you turned your head.

When I think back on these things, I wonder what made Pappy Maberry so "bullheaded" about religion. Was it that because he believed that possessing the knowledge of God's Love, excused him from practicing it, or was it simply that he felt he was right doctrinally, and therefore needed to speak out? There is a saying that we hear today that goes, "People don't care what you know, until they know that you care." It is of course, not mine to judge his motives, but I hope I can internalize a lesson from Pappy Maberry – and not try to substitute knowledge of the word for implementation of its principals.

4. <u>Remembering a Community of Faith</u>

Yesterday, while rummaging around some long stowed away files I wanted to use in a project I am doing for General Motors, I came across a Carthage Church of Christ Directory. In it were listed the charter members of that church so dear to my heart. May McClard, Sam Lee Kirby, Mrs. J. C. "Ma Jinks" Jenkins, Miss Clester Huffines, Mrs. Beulah (Aunt Boo) Matthews, and Bob Lee Dudney, were a few of the names that jumped off the page, among the 25 or so that signed a card wishing to be charter members of that congregation being newly organized under the watchful eye of the elders of the Chapel Avenue Church in Nashville.

That first meeting of the Carthage church was on the afternoon of March 31, 1946 in a "dwelling house," as we always called it, I suppose to differentiate from a building built as a "Church or Meeting House." The property had been purchased from one John Meador, and it is the location where the present church now stands at 707 North Main Street. Reports are that 150 or so people had shown up for the first assembly, although most may have been from Nashville in a show of support.

Chapel Avenue Church assisted in the purchase of the property, and engaged Brother Frank D. Young, who along with his good wife Gracie, and their small son Paul, (Janet would be born some time later) were to be an integral part of our lives for the next nine or ten years.

We came to Carthage in the winter of 1948, and the church was in regular meeting each Sunday at that same dwelling house. Most of the charter members were still in attendance when we arrived, and had been joined by a number of others. With the passing of Sam L. Kirby, the last of the charter members appears to have gone to their reward. If I am wrong, please let me know.

Within a few months of our arrival, the church had grown to a size that could no longer be accommodated by the old house, which also served as the home of Brother Young and his family. The Robert Wright extended family, and the Fred Evans Family, had also arrived in Carthage and were in regular attendance when I can first remember. Of the group that was there when we arrived, I believe that only Hale Wright, and Patty Evans Piper remain in regular attendance. Again, if there are others, I apologize and invite you to correct my thinking by a giving me a call.

With the economic aid of a number of area churches and many individuals, a new church building was started and completed sometime prior to the fall of 1950. Brother Vollie P. Moss, a charter member and also an accomplished builder, oversaw the work and much "in kind" contribution went toward the erection of the building in the form of back-breaking labor by the members. While the meeting house and apartment for the Young family was in progress, we assembled in the old Princess Theatre, which sat just to the north of Ray's Market, and was long ago destroyed by fire. I can vividly remember hoping that by some miracle of mistake, Bambi, might appear on the screen instead of Brother Young to deliver his sermon – it never happened.

Prior to 1946, the church of Christ had met in the church building across the street from the theatre. The old church had become a Christian Church as a result of the division which occurred between the Churches of Christ and the Christian Churches that primarily centered around the use of instrumental music in worship. It was renamed a Christian Church in about 1946 and later became a church of Christ again when the Christian Church folded, apparently "due to lack of interest." Most of the Churches who were going to introduce instrumental music had done so much earlier than

1946 and there had been a great push by a certain faction of the membership in Carthage to follow this trend; but Mr. Bill Reed's mother, a patron influence on the church, had announced that this congregation would accept instrumental music "over her dead body."

As the story goes, an instrument was brought in so quickly following her death that it was nearly literally "over her dead body."

Christian Church – Carthage Tennessee

A few years ago, this lovely and storied old church was destroyed by a devastating fire which tragically took the life of Mr. Edward Stallings, the warm, serving, and beloved fire chief of the town. Today the now vacant space remains a park in his honor.

The new building was finished and we moved into the little red brick building sometime around 1950, about the time the Chaffin family was moving into our new home in Carthage. From that day forward, our lives revolved around the people and events of the little red brick building. It was the center of our universe, and those people and that sharing of like precious faith, was the measure by which we defined ourselves.

Tom Holland, a noted church of Christ preacher, once authored a book called, "All I ever needed to know, I learned on the farm." As I shared my growing up-years with Hale Wright, Bill Ross, Larry Bussell, Jimmy Young, Larry Dudney, and Richard Wright, it seems that all I ever "needed" to know, I learned in that red brick building. Faye Wright, Patty Evans, and Elaine Ross, were like older sisters and Jane Bradley, Miss Clester Huffines, and Mrs Beulah Mathews, with her weekly tribute to the color red, were teachers that shaped my life in enormous ways. Bryant Lee Kittrell, Bob Lee Dudney, Elmer Massa, Horace Wright, and others were mentors that taught by word and example what it meant to be a Christian man.

Frank D. Young, will ever be in my mind, leaning over the pulpit and delivering a sermon in that rapid fire style common to Freed Hardeman graduates, while his son Paul and I sat on the front seat, trying not to go to sleep. Mrs. Gracie Young will long be remembered for the rides to Brush Creek where she turned the car into a roller coaster and made your stomach lighter than air, and all of these thoughts bring a warm glow to my memory.

It was a good community of believers to grow up in, and I pray that each of my grandchildren can experience the strength that comes from the love and support of such and extend church family.

I am at a lost to understand why any parent would not want to provide that love, support, and experience for their children.

> Time is filled with swift Transitions
> Naught of earth unmoved can stand
> Build you hopes on things eternal
> Hold to God's unchanging hand.

I'm not sure what the moral of this story is, but the little church out on Main Street North has been a touchstone for me as it moved from white dwelling house, to red brick building, to white brick and stone. Like me, it grew and expanded – I'm talking about my mind, of course – and it hardly looks at all like the place we started, but in my heart, the location is precious and will always remain so.

I am indebted to Miss Inez Stallings for a 1946 Gospel Advocate article she graciously gave me, giving account of these events, and to Daddy and Lovell Wilson Chaffin, who had kept the directory and the ledger book denoting the charter members and the events of the building of the Carthage Church of Christ.

5. <u>Crossing The Cumberland on the Jere Mitchell</u>

When there was little else to do, and gas was 25 cents per gallon, our family, like many of yours, went for rides when we had leisure time. In fact, Jan and I still like to get in the car and just cruise around to places we don't often get to visit. Much of the time, there would be family somewhere on the route and we would stop while Mama and Daddy visited for what seemed like an interminable length of time. It was probably much shorter than it seemed to Donnieta and me, but our limited attention spans created their own perceptions. Occasionally however, there was not a destination, it was just a ride.

I liked those best of all, because we went to places like Bug Tussle, Wartrace, Hardscrabble, Step Rock Hill, or the Bloody Eighth District; we went around Devil's Elbow, passed through Difficult and Defeated and rolled on to Nameless and just cruised around in general.

Occasionally we would ride down to Rome, cross the Dr. James Fisher Bridge, and take the Jere Mitchell across the Cumberland to Beasley's Bend. Then we would work our way out to Dixon Springs, and stop for a Co-cola at Taylor's Store in downtown Dixon Springs.

Crossing the ferry was pretty exciting and the Jere Mitchell was big and modern by the standards of the day.

Even after Jan and I married, there were several places on the route to Detroit where we had to cross a ferry, if we "went through the mountains." By going through the mountains, I mean going north from Cookeville to Livingston, through Byrdstown, into Albany, Kentucky then north through Somerset and on to Renfro Valley (the little town that launched the careers of Red Foley and Homer and Old Jethro). The mountain route took you down into the river gulch east of the Dale Hollow Dam, across the Cumberland, and up a switchback road chiseled into the hillside. Depending on the road one followed, there might be one or two ferry crossings. In one the boat was shackled to a cable that stretched across the river and a rigging of cables and pulleys used the river current to provide power coming and going. At the other, the ferry barge was shunted across the river by an open johnboat with an outboard, affixed to the barge platform. There was no cable so a degree of skill was required by the ferryman. Obviously the cable arrangement would only work on rivers small enough that no traffic up and down the river would be hindered by the cables.

The Jere Mitchell, the last of the Rome ferryboats, was a sure enough ferryboat however, and still sits forlornly drawn up on the bank beneath the Fisher Bridge just east of Rome. It can be easily seen by pulling down into the area provided by the Corp of Engineers for launching pleasure boats at Round Lick Creek at the head of Old Hickory Lake. There is talk of restoration and of reactivating the boat, which would probably be a real treat and an oddity that would attract attention today, but a captain with a river pilot's license is required for operation, is my understanding, and finding one that wishes to spend his time at the Rome Ferry is quite difficult.

The Rome Ferry was at first a much cruder affair, as can be seen by the picture below, but this more elaborate boat was named after Jere Mitchell, a Smith County native killed in World War II, and was one of the last two ferries remaining in operation on the Cumberland. It was privately owned by Comer Haley of Beasley's Bend, who provided the ferry and its landings to the county in the late 1920's for one dollar, and was to operate until a bridge was built at this location, according to an agreement with county officials. The old ferry was placed on the National Register of Historic Sites in 1987, and is at River Mile 292.4. I don't know when it was last in operation so if you do please let me know.

Our excursion was completed when we wound our way back up highway 25, past Cox Davis School, past the old Tanglewood Road (a favorite parking spot for teenagers – or so I heard tell) and past the Bloody Bucket. (The Bloody Bucket was what was locally referred to as a *knife and gun club* – they checked you at the door and if you didn't have one or the other, they gave one to you.) Passing back through Beulah Land, we made a left at Jefferson Avenue, and we were home again. It was now time to quickly eat Sunday dinner leftovers, which had been left on the table with a cloth spread over them, and then back to church.

Our Sunday rides were a microcosm of our lives themselves, starting out down a road of choice, then winding our way through both expected and unexpected circumstances, familiar and unfamiliar territory, sometimes meeting or making friends along the way, occasionally encountering a detour, and often making difficult, if not outright dangerous, crossings.

Eventually, we would arrive back at home, ready to meet again with God's people. Enjoy the journey, endure the crossings with care, enlist the help of others when the detours come, and always keep the final destination in mind.

6. <u>**Sometimes even an Old Crank can be Fun**</u>

No one makes homemade ice cream any more – at least not in the old fashioned way. I suppose the reason is that it is quite a chore and with all of the labor saving devices each of us has these days, we have no time for anything that is not instant. The more time we save the less we seem to have – how does that work?

We had one of those old hand crank, wooden bucket, cork in the hole, ice cream freezers that was common back in the 1950s, and it was a real treat when we made ice cream. As long as my grandparents lived on the farm, we made it with whole raw milk, with lots of rich Guernsey cream still floating on the top. The ice came from the ice house behind Hughes Motors, the old white building between D.T. McCall and the Post Office. It was an ammonia style ice house and we would buy 25 pounds of ice and chip it off with an ice pick. I don't suppose you could buy a 25lb block of ice today and if you did no one would have an ice pick with which to chip it up.

When Mama had made the ice cream mixture (each lady had her own recipe) and dropped in those tablets – I think she called them junket tablets – she would pour the liquid into the center container being careful not to spill an ounce of the precious liquid. Daddy would then begin to pack a layer of ice, and a layer of rock salt, a layer of ice, and a layer of rock salt, until the whole mixture rose to just about three inches below the top of the cylinder – had to leave room for expansion of the frozen mixture.

Turning the crank was a job just made for little boys, and away we would go, seeing how fast we could turn the thing until our daddies would say – "slow down, you don't need to go fast, just steady does it."

Pour in a cup of water to start the melting process now and then, be sure the cork is out of the hole in the side of the bucket, so no salt water would get into the center ice cream container, and crank. Crank until your arm felt as if it were going to fall right off. Finally it would get too firm for me to crank any longer and then Daddy would take over, giving it those last few turns to bring the whole thing to perfection.

Mama would then enter the process again, taking the paddles out of the cylinder that was holding the nearly frozen mixture and sometimes letting little boys or girls lick the paddles when she had spooned most of the ice cream off and back into the cylinder. I am sure she left just a little for that very purpose.

The bucket would be packed to the top in ice, a quilt wrapped around the whole wooden bucket, the bucket set in Mama's aluminum dishpan, which I still use to gather tomatoes, and into the trunk of the car it went.

When we arrived at the church building, the Wrights, the Evans, the Dudneys, and other families were also unloading ice cream freezers. Some had used fresh peaches, some had broken peppermint candy sticks up with a hammer, some had used strawberries, and on and on the inventiveness went with each "church lady" trying to out-do the other.

When Sunday night worship had finally (emphasis on finally) finished we would all gather around back and the freezers would be unwrapped and opened. The preacher would say a few words about "dwelling together in unity," which I think was to make it acceptable for him to be first in line; and we would all enjoy the taste of the closest thing to manna from heaven any of us were likely to enjoy this side of the pearly gates.

Little boys were allowed to eat as much as they wanted, which was a lot, and no one told them they were going to be sick or get fat. In fact the adults reveled in watching the children enjoy the treats set before them. Those without freezers had brought cookies or brownies and it was a precious time of fun and friendship (which is called fellowship if you are at church). It was a jewel in the crown of spiritual family love.

As I stood this week at the head of a casket, holding the funeral of a friend who had died an untimely death, I wondered how anyone faced such tragedy without a church family. I also wondered why anyone would not long for the love and support that comes from the deep relationships a church family provides. God does not ask us to congregate for His benefit, as we sometimes suppose, but for ours. He knows our needs in a way that no one else can, and has provided for us in a unique fashion. It is beyond my comprehension why anyone would not take advantage of his goodness.

Ice cream suppers have, for the most part, passed into antiquity, but the friendship/fellowship, love, and general joy of being with others who genuinely treat you like family out of sheer love will never go out of style. God is all good, all the time.

7. <u>Coming to terms with Man's Mortality</u>

When my mother passed away, as my sister and I undertook the daunting job of sorting through her things, I came across an old Gospel Advocate dated March 28, 1957. In my mother's hand was a note that said, "Very important – Valuable – Bro. Parker's Picture inside." She did things like that to keep Daddy from having a "pitching fit" in which he pitched out valuable things. Upon contemplation, it seems to me that she particularly labeled things after she knew her life was going to be cut short by pancreatic cancer – now that is a thoughtful person!

The GA article had been written by the late Willard Collins, one time President of Lipscomb College and in it, he noted that Hollis Parker had passed from this life on February 21, 1957 and other facts that might lead the casual reader to believe Hollis Parker was a mundane guy – just another bubba on the block, but I remember Brother Hollis differently.

In the days I was growing up, death was a highly experienced part of life. No one that I knew would have thought about not taking children either to a funeral service or to visit the family of the deceased. Bodies of loved ones were often kept at home without benefit of special funeral home lighting or ambiance through the 1950s and funerals were much more bathed in stark reality than in this day and time. The whole experience was generally a throw-back to the Scotch Irish roots shared by the preponderance of the Upper Cumberland Area's inhabitants and contained elements of both the Irish Wake and Keening. By the time I was 12 or 13 years old, I had become quite acquainted with death – or so I thought.

It was about this time in my life that I was to come into contact with death in a whole new and lasting way. The church at Carthage had hired a new preacher in the person of Hollis D. Parker in 1955 and he was a delight to everyone in the congregation. His family was picture perfect. A beautiful, gracious, wife named La-Murle, and two beautiful young daughters, Lynn and Mimi. The girls were about 5 and 7 when the family moved to Carthage and I loved them dearly.

The Parker Girls – Mimi and Lynn, Note my bicycle parked with care on the lawn and the big metal lawn chairs and heavy porch rockers. The Nashville Banner is spread on the ground for evening reading.

We lived close to the church building and my mother was the picture of Christian hospitability. Our parents always made a special effort to be a comfort to whatever family was doing full time ministry in Carthage. We kept their big collie dog when they traveled, and Hollis' little brother John visited with us and played "army" with me in the fields and pastures.

La-Murle was not only beautiful, she was accomplished, outgoing, and generally a joy to be around and was the immediate role model for my sister, Faye Wright, Patty Evins, and all of the other young girls in the congregation.

Hollis began to teach the teenage class on Wednesday night and although I was not yet a teenager, the sixth, seventh and eight grades were included in the class. We had the beginnings of a "youth group," something none of us had ever even heard of prior to this. There were trips to Sulfur Dell to see ballgames, and weenie roasts at Sampson's Mineral Wells (the sulfur well). The bible classes were stimulating and interesting and it was as if a whole new world had opened up to all of us. He and I personally walked down through the semi-dark church basement every Sunday and Wednesday night to shut down the big furnace. It was our time.

When Hollis and La-Murle went away to the Freed Hardeman or David Lipscomb College Lectures, the girls (Mimi and Lynn) stayed with us and I felt as if they were my own little sisters. I adored the girls and life had become perfect in a whole new way.

Then tragedy struck, Hollis became ill and the local doctors were not able to make him better or even find out what his illness was. Finally, he was diagnosed with a terminal form of kidney failure. How could it be? This perfect family that God had graced us with was going to be taken from us, and there was nothing we could do but pray for God's peace on them and us. Finally it was over and I could hardly deal with the grief.

I felt so protective of the two girls and overcome with a feeling of the need to do something that I secretly wished that I was old enough to offer to marry the lovely and grieving La-Murle and just be good to the three of them for the rest of their days.

Finally, as it does, life moved on and our grief lessened and La-Murle gave me a few of Hollis' things when she was cleaning the closets preparing to move back to Jackson, Tennessee where she was to live with her mother, Mrs. Jarrett.

For many, many years those articles were precious memories of a bright light, a nova that had brilliantly and briefly burned in my life. I could never bring myself to wear or use any of the things I was given, but I kept them for many years, looked at them, and remembered the long walks through the dimly lighted basement to turn off the lights and shut down the furnace; our time – our brief moment together.

Today the girls are talented and accomplished and have long ago become women with children, and perhaps grandchildren of their own. La-Merle is now a friend of a friend, after many years she remarried, and through our common friends I have been able to catch up on her life, but I doubt that any one of them ever suspected the impact they had on my own life, that of my family, or on the community of believers in Carthage.

I puzzled over how God could take one so useful and dedicated to His service so soon in life, for he was only 28 years old. I have come to the conclusion that some things in life (actually many things) are beyond my understanding, and

He gets to be God, and I do not; that His vision and view of life is much bigger and grander than my own. I did however, learn that one must live carefully, for none of us knows how our life may influence others, no matter how fleeting the relationship.

Hollis' brother, John Parker, is a professor at Lipscomb University.

8. The Women in My Life

I have had many women in my life and as much as I am hesitant to talk about it, I need to come clean with the world. So here goes, this is the story of the many women in my life.

Our lives are blessed with many things and God touches us in unexpected and sometimes, at first, unperceived ways. Often, when we begin to look back we find that something will come into focus in hindsight that was less than clear at the time it occurred. With me, that is the case with the women that either fate or God has placed in my life; I choose to believe that it was God's providence. Whichever the case, I have been shaped and molded by a number of wonderful women who probably had more to do with me being who I am than even I would care to admit.

The first was, in the words of Abraham Lincoln, "my angel mother." She was without question the most selfless, and giving person I have ever know. A couple of years ago Terri Hatcher authored a book called *Burnt Toast* in which she extolled the virtues of the new woman who no longer accepted the leftover "burnt toast" for herself, while providing the best pieces to her family. It was a "taking care of number one" kind of book that seems to be popular in our culture since Dr. Wayne Dwyer penned *Pulling Your Own Strings* in the seventies. I noted that Amazon now has a number of copies of her book available for less than one dollar. I don't know Ms. Hatcher, and being an empathetic author, I hope everyone's books sell – especially mine – but it is evident that she did not know my mother, for she was a "burnt toast" kind of woman.

If there was a scarce amount of anything on the table, her "stomach wasn't feeling just right so I don't think I'll have any."

If there was only a couple of extra pieces of chicken left after everyone had taken one, she had, "been snacking while I was cooking and just spoiled my appetite."

Mama, Donnieta, and Me – about 1946
Gainesboro, Tennessee

Not that I was aware enough in the moment to realize her sacrifices, it is only in retrospect that the lens has cleared.

She was filled with energy of the kind that is almost irritating. When the 4th of July came and everyone else was celebrating, she was up to her elbows in canning green beans, or cooking and preparing a picnic lunch for everyone else. One of the great works of her life was always supporting my dad and making him look good. It was only after her death that it became apparent to my sister and me how much he depended upon her.

Next there was the other mom in my life – Great Aunt Ada Berry, or "Adie" to Donnieta and me. She was the very personification of "if you can't say anything good about someone, don't say anything at all." She was a widow who, as a young woman had married the widowed head of a large family. Mr. Berry, as she always called him, was much older than she and had "boys" almost her age. A couple of years ago in talking to one of the step grandchildren, Gilbert Berry told me that one of the vivid memories of his life was how he cried when he found out that "Granny" was not his real grandmother, but a step mother to his dad.

She moved in with us when we left Jackson County and was a wonderful addition to our family from whom we learned much – and from whom I developed a love for local history. It was the time when there was no paid custodian of the church building. Rather, various families took responsibility for a month at the time. When it was our turn, one of the things Adie did was to wax the hardwood floors; on her knees, under the benches (we were too small and too country to have pews), and then to buff those floors by hand with old towels. She was a true servant who filled our life with encouragement.

Ma Ma Maberry, my mother's mother was a smart, articulate, and savvy country woman and the Americana picture of a farm wife. She kept the kitchen garden, fed and cared for the chickens, milked the personal milk cows, churned, worked, molded, and sold rich creamy butter, and filled the cellar with good things to eat before winter overtook her family.

My Aunt Thelma, Daddy's oldest sister was a quite and gentle spirit who spoke softly and served others and treated me as if I were one of her own. She had been the oldest sister when her widowed mother passed away and was the mature sensible influence that held the family together. She was much closer than an Aunt, and I remember well walking into her house when I was a college student and hearing her say, "Well, here comes my third boy." There is no replacement for that kind of expressed love.

Even my sister Donnieta, four years older and enough of a model student to create unrealistic expectations of me by my teachers, was of unfathomable influence on my life for good – which only somewhat offset the influence for bad of others associates, I must confess.

Finally there is my sweet wife Jan, the brown eyed girl, who, like Aunt Thelma, is the embodiment of a "quiet and gentle spirit," and possesses few faults outside her poor taste in men. We have moved 18 times in our 45 years of married life, built six new houses (if you can build even one new house without coming close to divorce, your marriage is probably strong.) raised two boys, with all of the attendant difficulties, while she tolerated a husband who traveled often and sometimes worked 16 hours a day.

I remember once, when GM was in the midst of yet another reorganization (rearranging the deck chairs on the Titanic) and I was working crazy hours. The brown eyed girl was discussing the trials of my absence in a ladies bible class in Rochester, Michigan and noted that on one particular night I had worked until 2:00 a.m. came home took a shower and went back to work. One of the more mature ladies in the class, Mary Utley, spoke up and said, "Honey, if I were you, I'd be checking up on him."

A woman that will move with you 18 times and each time take the attitude that, "we are really going to be happy here" then work to make that prophecy a reality, is a Keeper. God really knew what he was talking about when he said, "It is not good for Man to be alone." Every father of boys of marrying age knows that to be true.

Dr. Paul Southern, when he taught at the late Michigan Christian College (now Rochester College), would always tell the boys aspiring to be preachers that what they needed was a P31. Referring of course, to Proverbs 31 – "For who can find a virtuous woman, her price is far above rubies, and the heart of her husband trusts in her."

Indeed, Dr. Southern, Indeed!

9. <u>Wood Fires and Going to Church</u>

One of the real pleasures of life in days gone by was a wood fire. My family had moved beyond the wood fire by the time my memory is clear, and had installed the new, more modern and efficient, coal grate. That meant sealing up a portion of the old huge wood fireplace and inserting an iron "grate" which held the coal about nine or ten inches above the floor of the fireplace. The ambiance of the wood fire was gone since coal looked different and certainly smelled different. The smoke from a coal fire was laden with sulfur and one could taste it in the resulting black smoke, which covered everything in the house.

Even when we moved into town, the house was heated by coal – big chunk coal that was delivered once a year – or more in a really bad winter – and dumped into the basement coal bin. The last job on cold winter nights was for Daddy to go down to the basement and shovel a sufficient amount of coal into the monster of a furnace, then "bank" it with ashes from below so it would burn lower and slower and last through out the long winter night.

Of course, with the change to coal, the farm family moved one step further away from independence – coal was one more thing that required always scarce cash. Wood had been available in the tree stands around the farm and, in fact, was a by-product of the continual clearing of the land. On the other hand, as cash "public works" became more available in the Upper Cumberland, the family began to swap its labor off the farm for cash and had less time to spend in the woods, preparing for winter.

Since this is a hot August day in Tennessee, wood fires may seem like an unusual subject to be thinking about, but my mind had been on the old story about the preacher who was visiting a back sliding brother. The old brother had been absenting himself from the assembly and the preacher was there to encourage him to congregate with others. As they talked, the old backslider droned on about how he didn't really need the company of other Christians and could find God in the woods (along with his squirrel rifle, no doubt) and that going to church really didn't really do him any good.

As they talked, the preacher picked up the tongs leaned against the big fireplace and pulled a burning chunk from the roaring wood fire. The old fellow continued his monologue about the advantages of solitude. Soon the burning piece began to cool, and having no synergy from the fire around, it dimmed and soon became a smoking ember on the hearth. The preacher picked it up and threw it back into the midst of the body of the fire and it roared to life again. "Well," he said, his point made by the fire, "we will still be looking for you next Sunday," put on his hat and coat and made his exit.

Next Sunday the woods were minus one squirrel hunter.

10. Religion – Idols with no gods Required

Today it occurred to me that we may have become more like those idol worshippers of old than we care to admit. When those men of old first set up the stone or metal idol, it was not their intent to worship the stone or metal, there was a supposed god somewhere behind it, and the idol was simply a reminder. Over time, they began to focus on the idol itself and forgot that it only represented a god and the chunk of stone or wood became the center of their adoration.

We in popular Christianity today, have fine tuned worship to the point that it may have become like the idol of ages past, an end in itself.

Complicated and entertaining worship services begin to look like an NFL playbook, with producers, directors, musicians, and preachers who all must play their scripted part on queue.

The worship service itself has become an end and we feel that if it can just be professional enough, if we can just get it right, we will have earned some greater favor with God – besides it brings out the crowd.

Somehow, I suspect He would rather have our hearts involved than have a speaker that moves us to tears, boosts our self-esteem, and leaves us with a warm and fuzzy feeling. I am also suspicious that He would prefer us live each day being kind to our spouse, children, and co-workers, than have a praise team that sings in perfect pitch and time, and be able to execute the rigors of passing the Lord's Supper within the allotted time; that He would rather have us stop and think of Him in the middle of a hectic day, than have the weekly "performance" go off without a hitch.

Don't get me wrong, I am not against doing your best at anything, particularly presenting corporate worship to God, but my understanding is that it is the worship of our lives he desires above all else.

"Let Justice roll down like rivers of water, and righteousness like an ever-flowing stream." Amos 5:24

I don't know – maybe I am wrong, but that is how I am feeling today.

Chapter II
Country Boys Do Survive

11. <u>More fish Tales than Fish Heads</u>

When I was about 9 or 10 years old, I saved my money and bought a Johnson Century closed faced spinning reel. It was that special emerald green and I was able to also afford a jointed fiber glass rod with a spring loaded push button so I could change from one reel to another in a flash. Of course, I only had one reel and this feature, although a real drawing card, was really not much use to me. It had cork handles and the ferrules were wrapped with a real spiffy orange thread. I had never had anything like it and lots of work and saving went into its purchase.

The Game and Fish Commission (TWRA) had begun to stock rainbow trout just below Center Hill Dam, taking advantage of the cold clear water that came from the bottom of the lake through the generating sluice. Enough time had passed that people were actually beginning to catch keeper size rainbow – a thrill that will make a boy out of even a grown man. Daddy and I had ridden up to the dam, passing through Gordonsville, the Lancaster Community and parking beside the little forty just below the dam where the concrete tower stands at the rivers edge across the field.

It was February and cold as a pigs snout with about a two inch skiff of snow on the stubble and we were wrapped up in our warmest coats. No one had any idea that a light coat could actually keep one warm, so heavy and bulky was the order of the day. Mine came down to about the seat of my pants, was an inch thick, and had knitted cuffs to keep the cold from shinnying up my arms.

As we began to fish, I spotted a dead tree that stuck out over the river and decided that if I could get out on the old white tree trunk, I would get a better angle from which to cast that new Johnson. It would be just the edge I needed. I lay down on the white, slick, perpendicular trunk and began to inch my way out, allowing my legs to hang down to lower my center of gravity. I had just gotten comfortable and was about to make that first real cast, when the tree trunk broke right at the bank and the whole log went straight down into the water.

I hit with a giant splash and felt all the air go out of my lungs in a rush as I went under the freezing water "head and ears". After what seemed to me an eternity, I surfaced sputtering and spitting, nearly overcome with the all pervasive burning sensation that comes when plunged into ice cold water. My dad was hollering at me, trying to talk me out of the water, and extending a long stick for me to grab. I got a hold on the stick and started up the steep bank which lurked under the water, but the weight of the boy and the now waterlogged coat was too much, and the stick snapped sending me down for a second time. When I came back up again, now a little further downstream, Daddy was extending his own fishing pole, which was thankfully an old fashioned one piece job and he was telling me to grab the pole. I did and this time he managed to walk me up the steep river's edge and onto the snow covered bank. When I got my breath, I realized that the Johnson Century and the new ABU Garcia rod were in the river.

Oh no, this can't be happening. How can I lose something I had worked so hard for? I pulled off the big coat and in a master stroke of debating ability, convinced Daddy that I would be fine to go back into the river and get the rod and reel, which is exactly what I did. Daddy would tell the story and say, "Of all the dumb things I ever did, that might be the dumbest." Mama usually used that as an opportunity to remind him of a few other bad choices, like trading our milk cow for a T Model Ford, with a new baby in the house – but that is another story.

I suppose all is well that ends well, but I can tell you for sure that it was a long cold walk across that river bottom to the old '54 green Buick. And I can further assure you that one is warmer without a coat than having the water soaked thing on your body.

The Johnson Century was saved, snatched from the jaws of destruction by yours truly, and I was safe, snatched from the jaws of destruction by Big Bob. We got home with no fish heads on our stringer but a great fish tale on our lips, destined for a flock of disapproving looks from Mama as the story unfolded.

I was willing to go to great lengths and considerable pain to rescue from destruction that which I had bought with a great price, and Daddy was willing to go to great lengths to save the one to whom he was father. Is it any wonder then that God so loved the world? First he made us, and then he bought us with a great price. We are his and he does not want to lose us again – oh, by the way, I still have the Johnson Century!

12. Face Your Problems or Cut and Run.

All of these rainy days lately remind me of how much I liked a rainy summer day on the farm. It was generally a day off, particularly if it rained for more than a single day. You could clean stalls, repair harness, or clean out the gear shed for a day, maybe two, but eventually Pa Maberry was going to run out of something for you to do and Billy and I would take off fishing.

42

The word was that fishing was good when it rained, everyone said so, and it made a good deal of sense. The water, which had grown stagnant during the hot summer days, would be re-oxygenated by the rain, a lot of worms, bugs and other fish cuisine would be washed into the creek, waking up the lethargic fish, and the muddy water would make for good cat-fishin' since the whiskered night feeders would now be cruising the bottoms during the day, what with the water that deep brown muddy color.

I remember one particular afternoon when the rain had started earlier in the day driving us out of the cornfields about 10:00 a.m.. We had been doing battle since sunup with the Johnson grass that had sprung up during a particularly wet season in Middle Tennessee, using gooseneck hoes as our primary weapon. It was about to "take" the corn crop. "Boys, that Johnson grass is going to take the corn if we don't get in there with them hoes." For some time, it had been too wet to get the tractors into the field and use their cultivators to wrap the immature corn plants with a good layer of dirt, and "bust them middles." Now the Johnson grass had grown to half knee high and the cultivators would no longer do the job. We had no clue that one day herbicide would be used to inhibit the growth, and the gooseneck hoe was our last line of defense. Step, chop, chop – step, chop, chop – and so it went from one end of those mile long corn rows to the other. The big ball of sticky mud that accumulated on each foot made every step a struggle, and the sun drew up the moisture from the wet ground, creating a steam bath effect in your world of mud, heat, dampness, and corn.

When the rain finally began, it was a welcome relief from the heat, and as it picked up momentum becoming more

43

and more of a downpour, and finally the ground got so muddy that work mercifully became impossible. We were soaked to the skin when we finally piled in the old army surplus jeep we used to shuttle to and from the fields and headed back up to the house. It looked like an afternoon of fishing to me.

After catching John McDonald on "Noontime Neighbors" and listening to the weather on the big old console radio, the rain was still coming down steady and heavy and it was evident that work for the afternoon was not in the cards. Billy and I gathered our fishing gear together, Pa caught a ride with us to the City Café to "open his office," as we called it, and we headed across the bridge, and down Gordonsville Road for Mulherin Creek.

We fished the afternoon away, caught a few decent eating size fish, and jumped in the old green Chevy Truck and started home just before dark was to setting in.

As we twisted and turned around the old Gordonsville, Road, we hooked the curve at Mr. B. D. and Mrs. Ruby Wooten's place and saw a car traveling at a high rate of speed headed our way. The car began to slide, spun out of control and careened past us climbing up the high bank through which the road was cut, coming to rest against a telephone pole with a sickening "thump." Immediately steam and smoke began to rise from the front end. By the time we could get stopped, pull to the side of the road, and run back to where the old 52 Chevy sat with buckled hood, flames had become clearly visible in the deepening twilight of a rainy evening. We climbed the bank the old Chevy had sledded up and started to look around for the occupants. We saw not a single person, and began to search the area around the now fully blazing car to see if anyone had been thrown from the vehicle. Nothing, no one, what we did find was beer and an open whisky bottle with some of the dark brown liquid still inside. The heavy smell of whiskey made the whole area smell like the proverbial brewery.

When it became obvious that the occupant or occupants had abandoned their car in favor of leaving the scene of an accident, we simply turned around, walked back to the old Chevrolet pickup, and drove silently on home, discussing whether we ought to do something or not. We defaulted to not, and never learned more of the accident. I have often wondered over the years if some young husband had to go home and confess to his wife that he had wrecked their only car, or if a teenage boy had to go to his father with some cooked up story about how two crazy guys in an old green pickup had forced him off the road and how in the moment he had left the scene dazed and confused.

We never spoke much of it after that, since we ourselves had left the scene, but I will never forget the sight or sound of that vehicle flying up that embankment and striking the utility pole, as the hood crinkled and both doors flew open.

Sometimes we think that running away from our problems is a better answer than facing them, and we act accordingly. I am suspicious however, that running away is never the answer, nor the end to our troubles; only the beginning of a whole new set of difficulties. Our maker encourages us, in fact instructs us, to face our troubles, but then tells us that we do not have to face them alone. "Draw near to God, and He will draw near to you." "Bear you one another's burdens." Life is far too scary to face our troubles alone.

13. <u>Skinny Dipping at a Baptist Picnic</u>

When I was growing up, my Uncle Tom Kittrell and I often fished in Mulherin Creek. The creek was just off the road that ran twisting and turning between Carthage and Gordonsville, until it crossed the creek about halfway between the two towns. The old bridge crossed the creek four or five miles up from where it finally emptied into the Caney Fork River and it transformed itself from a shallow little creek at the bridge to a sizable body of water in that few miles. It was beautiful to the extreme in those days and only an occasional car would cross the narrow old bridge. Each twist and turn of the creek opened onto a vista that was more picturesque than the one before. Kit, as I called him, was a fly fisherman and used a split bamboo rod, an item which today would grace an antique shop. He carried a willow basket creel with a double barreled, pearl handle, derringer pistol inside and he loved to roam up and down the beautiful creek bank almost as much as I.

He and my Aunt Gene, Daddy's baby sister, would often come up from Nashville on Sundays to visit, and while the rest of the family sat and talked, he and I would head to Mulherin Creek. I suppose the strain of being a struggling Nashville lawyer would all wash away in the creek and he would be completely relaxed. Starting at the bridge, we would wade in jeans and army surplus tennis shoes, down the creek taking a few largemouth, smallmouth, and warmouth bass, as well as a large number of those big fat black backed brim that filled the little creek. There were no industrial plants nearby then and the lumber yard would not come for years, so it was just the peace and quiet of the farm land around us. The farms belonged to Mr. Bill Young and Mr. Colman Wright, both of whom attended church with us at the little church of Christ in Carthage, and each of whom had a boy just my age. We were welcome in the creek and on the farms, and had the run of the place.

The Tennessee Central spur line that ran from the Junction at Gordonsville over to Carthage crossed the creek on a high wooden trestle bridge above the creek. Crossing the railroad bridge was a test of courage since it was narrow, quite high, and was open between the cross ties. If one looked straight down, the view was the rock strewn creek bed some fifty feet below. It took a fair amount of time to carefully cross the trestle, as the ties were too close together for a full step, and too far apart to take two at a time; and since the space between the crossties was wide open to the fifty foot fall to the creek bed, considerable care was given to each step. The chance of a train actually coming while you were crossing the bridge was probably remote, since the main traffic was coal coming into Carthage, and tobacco hogsheads going out, but it was the chance that one would come while you were crossing and the penalty for error that made it interesting. We would lie down and put our ear to the track, following the popular myth that one could hear the wheels of the train several miles away by that method. After all, that is the way the Indians always did it in the cowboy pictures, and it worked for them.

Another interesting feature of the creek was the "millpond" a deep hole where years ago a water mill had stood and a dam had provided fall in the water to drive the water wheel. It was at the millpond on a hot Sunday June afternoon, that Kit got the big idea that a hot as it was, he and I, "ought to just shuck off and go swimming – Jay birdin'." Skinny dipping, they call it on TV but we just referred to it as "shucking off and Jay birdin" Well, we shucked off, and laid our, already wet, britches and tee shirts under a bush sticking out over a flat rock. The water was cool and refreshing and we were floating and paddling around when we suddenly hear voices from just up the bank. There were a bunch of people coming through the field, and they were almost on us. No time to get out and get dressed as the local Missionary Baptist Sunday School picnic headed our way. We clung to the bank closest to them with nothing but our heads sticking out of the water, and those concealed as much as possible by the protruding ledge. All was going well until I saw a water snake, disturbed by all of the squawking of that bunch of Baptists, drop into the water from a low limb and begin propelling himself toward us in that creepy S shaped way snakes move through water. Just as I was about to give the Baptists a little uplift to their picnic and the snake the creek, Kit smacked the water with his hand, and the snake changed directions. I never thought more of a man than I did him right then. A couple of the good brothers and sisters looked over the bank in our direction but must have decided it was a fish because they kept on moving toward some picnic spot unknown to us.

Eventually, the Baptists moved on down the creek and we retrieved our clothes, hardly worse for the wear, but the episode had taken the edge off our desire to be in the creek any longer that day. We hiked back up the creek out on the dry bank laughing uncontrollably but Kit suggested that it would be better if we just kept this to ourselves. I agreed, and never spoke of it until I was asked to speak at his funeral.

He was, as my sister so aptly phrased it, "the pied piper of fun," and managed to remain a boy for the greater part of his life. It would have been difficult to watch him, a criminal trial lawyer, defending an accused man in court, and imagined him swimming in the buff in Mulherin Creek, but all who knew him well, knew just how possible that was.

None of us are ever exactly what we appear to others — or even ourselves, and each of us has many sides to his personality. We appear one way in some circumstances and another way in others, but there is One who sees us as we are. One from whom we cannot hide our nakedness though we may tuck ourselves in the cleft of the rock. One who looks beyond the masks and disguises we wear in the world we exist in and sees us as we are and shall be. Boy, that's a sobering thought, isn't it?

A day's catch on Center Hill in the Good Old Days

14. <u>Sweat Bees and Sweet Serendipity</u>

It seems that one fishing story just leads to another, doesn't it? I have had a couple of other life events that have been on my mind since yesterday when we talked about fishing the Mulherin Creek. One was when Daddy and I went fishing on Smith's Fork Creek one Saturday afternoon. We rode up toward Center Hill Dam and detoured up Smith's Fork because we had heard that the little silver stripers were just wearing little ¼ ounce ABU's out at a particular place. It was a hot afternoon in mid summer and I was appropriately dressed, me in standard uniform of blue jeans and a T shirt, and Daddy in the perennial short sleeved Kaki Shirt and Steven's Work Pants that he wore daily.

The road was a good ways above the level of the creek, and we stopped at a place where fishermen had shinnied up and down the steep bank until they had worn a dusty slide that looked like a bear might have been working a laurel thicket. When we finally got all of our tackle firmly in hand, we started down the bank, so steep that we had to sit down on our feet, and slide down the embankment. We would worry about getting back up when it was time to go home.

We had our rigs together and were actually having a bit of luck when what looked like a black cloud above the water came up the creek. It was an enormous black swarm of sweat bees, so thick they looked like smoke and were moving our way. You might not know what a sweat bee is, but it is only a little larger than a gnat, looks like a flying ant, is hard as a bb pellet, and stings like fire. If you even touch the hateful creatures they will sting. They get in the crease of you neck, under you shirt, creep into your underarm, snarl themselves in your hair, and are generally a pain – quite literally.

Never in my life, before or since have I encountered such a quantity of these critters. The black cloud moved in and engulfed us and they were as thick as the gnats on the riverbank at Savannah, Georgia. Having had a bit of luck, and being unused to fleeing from the elements of nature, we kept on throwing the ABUs but I was pretty soon in near panic mode, as they were inhaled up one's nose, made exploratory expeditions into my ears, and flew into my mouth, if I dared open it. Finally, to my everlasting relief, Daddy said, "Come on son, we got to get outta' here," and started up the steep bank. Two steps up, three steps back; he couldn't get traction to get up the bank and I couldn't get around him. Two steps up, slide back, slapping, waving our arms, and grunting as the little demons made whelks all over us. Finally, I took to the bush and went over rocks, briars, and, clawed my way up the loose gravel to the top. I grabbed a paddle out of the trunk of the car and poked it down to Daddy and held on for dear life as he extracted himself from the death trap below. We jumped in the car, still slapping and brushing bees from our bonnets, and sped off down the road, rolling the windows down to suck the remaining bees out. In a few minutes we started laughing at ourselves and hee hawed until our sides nearly split.

I never knew what the deal was with that enormous swarm of bees, but to my memory it was the last time we fished Smith's Fork Creek. We never again passed the spot without breaking into laughter.

A month or so later, he and I went to the old Cove Hollow Boat Dock and rented one of those flat bottom green wooden boats, which was all they had for rent in those days.

Daddy had borrowed an outboard motor from someone, don't remember who. They did not rent boats and motors in those days, or if they did we could not afford to rent the whole thing. Everyone I knew either had a little boat on a trailer, or a motor which they carried to the lake in the trunk of the car. They were mostly little 8 horse Johnsons, maybe a little bigger, but not much, because you had to tote the thing down to the boat dock and back up to the car. I remember Brother Eddie Pinkley, our preacher, had a 3 horse. But an 8 horse was plenty big, because no one thought you had to be in a hurry to get across the lake in a 200 hp Bass Boat. Fishing was a leisure time activity to be entered into in a leisurely way and not a time to rush to get anywhere. I always wonder where those guys are going in such a hurry.

We were working the banks of Indian Creek and I was in the bow of the boat with the short paddle, sculling close to the bank just like Horace Wright from our church had taught me, when the sky began to darken and turn from grey to black to green. Daddy decided we needed to get out of there and pulled on the starter rope – and it pulled right out of the motor and fell into his lap. When he pulled the cover off the motor, the parts of the spring that returned the rope when it was pulled on, fell into the boat. It was supposed to be in one piece and this whole thing was not turning out as planned.

I beached the boat near some rocks at the head of a little creek we were working and got out to hold the boat steady. As I stepped out, I noticed something in brown, heavily waxed paper lying on the rocks. It was heavy, and had obviously been laying there for a long time since the paper on the side exposed to the sun was extremely faded. I started to open the now fragile paper, and found a spring inside, with hardly any rust due to the heavily waxed wrapping.

I asked, "What is this daddy?" and he looked up, scowling at being interrupted.

"What's What?" He asked.

"This looks just like the piece that is broke, Daddy."

"Let me see that. Where'd you get this thing?"

"Laying there on the rocks."

And wonder of wonders, it was the exact piece, down to the part number, that had broken on the motor we were borrowing.

"Was this in the boat somewhere?" he continued to ask.

But it had just been laying there on the very rock I drew the boat up to – waiting for some kid to rescue it.

Daddy used the pliers and screwdriver he kept in his tackle box for just such emergencies and repaired the motor. One pull and it started up, and we motored back down to Cove Hollow, tackling some pretty scary waves for a flat bottomed wooden boat.

About the time we got to the dock, and into the little store there, it cut loose and rained in sheets of water, complete with wind, lightening, and crashing thunder.

Isn't it funny how life goes? Some days are filled with sweat bees and all you can think to do is keep you mouth shut, and keep on moving until you're out of the cloud. Other days, just when it looks like disaster is going to be your lot, some twist of fate brings unexpected and unexplained good fortune and you are filled with a sense of serendipity. Now I know that a lot of people would think that the spring was a minor miracle, but I have to wonder if the God of the Universe doesn't have more important things to do than repair outboards to keep me dry.

I do understand though, how fragile is the moment and how life's sky can change from grey to black to green in short order. But through it all, we place our trust in a God who loves us and has sought a relationship with those he created. And whether life is filled with sweat bees and stings or sweet serendipity; we can say with confidence – *It is Well With My Soul*.

15 **The Path We Choose**

I just watched a TV special about the "miracle on the Hudson" when Captain Sullenberger set a flamed out airliner down in the Hudson River without loss of life. It has been one year ago that it happened and some of those involved were speaking of the impact of the event on their lives. Sully's wife was asking, "why us", "why did it happen," when Sully answered, "because I was assigned that flight on that day, it's just as simple as that."

I was remembering finishing up my tour of duty in Korea and getting to Kimpo Airbase for the flight home. As unbelievable as it may seem now, we were not given transportation to Kimpo, we were simply told to get there the best way we could and not be late, if we didn't want to miss our DEROS (Date of Estimated Return from OverSeas). I had bought a train ticket well in advance, wanting to make sure there was room for me on the often crowded Korean Train, but the morning of the day I was supposed to leave, a couple of

MP buddies of mine phoned and said there was a U21, reconnaissance plane leaving K21 airbase and the crew had room for a passenger. The MP's had convinced the pilots to hold the aircraft for a few minutes, but I had to leave right now if I want to catch it.

In a few minutes an MP Jeep roared up outside my workstation with siren blasting full and, I threw my duffel into the back and climbed in and we roared through the streets of Taegu running Papa Sans, Kiamichi wagons, and honey dippers in every direction.

Reactionary Force in Korea - 1968
I loved that soft cap and avoided the "brain bucket"
I still love the soft cap

Sure enough, the plane was sitting on the runway with the props already spinning, but the pilots taxied back in and I climbed aboard. About 100 miles outside K21 I noticed one of the Army Majors flying the plane, lean forward and peck on one of the dials. He then shook his head and punched the copilot and pointed to the dial. The second officer also leaned forward, squinted at the dial and likewise gave it a thump. As if directed by some invisible string, both of their heads turned toward the left side wing in unison. Now I'm not much of an aviation expert, but I knew enough to know that this was not a good sign. I shifted where I could also see out the left side and a small trail of oil and smoke was streaming from the left engine. The pilot then leaned forward flipped a switch and the left engine began to slowly come to a halt like a ceiling fan that has been switched off. He then turned to me, removed his headset and said, "We've lost oil pressure in the left engine and looks like there might be a little fire there. I have feathered the engine and we are returning to K21."

Immediately, I began to look around for a parachute, and finding none ask the pilot if one was stowed under the seat or somewhere.

"Are you crazy," he shouted, "that tail would cut you in two the minute you stepped out the door."

Thinking of other possibilities, I asked, "how far with this thing glide?"

"Don't know," he replied, "how far do you think it is from here to the ground?"

He then said, "sit back and relax kid, and we'll get this hunk of junk back to K21."

Well I sat back alright, but the rest of the instruction was impossible to follow, so I worried – a lot. I thought to myself, "I had a train ticket, why didn't I just take the train? How could I have been through all I have been through and now I'm going to die in an inglorious manner on some barren mountain side in South Korea – what a bummer."

While I kicked myself for the next hundred miles, the pilots seemed rather calm, but just as the runway came in sight the copilot told me,

"Look kid, when we get this thing down, you get yourself out that door in a hurry, this thing could go up like a torch and I don't want you in my way."

My anxiety was heightened by the full compliment of firefighting equipment and crews that I could see on the runway and when the plane stopped rolling, I started to grab my duffel and get out the door, but the Major was faster. He grabbed me and threw me out the door, about a six foot drop which seemed like twelve. I landed on all fours on the tarmac bruised and battered as the fire crew shot the left engine full of foam.

I gathered my gear and headed to catch a cab to the train station. I still had a ticket, the train had not left and I had only one thought in mind. Get to Kimpo and on the Red-tail that would take me home.

"Hey kid, we'll have this thing fixed in a little while if you want to stick around,"

"Thank you sir, but I have alternate transportation."

As I hear people surmise that they know how God is working in various events of the earth such as the earthquake in Haiti or the tsunami in Indonesia, or even so simple a thing as why I am on a certain flight, it seems to me they have forgotten a few things.

First, it is not within us to understand the ways of The Creator of the Universe. His ways are not our ways and his view is somewhat different than our own. For instance, I might look at a nuclear reactor but that certainly doesn't mean I understand the subtleties of how it works. Even so, as we look upon God, there are likely a few subtleties of His nature we cannot grasp.

Second, this is not heaven; it is not the place of perfection that God longs for us to yearn to inhabit. Those mansions are still, "just over the hilltop" and we not only are not there, but cannot even clearly view them. If this were the place of perfection, to what would we aspire?

Finally, we are clearly taught that the workings of this imperfect world filled with sorrow and pain will not cease; rather that wars, famine, death, and natural disasters will continue while this world stands.

So, let us be kind, loving, and lend help to our neighbor, while longing for the city that is built foursquare.

16. <u>Frog Kissing and other Contact Sports</u>

And then there was the time my sister and my cousin Marva came home from Lipscomb for the weekend and brought their boyfriends. There was nothing particularly unusual about that since they came to our house for the weekend often; but this time was special. I had been engaged in the fine sport of frog gigging for a couple or three years and had mentioned it to Bob White and Borden Nettles, the respective boyfriends. They, being from up north, but wanting to prove they were as rugged as the good old local boys, decided they would like to go froggin'. I explained that it was pretty rough getting around in Mulherin Creek at night, but that only stiffened their resolve, and the girls, wanting to seem like outdoorsy, girl next door, good sport, types decided they would like to just go along. Now neither of them was either outdoorsy or good sports about such things, but one out of three is not too bad. (Girls do that you know, pretend to like football, hunting, fishing, and camping, until they have you firmly in hand, then you learn that their idea of roughing it is staying at a Holiday Inn without room service.)

To be fair, we guys are just as bad, acting like we love their cats, are interested in shopping malls, and feel ballets are educational, until we think it is safe to eventually burp in their company.

Well sir, I dragged out the frog gigs and the old grey brakeman's lantern and off we went out Gordonsville Road toward the creek. It was late in the fall and so was getting dark early and we arrived at the creek when black dark had fallen. Now, if you have never been out in the woods or on the creek bank in black dark, it is hard to imagine just how dark, that dark can be. It is also hard to explain how disoriented one can become when robbed of the landmarks used as guides during daylight hours. I knew we had a slight lack of communication when they begin to ask about the boat; no boat, I explained, we were just going to wade through the creek and stick the critters where we found them.

After some discussion, the girls decided they actually needed to stay close to the car, and would just wait right there on the creek bank until we returned. It was too dark for them to walk back to the car alone, we did not have an extra light, and I was a 14 year old boy who was already pretty put out that they had wanted to come, so I was not in a chivalrous mood. Bob, Borden, and I slipped into the cold creek water and started wading down the creek watching for frog eyes shining back as the light searched the water's edge on both sides of Mulherin. We had not gone far when we began to see the snakes dropping from the tree limbs into the water, as snakes will do when disturbed at night. I took only a few of these incidents for the guys to decide we probably ought to get back to see about the girls since they might be afraid. Yeah, I'm sure that was it! I don't remember if we had actually taken even one frog or not, but needless to say it had not been a banner night.

An Unlikely Crew for Froggin, Donnieta, Bob White, Marva Mabry, Borden Nettles
The brown eyed girl and I still try to have a week with the six of us each year.

When we arrived back, the girls were less than happy. They had been too scared to stay where they were and too terrified to return to the car, which they probably did not know how to find by that time. It was not a happy night for the boyfriends and not a pleasant ride back to Carthage. But eventually a slice of Mama's coconut pie and a big bowl of popcorn brought peace to the camp.

I guess we always think we want things that are new and different, until we find out what it is all about. You know, by the time we have the experience to know what not to do, we have already done it!

One often wonders why God gave us the latitude to make mistakes to the degree He does. And I often wish He had held the reins a bit tighter. Still, His desire is that we would recognize that His way is best of our own accord, at first through experience, and then later by Faith. I suppose we eventually just learn from experience that His way is best, and do not have to experience each mistake to know which to avoid. We take His word for it.

The child first must learn the cost of disobedience of a mother's direction, before it can develop the faith that mother knows best, and has their best interests at heart. When that happens, a great step toward maturity has been taken.

Every person mature in Christ was Paul's wish for the early church, (Col 1:28) and a better prayer I cannot imagine.

17. Uncle Hick and Aunt Mary

Now Uncle Hick and Aunt Mary were not married or even related in any way that I know. In fact, neither was more than marginally related to us, but, in the way of Roaring River, we called them Uncle Hick (Loftis) and Aunt Mary (Petty) because they were older neighbors and that is what older people who were part of the "shirttail relatives" of extended family were called.

Uncle Hick was a story teller, and tall tales bordering on lies, was his specialty. For instance he once told that his best old mule had so much heart that when she was trying to pull a stump and didn't have quite enough "oats" to make it happen, she hooked her chin on a nearby sapling and gained just enough leverage to "jerk that stump out'n the dirt."

Aunt Mary was an old lady who lived in a little house down the road that had neither running water nor bathroom facilities, and she could be seen almost any morning or evening carrying a bucket of water from a neighbor's place about a mile down the road.

Mrs. Kate West's general store was about a mile and a half down the road from Uncle Hick's house, and Aunt Mary's little house was between him and the store. The store had a big front porch where all the local loafers sat and passed the time of day talking about the weather, politics, and religion – all in equal proportions of shared ignorance.

One day when Uncle Hick was passing by the store one of the "boosters" on the porch called out,

"Morning Hick, come in and tell us a lie."

"Can't do it," remarked Uncle Hick, "Ain't got time. Aunt Mary Petty done died, an I gotta go and holp the ol' woman lay her out."

Well the loafers were shocked, and began to talk among themselves about what they needed to do, since the community was expected to rally on such occasions. They decided that they needed to get over there, get some wood in, and see what food was needed and who was going to build the coffin, dig the grave, and so on.

As they started down the road toward Aunt Mary's house, here she came, carrying a bucket to fetch some water – just as alive as any of them.

Uncle Hick had done just what they had asked; he had told them a lie.

Today many of us are like the loafers on the store porch, wanting for someone to tell us a lie and ready to believe it, even when we know better. Perhaps the most prevalent form today is the internet, where videos and e-mails that are filled with lies of various kinds are perpetuated by good people who fail to stop and think about their responsibility toward gossip and false witness. We need to stop and check at least three things before we pass on what is forwarded to us:

1. Is it the truth, the whole truth, nothing but the truth?

2. Will any good purpose be served by me passing this on?

3. Does forwarding this bit of information, or misinformation, make me more or less like Jesus, and bring Glory to God?

If the answer to all or part of the three tests above are "no" then we should refrain from passing the talk along. As Adie would have said, "If you can't say anything good about somebody = don't say anything at all."

18. <u>Of Wells and Springs</u>

When I was a child every farm home had either a well or a spring. The wells either required a pump, which demanded a little water be left in the bucket each time it was filled for "priming the pump," or had a "well bucked" that was let down by means of a long rope, filled with water and then drawn up again. Springs required no pumping, but the water had to be carried from the spring to the house – which was generally a considerable distance from the spring. (A few minutes thought about the absence of indoor toilet facilities will soon cause you to realize why the two were prudently not located closer together.)

One thing was sure, whether spring or well, each family thought that the source of water on their place was the coldest, purest, best tasting of any water source in the county. Now there was no empirical evidence to support this, nor did anyone seek such evidence. The fact that they thought this was the truth was good enough for them, so you would often hear, "yes sir, six steps from my back porch is the coldest, purest, sweetest well water in this state."

We often are the same way about our religious beliefs; we believe them to be the purest, sweetest, and most pleasing theological ideas available, and often without a wealth of empirical evidence. Now it is not that empirical evidence is not available, it is just that it is so inconvenient to determine the evidence, or perhaps there is fear that the evidence will repudiate our intuition. While it was fine for each of us to believe as we wished about our water source, more analytical searching is required to determine the purity of our theology. Search for the evidence.

Chapter III
Changing Seasons

19. For Everything There is a Season

Having returned home after 16 days, I appreciate the beauty of Middle Tennessee more than ever. It seems to me the best part of any trip is when you first catch sight of your own home after being away. Following a 26 hour trip through two other countries to get to Rome, Italy – 14 days on a ship doing 4 countries and 9 Cities, and a seven hour time change to give one a monumental case of Jet lag, I rounded the corner and caught sight of our house, and it looked better than Mussolini's summer palace, St. Peter's Basilica, and San Marco's Cathedral all rolled into one.

I was pleasantly surprised that fall had come in earnest to the Upper Cumberland and my trees were beautiful shades of gold and red and that mixed with the still green grass and a bright blue sky to paint a background that would pale Michelangelo's Sistine Chapel ceiling. Nobody does artwork better than God, and, in my opinion, some of his best work is right here in Middle Tennessee.

Looking at all of the glory of fall reminded me of the days gone by when we started to buttoned things up for the winter on the farm. The days began to get shorter and by 5 o'clock the shadows were long and the sun was starting to retire for the night. The ubiquitous cornfields were drying to perfection, ready for the day when Daddy and Pa would hitch Kit and Bell to the wagon, put the sideboards on and the tailgate in and begin corn gathering. The gardens were turned under, waiting for the spring and the stalls had been cleaned and the loads of aromatic manure spread on the tobacco patches in preparation for next years crop. Last years crop was hanging in the barns drying, waiting for foggy mornings when the leaves would be stripped from the stalk and graded into; trash, bright, red, and tips.

Little boys stripped tips because the stalks were light and all of the other grades gone, so they did not have to make judgments about where their grade started and ended. Much of the kitchen garden had been disc under and planted in turnip greens which would provide good eating late into the winter and bring a precious source of iron into the farm family diet. The exposed rafters of the attics were hung with strings of red peppers and "leather britches" beans, and bags of sliced apples had been dried on the roof hung in flour sacks by wires from the rafters to keep the rats and mice from getting to them. Down in the fruit cellar, Ball and Perfect Mason jars were filled with green beans, blackberries, peaches, tomatoes, and tomato juice, and jars and jars of sour kraut.

Only the smokehouse stood empty, waiting for the first cold days that would come around Thanksgiving, when the weather would be cold enough for hog killing. The weather had to be cool enough for the meat to resist spoiling while it was curing in salt and smoke, yet not cold enough to freeze and stop the curing process.

A farmer had to be a weather man on top of all of his other jobs.

Just before frost – sometime around Halloween – the "hog punkins" would be gathered from the cornfields. What were not used by Mama and Ma Ma Maberry for canning and making pies, were stacked in the barn to be cut up with an axe and fed to the hogs. For several years I took a wheelbarrow loaded with pumpkins up and down the streets in town trying to sell them just before Halloween, but with little success. Most everyone knew a place where they could get a pumpkin free and no one would pay for what they could get for a little trouble in those days.

By the time really cold weather came, the fat hogs had been killed and hams, shoulders, middlin' meat, and sausage hung by wires from the cross poles in the smokehouse. Little remained to be done and the, up until then, frantic pace slowed considerably.

Still there was wood to be chopped during the cold days and left to cure for next season, while wood cut last season was split and ricked in preparation of providing heat in the big fireplace for this season. The last two weeks of December were primarily dedicated to getting the, now stripped and booked, tobacco to the warehouse for sale and for sitting by the fire. When Christmas had come and gone, January was the slack time. A few wood lots might be cleared with axe and crosscut saw and wood was carried in to the fire; hay carried out to the cattle, and a significant amount of time was appropriated for just sitting by the fire warming and planning next season.

The cycle of the seasons on the farm seems to me like the cycle of the seasons of a man's life. If we sow the seeds of service to others well, and the early and late rains come, we can expect a plentiful harvest of good will from our friends and neighbors in the winter of our lives. If we sow devotion to God in our youth and are diligent to work the crop until harvest time, we can expect the harvest to be bountiful. We can count on being filled with God's Mercy and Grace when the weather is stormy and winter winds blow and the darkness approaches early.

It was a favorite time of year for me. I didn't mind the cold, for it meant the warmth of the fire would be that much sweeter, and the grey and barren days of winter would accentuate the beauty of the green and yellow of early spring.

"For everything there is a season, and a time for every purpose under heaven." Eccl. 3:1

20. Managing Expectations when the Mercury Dips

This year has been one of those unusual years when the roses were blooming one day and the snow flurries were flying the next. I mowed the yard in November just before Thanksgiving, and then it turned cold and I had to scurry around making sure no garden hose was connected to an outside water spigot. I learned the hard way that leaving a hose pipe connected all winter in the state of Ohio is a good way to cause a pipe to break, in fact, if I wanted to cause a pipe to break that is the way I would choose. Tomorrow, I will need to feed the cattle, and I wonder if the diesel tractor will start in this weather. I may be toting square bales out to the big black mamas tomorrow. This kind of weather is a piece of cake in this day and time, compared to the days I can first remember when houses were heated with wood cut the prior winter when ground was cleared, or heated with chunk coal delivered from the coal yard in South Carthage. Prior to living in town, the houses we lived in were totally without insulation in either wall or attic and for the most part the residents were at the mercy of the ambient temperature. I can best remember the house my grandparents lived in on the Turner Farm. They typically kept a fire burning only in the kitchen and kept the other rooms (four rooms in all) shut off from the source of heat in order to conserve. There was no need to worry about the pipes freezing since there was no "running water" in the house and even the water bucket would freeze if it was set too far from the fire (or too far from the "far"). Along about 6:30 or 7:00 p.m. my grandmother would open the door to the bedroom that she and Pa slept in and let some of the warmth seep into that room before they retired at 8:00 (or sometimes earlier). The bed was piled high with two or perhaps three quilts and a woolen blanket, and the position one went to sleep in was the position one woke up in, because turning over under that pile of quilts was not an option.

I remember when we lived in the big white house up on 70 Highway (Cookeville Highway) we had a "Warm Morning" stove – often called a pot bellied stove. A stove did a much better job of warming a house than a fireplace since it did not suck all of the heat up the chimney, and many people closed up their fireplaces in the 1940s and cut a flue hole into the brick chimney for the stove pipe to enter. For some reason my grandparents never took this step, perhaps because the house did not belong to them, since it was a house provided to them as part of the deal to oversee the farm.

When it began to stay below freezing for several days, the ponds would start to freeze but cattle still needed water. The smart farmers often put a tobacco stick in the edge of the smaller ponds and used that to slosh the ice back and forth breaking it up along the sides. If one were lucky, their pond was spring fed and the 55 degree water running steadily into the pond would maintain the water temperature high enough to keep the pond from freezing solid. I am hoping that will be the case with our current spell of extended cold weather since creeks and springs are running big, given the abundance of rain we have had lately.

Even these days, when the brown eyed girl and I visit older relatives living in the country and without central heat, it is not uncommon to find women inside the house wearing a head scarf and pants under their dress, not as a fashion statement, but simply as a method of keeping warm. The little natural gas or propane heater will be running full blast, but the drafty little houses with no insulation, let out as much heat as the heaters generate.

A few years back, everyone had stock to be fed, chickens, milk cows, mules, and hogs and the animals did not want to wait just because a farm family was ill equipped and ill dressed to deal with below freezing weather. So it was jump out onto the cold floor, grab your britches, and out into the dark morning with the old coal oil lamp, leather work gloves, a denim jumper lined with corduroy, and brogan shoes which kept out very little of the cold from the frozen ground. The one haven was the barn, since the body heat from the mules and other barn stock kept it warmer than the outside and it actually seemed warm in contrast to the outside when a little boy walked in.

The watering troughs froze with four or five inches of ice and had to be busted up several times each day with sledge hammer or single bit axe so stock could get a drink. Then there was the matter of the amount of feed required to keep stock warm in that weather. It required unusually large amounts of feed to give them the protein needed to generate their own body heat.

The standard operating procedure in the short winter months was to get out each morning, do the milking and feeding in the dark, then rush back in to sit by the fire and get a big breakfast down before going out to break ice on ponds and troughs so the beef cattle could drink.

Back in by the fire to warm and thaw out fingers and toes, then back out to shuck and/or shell corn for feeding chickens, hogs, and milk cows. While you were out this time, square bales of hay were tossed down from the loft onto a wagon and taken out for feeding the pasture animals.

Back in by the fire again to try to thaw out and have a hot noon meal, then make the rounds of ponds and troughs to break ice once more, which invariable led to getting into ice cold water over "shoe mouth deep" and having to slog along until you could get back in again to dry feet and change socks. The one good thing however, was that the muck and mud of the barnyard was frozen solid and generally did not cause the usual problems of getting from point A to point B without ending up to your knees in barnyard mix.

Finally, it was time for milking again, also by lantern light as dark fell at 4:30 and eventually, the evening feeding and milking done, inside to supper and time to sit by the fire and listen to H. T. Kaltenborn give the news on the old Sears Roebuck console radio on Clear Channel 650, WSM, *The Air Castle of The South.*

So when I braved the cold today to put a forty watt light bulb under the cover for the backflow device of my lawn irrigation system, and started the little heater in my small motor home, I found it hard to complain.

I listened to a preacher today talk about making a New Years Resolution to maintain a grateful attitude for all God has given us, and noting that it starts by lessening our personal sense of entitlement, and managing our own expectations. His point was, we are not entitled to have every day sunny and 75 degrees, nor are we to expect that central heat, warm clothes, and insulated boots, are a birthright. I learned during a 13 months tour of duty in Korea, that such is not within the idea of entitlement, nor expectations of the inhabitants of a greater part of the world.

Sometimes it takes a 24 degree day to make us grateful for the 75 degree days, and sometime it takes a little cold, bad, weather to remind us that we need to keep our expectations in check. Then we are truly able to "in all things…give thanks."

21. <u>First Kill</u>---

I just ran into Tom Hoffman in Kroger. He was there with his wife, Margie getting his H1N1 Flu shot and he mentioned that he liked a certain hunting story that I published a while ago. Tom, like me, enjoys hunting and fishing and grew up doing plenty of both. Talking to him started me thinking about those first days of being able to carry your own shotgun, and finally making your first kill.

Daddy gave me a little Iver Johnson, single shot, hammer type, 410 shotgun for my twelfth birthday and I don't think I ever received any gift that I though more of than that one. I still have it, but it is much the worse for wear now;

evidence that it has seen plenty of action, and I treasure every scrape and scratch on the little gun.

When I got big enough to carry a gun, Daddy bought us a couple of small size beagle dogs from Jake Wright and named them Queen and Lady. They had spent most of their life in a pen when we got them and had never actually been hunted. We picked them up on a Thursday and by Saturday decided it was time to take them hunting, so we loaded them into the car and headed to Jackson County. Daddy had grown up on Roaring River and we often made the 18 mile trip back up to the river to hunt or fish or just visit Norman or Roger, Daddy's cousins who still lived on the river.

We pulled up in front of Norman Chaffin's house in Tally's Hollow and after the usual "howdy, how you keeping?" and other preliminaries, Daddy and Norman decided that the best course of action was to go up on the low gap opposite his house. There was absolute no thought or discussion of whether we were welcome to hunt on this land; since the river was a tight knit community and being with Norman meant we were unquestionably welcome, however, tromping those lands without a local was a risk.

We turned the dogs loose and off they went, beating the bushes and briar patches with their tails until they were tinged with blood. They soon raised a rabbit and the race was on, each dog singing in a slightly different tone and meter. They dropped over the west side of the ridge and we lost the sound of their bugling soon after. We never saw them again that day – nor for several days following.

Boy, we were dejected hunters, especially the 12 year old boy. Gone – the dogs I had waited a life time for were gone. After forgetting about rabbits and hunting for dogs until dark, we gave up and rode home in silence, not saying a word to one another. I was personally afraid that if I said anything, I would cry like a 3 year old girl – I think Daddy might have felt the same. The next few days were pretty gloomy, with me taking care not to walk by the empty pen we had built for Queen and Lady – the pain was too much to bear. A few nights later, a fellow by the name of West contacted us and said that a couple of bedraggled hounds had come to his house, and he had put them up having heard from Norman that we had lost two dogs. Daddy thanked him profusely and assured him that we would be there bright and early Saturday morning to see if the dogs were ours. "They have to be ours," I though, "They must be ours, how can I stand it if they were not?"

Saturday morning at dawn's early light, we headed for the river and when we arrived at Mr. West's place – sure enough, there they stood, looking like death row prisoners peering guiltily through the wire. Their feet were so sore they could hardly walk and their tails were a bloody mass, but otherwise they seemed only too anxious to load into the trunk and go home.

I spent the next couple of weeks letting them out in the back lot on a long plow line rope. When I called or whistled, I would reel in the rope and then give them a treat; until soon, they did not need the rope, they came on command. (Eventually they would learn to respond to daddy blowing through the barrel of his old double barrel, and if you opened the trunk of the car around home they would load in, invited or not.)

Three Saturdays later, we headed back up to Norman's and this time we let the dogs head back up the holler behind Norman's toward the old house in which his granddaddy had lived. We hunted the morning by letting one dog loose to hunt and keeping the other on a chain leash to make sure its mate came back to us. Hattie, Norman's wife, had fixed dinner (lunch) for us and I wolfed mine down, ready to get back on the hillside. Daddy and Norman ate slowly and talked leisurely, and then scooted up around the open wood fire in straight chairs, as old friends will do. It looked like they had settled in.

I asked Daddy if it would be alright if I took the dogs and went back up on the hillside. Queen was loose and Lady was on a leash at my side when Queen struck a trail and began to sing that lovely song. She worked slowly crossing over the rock fence that separated Norman's farm from the old Young Place, which had belonged to my great great great granddaddy, Littleberry Young. I sat down and leaned up against an old hackberry tree and waited as Queen did her thing. Pretty soon I saw him, a big old fat rabbit hopping leisurely along from briar patch to briar patch just ahead of the dog. He disappeared into a clump of bushes and briars just up the hill and I reached my thumb around the hammer and cocked the little single action 410, then sighted in that general direction, waiting for Mr. Rabbit to make his appearance again.

Then suddenly, there he was, hopping quickly toward the next dense cover. I was shaking like a leaf and just as I pulled the trigger; it occurred to me that the dead rabbit would be on the wrong side of the rock fence, the Young Place, not Norman's land. Too Late, I had squeezed (more like jerked) the trigger and Mr. Rabbit took an awkward tumble in the opposite direction from me. Now I was shaking all over and my breath was coming in short pants like I had been running up hill. I laid the 410 down on the ground, tied Lady to a little bush, and wondered if I was about to get arrested or shot for killing a rabbit on the wrong land. Not about to lose my rabbit, I mastered my apprehension, crawled over the fence and there he laid – my first kill. In spite of the tension, it was all I could do to keep from beating my chest like a gorilla. I had done it; I had killed one, on my own, by myself. I took out my pocket knife, cut a small twig and slit a small space in the rabbit's hind leg through which I ran the twig and affixed Mr. Rabbit (Mr. Dead Rabbit) to a belt loop where he bled on the new hunting pants – exactly as I had hoped he would.

The hunt was over; I took the dogs, Mr. Rabbit, and the 410 and headed to Norman's house. I laid the rabbit on the back porch, carefully tied Queen and Lady where they could not get at him and walked in; there sat Norman and Daddy still by the fire. I tried to appear casual, wanting to savor the moment, and Daddy said,

"Heard the dogs running, get something up?"

"Yes sir, I did."

"Heard someone shoot, that you?"

"Yes, sir, it was."

"Well, did you hit it?"

I didn't answer; I just turned my body in such a way that he could see the blood on my new hunting pants.

"Did you bring him in?"

"He's on the back porch."

"Well, let's take a look at him."

I have often thought what a good dad to let me go out on my own and then let me make the grand entrance, allow me to play out the drama, and savor the conquest. He could have kept me entirely safe by making me stay by the fire, he could have protected the dogs by demanding that I not take them, he could have rushed up the hill the moment he heard the race begin, or the moment he heard the gun fire. Instead, he allowed me to grow, to experience the hunt, to feel the thrill of victory, knowing that there was some risk involved.

I suppose God could take Christians the moment the put Him on in baptism and wrap them in a protective bubble. He could take from them the ability to make decisions, right or wrong. He could treat us like toddlers for all our existence – instead He allows us the freedom to achieve, to grow, to mature, knowing that with freedom, comes the risk of failure.

What a good Father.

22. <u>Snow on the Pines</u>

Most of the days of one's life simply meld into the general memory forming good or bad impressions, but some days, for whatever reason stand out in memory as clearly as if they were yesterday. One such day for me happened about 1958 when I was a boy of 14. It had come an early snow, the soft and wet kind that sort of plops down on the countryside without warning or apology. It was early December, those days when the weather dips below freezing at night but usually hovers around 50 in the day. The leaves had fallen and only the brown of the oak leaves, waiting to be pushed off with the coming spring, interrupted the starkness of the woods. School was "let out" at about ten o'clock so the big yellow jobs could get kids from out in the county home before the roads got impassable and those of us who walked home were home early with conflicting thoughts of what to do next – there were so many options.

For me the choice was easy, I grabbed the little 410 single shot Iver Johnson Daddy had given me for my 12th birthday and headed out for the Cumberland River bottom land, about 4 miles from home. I was riding "shanks mare" and the trip was an hour, so the snow continued to plop down as I walked, passing a hillside stand of long needle red pines that we had planted four or five years earlier. They were weighted down with snow and looked like an old woman in a green frockcoat bent over from the weight of time. I made a pass through the pines but neither rabbit nor quail was flushed from their hiding place. Everything was setting tight.

As I continued on toward Upper Ferry Road, the only tracks I could see were my own since it was coming down hard now and covering lighter tracks nearly as soon as they were made. I crossed Upper Ferry Road in sight of where the new Wal-Mart is today, but in those days it was all farm country.

Judge Hubert Turner owned the farm that Pa Maberry ran, and Judge Turner and I had something in common – we both loved to quail hunt. As opposed to me, he was able to do something about his hearts desire and the Tennessee Fish and Game Commission (now the TWRA) often planted quail in those rolling bottoms to the north of the Carthage bypass. The bottom land had been laden with row crops a month before and grains of corn that had been left in the gathering, along with the native grasses provided ample food for the birds which thrived once released.

Traveling in the quiet that can only come with woods sound-proofed with newly fallen snow; I finally arrived at my intended destination – a long curving slough that only held water when the Cumberland was rolling big in the springtime. It threaded it's way through fields of gathered corn, cut oats, combined soybeans, and other quail delicacies, and provided the kind of cover that always seemed to appear only in *Sports Afield Magazine*.

It had become my own private hunting preserve, my sweet spot where I was always sure of getting at least one rabbit or quail in season, or perhaps a groundhog or crow when other seasons were not open. It was like stepping into a whole different world from the neatly rowed fields, and in the dark of the slough, critters of all sorts held sway. The area was usually full of life from the tangle of honeysuckle vines at my feet to the bunched up squirrel nests at the top of the tall slender poplar trees which tucked their toes into the moist rich earth of the slough and reached for the sky above. But today it seemed like another place, quiet, so quiet you could actually hear the giant snowflakes hit the four or five inches of wet plump snow that had fallen. Not only did it sound different, it looked different. Something about the light changes when the snow falls and the shadows against the stark white make the whole place seem surreal.

Finally the snow stopped, and in a little patch of short river cane I found what I had been looking for; bird tracks close together and sort of messy looking in the snow – a covey of quail. I followed the trail slowly, then, was as always, startled when the plump bobwhites sputtered into the air – first one, then three, followed by another pair, and a final single. Just as I cocked the hammer on the little 410 single shot, another single came up right from under my feet. It was all I could do to carry out my original intent and draw down on the first single, instead of swing toward the last bird to flush. It was their plan I think, some sort of collective instinct to survive that causes them to flush the way they do; coming up in ones, twos and threes, causing you to instinctively lose concentration just as you are about to squeeze off a shot. But you must pick one and follow through on the shot, particularly if you are hunting with a single shot. Otherwise you find yourself pointing in many directions, but never pulling the trigger; always distracted by the latest thing to come up, never following through on your original intent.

It is a good lesson for life, in my opinion, pick something and follow through. Too often we try to do all things, to shoot into the covey, rather than picking one thing and concentrating on mastering that one, then moving on to another if you are so able and so inclined. Too often we think we can learn new skills, solve problems, or clean up our lives by "shooting into the bunch," and then find ourselves disappointed when we have wasted the shot.

As with quail hunting, in life we need to pick something and actually follow through on that one thing, then move on to another thing we need to master. But unlike quail hunting, in life we are not on our own – not dependant solely on our skill and ability. In our Christian lives, we have aid and comfort from The One who lives inside us.

"But if the Spirit of Him who **raised Jesus** from the dead dwells in you, He who **raised** Christ from the dead will also give life to your mortal bodies through His Spirit who dwells in you." Romans 8:11

Still, it is a good idea to take your grandmother's advice, "One thing done and that done well, is a very good rule, as many can tell."

23. <u>Agnes, I've had a Terrible Day</u>

About 1980, when I worked in Grand Rapids, Michigan, we lived in the little village of Ada. Our claim to fame in Ada was that the Amway Company had been founded there in the garage of a couple of guys named Richard DeVoss and Jay VanAndle. Their now enormous factory for the worldwide organization was still located in Ada and Rich and Jay lived there in a compound much like the Kennedy's in Hyannis port. They were to Ada what Charlie Daniels is to Mt. Juliet and were a couple of the richest and most influential dudes in America.

Ada was 16 miles out in the country from Grand Rapids, and we lived in a very modest house at the end of a cul-de-sac. We had simply had an opening bulldozed out of the New England like, hardwoods that surrounded us to clear a spot on which to locate our house. Chris was in the fourth grade and Patrick in kindergarten when we moved to Ada and it was a place we all liked immensely. I always said that my family cried and wailed when I moved them there, and cried and wailed when I moved them away. The area where our street ran was basically through a hilly, hardwood forest and had a vista of farm land where the deer grazed alongside the cattle.

The village itself was very old and had an Orvis fly fishing outfitter, a little red one room schoolhouse that had been turned into an ice cream parlor, and a bakery with a solid stone floor, lots of atmosphere, and was run by a group of Franciscan Nuns who had a farm they ran nearby. Those sisters could bake up a storm!

All in all, Ada could have been any New England town that had been transported to the west side of Michigan by magic carpet; it was beautiful.

The boys learned to fish in Ada, and there could have been no better place. The village's center attraction was a covered bridge which crossed the Thornapple River which wound its way through the town, and was filled with largemouth, smallmouth, and at certain times of the year Coho Salmon. I remember on a certain day when they went to the little lake (pond) in the subdivision. They were allowed to go there by themselves since it was not very deep, but was stocked with some pretty decent fish. Since the weather stays much cooler there than here, the water stays more aerated and small bodies of water can be very productive. They had a pretty good morning, and returned with a catch of fish, but had other things to do, so Chris put the fish in their little red Western Flyer wagon, ran some water in on top of them with a hose and shut them up in the garage. It was June.

What he had not considered was the temperature inside the garage, nor the fact that the bed of a metal wagon is not water proof. When we discovered the fish a day or two later, it was less than a treat to the olfactory nerve. Since they had been told to catch and release, we ended up burying them under the shrubs like the Indians did in order not to waste nature's bounty. Made the shrubs grow nicely too.

There was lots of wildlife around, including a family of 5 raccoons (might have been more but they were difficult to get in one place to count) moved into the wood pile in our garage. Now they have been known to eat through walls if the wall is in their way, so we put a supply of pork chop bones outside to lure them out – then shut the door and kept it closed for the next month or so.

Our neighbors across the cul-de-sac were the Inman family – Bob, Audrey, and their son Dewayne. Dewayne came running over one night and said, "Mr. Chaffin, come right away, my mother needs help." I dropped everything and ran across to their house, only to find Audrey in a tizzy. Something was in her chimney, making an awful racket. She had been poking at it with a yardstick, filled the room with chimney soot and all to no avail. Bob Inman was at work and she was beside herself – a state in which Audrey spent a fair amount of time.

I got a flashlight, looked up the chimney past the damper the best I could, and saw what looked upon first inspection, like a giant snake with head reared in the air. "Oh man, why me" was what I was thinking, but what I said was, "I don't think it's anything to worry about, but I need a coat hanger, and you and Dewayne might want to stay back there in the kitchen." You know that when a man doesn't know what else to do he will order up a coat hanger or a roll of duct tape – it is to a man what bailing wire used to be.

I worked the heavy wire hanger into a shepherd's hook and finally snagged the head of the beast (by this time I had decided it was not a snake) and dragged it out onto the hearth. It was a beautiful wood duck. After a lot of flapping and quacking and floundering around, I finally got the duck by the wings and struggled to the open patio door. Once outside, I gave the bird a boost toward the blue sky and away it flew.

Can you just imagine when that duck got home? He probably staggered in, flopped down on the couch, and said, "Agnes, I have had an awful day. First this hawk got after me but you know how sharp my eyes are – I spotted a hollow in the top of a big tree and flew in – but Agnes, I couldn't get enough wing spread to fly back out. Then this woman and a boy started poking at me with a yardstick but I ducked down and didn't budge. Then finally this big, mean, savage looking man with a hook got it around my neck and dragged me into a big cave. He had duck kabobs in his eyes, Agnes, I though I was a goner. But when he grabbed me by the wings and got close to the opening of the cave, he loosened his grip for a moment, and I threw it into overdrive and flew away. I'm lucky to be alive, Agnes, and wouldn't be if it wasn't that I am as tough and fast as I am."

If only he could have known that I meant him only good, not harm. That everything I was doing was for his benefit. That he simply didn't understand my plan for him.

That is the way we undoubtedly are with God as we thrash about and flounder around, Him with one plan for us and we, intent on our own agenda. What He intends for good, we take as evil. What we believe we have accomplished by our own cunning, he is the author of.

Did you ever think what it might be like for a slug to contemplate a human being? You have to think there are a few subtleties the slug might miss! Perhaps this is the way it is with us as we try to contemplate the infinite nature of God — there are more than a few subtleties we are apt to miss.

Perhaps we need to relax a little and let Him take control of the agenda knowing the "all thing work together for good for them that love the Lord."

Chapter IV
School Daze

As a First Grader

24. Rocky Gap School Tales

My dad went to school at Rocky Gap, a one room school on the low gap of a ridge between Blackburn's Fork and Roaring River Communities in Jackson County TN. One of my favorite stories had to do with man's ability to fix himself – or at least his big toe.

It seems little Bob was walking to school with his cousin Layton, both barefoot as usual, when he hung, or "stumped" his toe on a root protruding from the hillside path.

So grievous was the injury that he knocked his big toenail completely off exposing the bloody nail bed and creating a painful injury. After saying a couple of the words his mama had told him never to use, he limped along the path toward school.

Layton said to him, "you know that if you go back and get that toenail, you can stick it back on and it will grow back, good as new."

Little Bob was in such pain he was willing to try anything, even though the remedy didn't sound exactly right to him.

He would then continue the story, "Well sir, I went back down that hillside to where that root stuck out across the path, and got down on my hands and knees and looked for that toenail."

I would interject, "Did you find it, Daddy?"

"Son," he would say, "There were so many toenails laying around that root, I never could figure out which one was mine."

I think we might be somewhat like little Bob, trying desperately to fix ourselves, and willing to take every suggestion, no matter how much our inner voice might tell us the "home remedy" is off base.

The only one who can "fix us" is the one who made us, and try as we might, man is incapable of "pulling our own strings," and expecting a good outcome.

25. **Howdy, Annette, and Our First Television**

Daddy bought us a TV when I was in the third grade and a whole era of communication and verbal entertainment in our family and other American families ground to a halt. As for us, like most others around us, many of the stories and lyrics Daddy had shared with us stopped as we became addicted to the black and white Admiral Console model. Watching TV in those days was something of a challenge since in Carthage, fifty miles away from the transmitters, we had to have two antennas, one to pick up each of the two Nashville stations – Channel 4 and Channel 8. Even with the two antennas, I often went out in the yard to turn one or the other right or left while my sister yelled instructions from inside. (humm, it suddenly occurs to me that I was always outside doing the work and she was always inside giving directions. Well, she always said she was smarter than me, and I suppose this proves it.) Another "fine tune adjustment" consisted of a big ball of aluminum, which we slid back and forth along the antenna wire to sharpen the reception. I also remember ordering a "Color TV Kit" from some "available only on TV" vendor and receiving a red and green film of plastic which adhered to the front of the screen. Color true enough, but bearing no semblance of reality. It was an experience which made me leery of ordering from TV advertisements to this day.

I rushed home every afternoon to watch Howdy Doody, Clarabelle the Clown, Buffalo Bob, and Princes Summer-Fall-Winter-Spring. Cowboy Ruff-N-Ready provided a B-grade cowboy movie each afternoon with heroes like Johnnie McBrown, and other cowboy favorites. The Lone Ranger and

Tonto, Hop-a-long Cassidy and Topper and Dale and Roy came to life on the giant 18 inch screen and some time about the fifth grade, I discovered the Mickey Mouse Club and Annette Funachellio, my first on-screen crush. Saturdays I got up early and watched the test pattern for at least an hour waiting for Mr. Wizard to wow all of us with practical natural science experiments and Sealtest Milk to present the Big Top where we could watch the high wire acts, jugglers, and trapeze artists right in our living room.

While that first TV brought wonders we could have never dreamed of into our living rooms, it also, in time, brought a sleazy side of life, standards of conduct, unacceptable lifestyles, and ungodly language of which we could never have dreamed. It was destined to impact the American family life in a way to which no other media even came close. It is a good idea to be careful whom or what you take into your home. Sometimes when the camel gets his nose under the tent, you find the whole beast soon inside.

26. <u>On Being Bad to Flog</u>

Around the barnyard, my Great Aunt Eva had an old red rooster named Ben Franklin, with spurs about an inch long on the inside of each leg and was "bad to flog" anything he came across, including small boys if provoked in the slightest. One day my dad and the local school children were passing the only basketball at the little country school when the ball got away from little Bob and rolled down the hillside path and into the barnyard. Ben Franklin, perceiving the basketball as some type of red, round, fat, rooster moving in on his territory, promptly attacked; flogging and spurring the ball with his long sharp appendages, putting a large hole in each side. This marked the end of basketball season at Rocky Gap and caused a considerable rift between Ben Franklin and the children of Rocky Gap School.

It seems to me that we have been that way in the Lord's church, "Bad to Flog" things that we are unfamiliar with, perceiving them as danger even when they pose no threat at all. A little restraint on Ben Franklin's part would have been in order since he soon ended up snuggled in dumplings, and we might take a lesson also.

27. <u>A Relationship with the One Doing the Choosing</u>

I had a friend in elementary school named Otis Collins. Otis was bigger and stronger than most of the kids in Mrs. Bridgewater's fifth grade class because he had been "held back" a year or two. It was not that Otis was not smart enough, he was perhaps one of the smartest boys in the room; rather it was that he had been required to help his parents in the fields and was kept out of school a good deal. We raised burley tobacco in Carthage, and on a foggy fall morning as many as fifty percent of the class could be at home stripping tobacco, 100% of the kids from out in the country.

Otis was my friend, the kind of real friend that is always on your side, no matter what; the kind of friend that will let you take his pocket knife home; the kind of friend that will teach you to carve a linked chain from a single piece of wood. Being big, strong, and athletic, Otis was often chosen as captain of the playground baseball team. Now there was no organization to our ball playing other than what little we brought ourselves, but the etiquette for "choosing sides" was not to be breached.

The two captains would each begin to choose, starting with their closest friends and those of outstanding athletic ability. Having little or no athletic ability myself, I was totally dependant upon relationship. When Otis was not at school and not captain, I endured the embarrassment of standing waiting until almost everyone on the playground was chosen before my time came. Ah, but when Otis was captain he choose me right away and I felt a deep sense of gratitude to my big friend.

It occurs to me now that the only reason I was chosen was because of my relationship with the one doing the choosing. It was certainly not because of any accomplishment of my own or because of any ability I possessed. My fate was in the hands of the one doing the choosing, and in my case that turned out to be the best option.

My life is much the same; I have a relationship with the one doing the choosing. And in life as on the playground, it is neither because of any special ability nor because of any notable accomplishment that I have been chosen. It is only because of my relationship with the one doing the choosing – Jesus Christ.

28. The Marble of Great Price

I love Christmas; and I love the season and the attitude of the people around me, but what I do not love it the fact I have so little time to do other things I love, especially write.

So I am always thankful when others contribute stories. This story is another that comes from Barney Smith, a long lost cousin in Texas, who has found that he not only has a knack for story telling, he also enjoys it.

All of us who grew up in the days of Howdy, Buffalo Bob, and Crusader Rabbit remember when trading was a way of life among the grade school set. The brown eyed girl, who loves to ice skate, also loves to tell of acquiring her first pair of ice skates by trading some other, now long forgotten treasure, for her first pair of figure skates.

Among the boys however, the marble was the coin of the realm and blessed was he whose pockets were bulging from a full tobacco sack of the round beauties; and anyone who knows what, "Playing for Keeps, knucks down, aggies, taws, steelies, and cat-eyes are, will enjoy Barney's story of playground days.

"The Fabulous Crystal Marble-----
I hate to always be looking backward in life, but who we are is, of course, a result of our life experiences. At nearly 70 years old, I am amazed at the technology that everyone younger than I seems to love so much. In my youth, not many family homes even had those big black ugly telephones; and now every kid above the age of eight has a tiny cell phone in his pocket and a stack of those bewildering video games in his room. I've noticed that county road workers, always famous for leaning on their shovels, are now also talking on their cell phones. The internet is a constant astonishment to me and I have developed a love-hate relationship with it; but I digress.
I remember a simpler time of no air conditioning or television, a time when a kid had to devise his own

entertainment and money was something that no kids and only a few adults possessed. When I was about ten or eleven years old, the boys in my small town played marbles. Each boy would keep a pretty good stash of marbles in a sock drawer or some other equally safe place, away from the prying eyes and fingers of little brothers and sisters; while we typically kept our "walking around" marbles in a Bull Durham tobacco pouch. Marbles represented the economy of our ragtag and nondescript group. Most of the marbles were cheap, dime store marbles, but each boy had his favorites, and trading marbles was probably as much fun as playing. He would usually have a taw (favorite marble) and an agate or two and maybe a "steelie" or two. A "steelie" was a ball bearing that some boys favored over conventional marbles, because they were rumored to be capable of busting another glass marble to pieces.

We played marbles by the hour and were subjected to many a sermon by our mothers and teachers about the sin of gambling with marbles. We were strictly forbidden to play for "keeps", a game where you got to keep your opponent's marbles if you won. Conversely, if you lost, you "lost your marbles," as the saying goes. Needless to say, although we nodded and looked serious during the "sermon," the lectures had little or no effect on us.

I was not a seriously good marble player but I had one marble that was unique and highly esteemed by the neighborhood denizens. This marble solidified my position in our social strata and I have not told anyone, until now, how I acquired this beauty.

In those days, I had a paper route which I worked by bicycle and stayed busy all over town delivering the "Amarillo Globe". On my deliveries, I took particular notice of the traffic signs of the day. Stop signs were yellow back then and most intersections did not have stop signs at all. There were one or two "red" lights in town but after seven o'clock in the evening they became blinking stop lights. What really caught my attention was "curve" warning signs. They were yellow and diamond shaped as they are today, but they were outlined by little clear marbles that reflected at night in headlights. After passing by this temptation countless times, I found myself alone on the road one day, and unable to resist further, took out my trusty scout knife and, with some difficulty and not a little damage to the knife, popped one out and put it in my "walking around" pouch. Except for the guilt over stealing the marble and damaging county property, I didn't think too much about the marble itself. Consequently, I was pleasantly amazed at the attention the crystal beauty received from the marble playing boys of our town. A Faberge' egg would have run a poor and distant second in our circle. It was a regular looking marble but was as clear as a crystal ball. I didn't tell the other boys where I got this marble because I didn't want to unleash a crime wave on all the signs of the town; and even at that young age I must have understood the theory of supply and demand. I figured that it would lower the value of my beauty if they knew how easy it was to get one of their own. "Little George" Richmond lived next door to me and coveted the marble and began a crusade to "trade" for it. He offered his baseball glove, a first

95

baseman's mitt (in seriously sad shape but still a baseball glove). I declined all offers and played the waiting game. Finally, about dark one day, he came over pushing his old bicycle. Would I consider trading my marble for the bike? I could hardly keep a straight face. The bike was old, had no fenders or chain guard, the handlebars were rusty, but the tires were fair and held air, and it was better than the bicycle which I currently did not have. I rode that old bicycle hundreds of miles and that may have been the only time in my life that I ever made a profit on anything.

Barney's story reminds one of the parables Jesus told about the Pearl of Great Price, or the Treasure Hidden in a Field, which when discovered became the sole desire of the discoverers. While "Little George" may have been less than discriminating in his choice of treasures, his actions were like those of the seekers in the parables. They were willing to trade all else for the single treasure.

The "good news" is that Jesus told this parable when telling what "the Kingdom of Heaven is like," and we are able to secure it while trading our sin and guilt and "to boot" receiving the abundant life promised by the one referred to as; Wonderful, Counselor, God With Us.

29. <u>The Trip up School House Hill</u>

I just talked with my sister who is on a driving trip to Washington State with her husband. She was in their Roadtrek Van passing Fort Lewis Washington, and I was doing my daily walk down West Main in Lebanon, TN. I had called her just to check that they were safely on their course and no bad luck had befallen them. Thanks to the miracle of the cell phone it was as easy as pie – it still amazes me.

She and I are the best of friends now, but it has not always been the case. Today, no child would start to their first day of school without at least one parent accompanying them to class, and more likely both, but it was a different time and my parents had built the Community Grocery across from the Cattle Sale Barn (the structure now owned by Joe and Robbie Oldham) and had a store to run. They left the chore of getting me properly enrolled to my sister, Donnieta – then just turned ten.

Ten years old in 1950 was much older that ten years old today – 60 years later – at least in terms of what we were expected to be able to accomplish. Ten years old must have seemed pretty grown up to our parents, who had been raised in a society where schooling came to an end for many children by the fifth grade. Boys were expected to go into full time farming and marriage for 14 year old girls was not unusual. By eighteen, most girls were married and at 20 they began to be considered candidates for becoming old maids. But as for me, in the reluctant custody of my ten year old sister, I began the long and often unpleasant marathon which would be my 19 years of formal education. It was truly a case of the unwilling, leading the incompetent, on a nearly impossible mission.

The walk to school in Carthage was an equal opportunity torture trip as this bastion of education was built on top of "School House Hill." No matter where you lived, it was necessary to pull up the steep hill with a heavy burden in the morning but one could return home at night with flying feet (or later flashing spokes) and a light heart. The post war baby boom had hit (actually, snuck up on) Carthage Elementary School by 1950, as those of us born at the end of WWII came of schooling age. I always suspected that the baby boom was as much a result of the prosperity which came when the war brought the great depression to an end, as it was the return of soldiers, particularly in my case since my father, a farmer, had not gone off to war but had labored on the home front growing crops and livestock to feed the country. Whatever the reason, on the first day of school there were more first graders than had been expected and I ended up in an "overflow room" which held both a second grade and a first grade class. It was an unexpected and troubling occurrence for me.

I sometimes wonder why my sister and I are such good friends now when we were a case study in sibling rivalry and discord in our growing up years. I suppose it is a testimony to the fact that shared hardship creates a bonding experience. Studies show, families who spend time camping together and traveling together bond, not only because of the good times, but expressly because of the shared hardships and difficulties. (If you are a camper who has experienced tent camping with a couple of small kids on a rainy weekend, you know what I mean, if not, well you probably don't understand.) Life is like that I suppose, it may be the valleys that bond us together more than the peaks and the rough sections of road which make us appreciate the smooth. The solace for those of us who are believers is that whether in the deepest valley or on the highest mountain top – He will never leave us nor forsake us.

We will talk more of this subject.

30. <u>Going on Strike at Carthage Elementary</u>

In the preceding story we started talking about the experience of starting school in Carthage TN in 1950 and ran out of time so let's continue with that thought. After my sister had delivered me to the first grade room, a tall lady whom I would later know was Miss Allen (we called them all Miss – it's a southern thing) announced that there were more first graders than had been expected – there was no kind of pre-registration that I remember. Therefore, the ones whose names were called would be sent to an overflow room.

Just being told I was being sent to an "overflow room" was scary to a youngster who was much more timid then that my personality in later years would have led one to believe. I didn't know what an "overflow" room was and my only connection with the word was that it was what the river did when the spring rains came too frequently – it overflowed. (There were Ridge Runners (people who lived on the hills and ridges) and River Rats in our society and I had always been a River Rat (those who lived in the low bottom land by the rivers). Knowing that the word, as I knew it, was associated with misery and sometimes tragedy, my first few days of school were something of a discouragement, and prompted by fear of punishment for something (I knew not what) that was not my fault, I went on a sit-down strike within a few days of school opening. My actions understandably sparked frustration and anger approaching rage, in my adolescent sister.

It all came about because on the third day of classes, Mr. Massey, the principal, explained that anyone making a mess in the new hot lunch cafeteria (the government funded pride of Smith County) would be promptly be sent to his office for a paddling. That was enough of that for me. Being against violence, particularly when directed at my personal body, I decided not to participate in this madness and simply skip elementary school. I figured I could just hang out at the store until time to go to high school, but I had not quite figured our how to explain this to my parents. At the risk of sounding like one of those old timers who talk about how much better is was in the olden days, and as incredible as it may seem in this day and time, in 1950, fathers explained to their children that if you got a whipping at school you were likely to get a second dose of the same medicine at home. It appeared to me that I was about to get beaten, not once but twice, as a result of my lack of fine motor skill development – which I considered to be genetics and therefore a technical difficulty beyond my control. It became the start of a highly honed sense of dislike for anything which I considered unfair, and the trait continues to this day.

As I said, I had not quite figured out how to break this to my parents so I was not sure exactly how to proceed, but on the day following Mr. Massey's speech, when we arrived at the Old Chamber's mansion at the top of school house hill, I sat down – announcing to Donnieta that I was not going to go any further, and assuring her that I would be glad to wait right there so she could pick me up on her way home.

Donnieta, now in Mrs. Bridgewater's fifth grade, had already developed a social life, (girls tend to be early social developers) and was already deeply concerned that Roberta Oldham, Ann Robinson, Barbara Stiltz, Elizabeth Ann Masters, or one of her other friends, would observe her walking her little brother to school, a plight which resulted in social ostracism. To see her having to deal with a little brother who was belligerent, and had opted for peaceful civil disobedience, was intolerable and added insult to injury. In her quest to get me moving again, she would move from asking patiently, to speaking sternly, to begging, pleading, and screaming, on up to crying and whining to get me going. She would cajole and threaten, with nothing working until she finally spun on her heel and started back home to get Mama. Then, and only then, with the clear and present danger of Mama's peach tree switch before me, when absolute certainty exceeded vague dread, I would reluctantly follow her to school.

This dance with no music, went on for several days with Donnieta reporting the infraction of the rules each night, followed by specific reinstruction by Mama – which we called "getting' a talking to" followed by promises on my part to do better tomorrow, proof positive that even the threat of torture could elicit a desired response from the one being interrogated. Despite my promises, the next day brought more of the same at the top of schoolhouse hill.

Finally, it occurred to someone to simply ask me what the problem was. I wept mightily, doing that snuffling thing, where you draw in a breath uncontrollably, and utter a word between breaths – "I" (snuff) "am" (snuff) "gonna" (snuff) "get" (snuff, followed by much snot wiping then wailing loudly,) "a whipping" (snuff, snuff) "and I cain't help it." The last disclaimer was the result, of course, of my perception of my clumsiness as an inherited trait and therefore not my fault. After a masterful combination of motherly reassurance and a firm parental reminder that the consequences to be suffered right there at home of such continued misbehavior, would surly posed a greater danger and ought to be feared more than any trip to Mr. Massey's office; I finally saw the error of my ways and resolved to go on to school and take what might come. You see sometimes children just need their parents to fully explain the ultimate consequences of their bad choices.

I know it isn't popular to talk about the wages of sin in our churches any more, but perhaps we need to be more like my mother. In her love for me, she was willing to explain to me the consequences of my bad behavior in a clear and understandable fashion. Why, because she wanted the ultimate best for me and realized that that would come from years of pulling up School House Hill.

God also wants the best for us, and has left it up to Christians to explain the consequences of bad behavior in a clear and understandable fashion. It is not popular and it can only be effective when it comes from a loving source, but it must be done.

31. <u>Miss Young's Fourth Grade Class</u>

This year our oldest granddaughter, Maggie, starts fourth grade. Her school is beautiful and we are always pleased when we get invited to Grandparent's Day, or Veteran's Day, or Author's Day or any other excuse to view her in her natural habitat.

It was 55 years ago that I started fourth grade, and as strange as it may seem, it seems like yesterday, at least in some ways. We went to see the movie "Time Travelers Wife" this weekend and I remarked to Jan that I felt almost like a time traveler, since it seems that I was in one stage of my life, and then – Poof – found myself in another.

It was always pretty hot when we started to school at Carthage Elementary since the August sun was still beating down and temperatures soared into the high nineties daily. There was no air conditioning, which was no surprise because in 1954 none of us had it at home either. The big old steel frame windows opened by swinging inward at the bottom panel which let in some air, but deflected the flow upward to keep from blowing the papers off our desk. The whole place smelled like sweaty little kids from late August until the middle of October and in those days most of us only got a bath on Saturday night and before Wednesday night church. Sometimes, if you were really crafty, you could even skip the Wednesday night ordeal, but not often. Trying to keep the paper you were working on dry was a problem, and Mrs. Young, our fourth grade teacher, taught us to lay a piece of tablet paper under our writing hand forearm to absorb the sweat and keep our hand-in work dry.

We sat in those desks that had been designed to be affixed to a wood floor by means of a large screw; you remember, the tops sloped and still had a round hole in the top, on the right hand side, which had been intended for the inkwell. Inkwells had already passed into antiquity by my school years, but the hole itself provided all kinds of amusements for 10 year old boys and with an old cigar box placed just right beneath it, could become an emergency repository for coins, marbles, arrow heads, and tractors made with spools from Mama's sewing machine – sometimes you had to get rid of that pesky thread which remained in order to put the spool to it's highest and best use.

The school officials had been called upon to improvise when we moved from the old building with its wood floors into the new, concrete floored building, and had attached the desks to long 1 x 4 strips of unpainted and unfinished pine. That kept them from turning over and allowed for military precision in lining the desks up. Since each desk consisted of a seat that folded down in front and the desk top behind, each student was sitting on the seat from the desk unit behind them, that meant that the front desk had a seat with no desk before it and could be used as the penalty box. If you talked during quiet time, or engaged in other infractions of the rules, a kid might be required to march forward and sit on the front seat where "Miss" Young could keep a closer eye on him, and where he could become the object of derision from other scholars. (No one worried much about our psyche in those days.)

We all started the school year with new clothes since we had worn out, out grown, or torn up, the prior year's school clothes. My wardrobe was always pretty much the same. Mama ordered two pairs of blue jeans from the Sears Roebuck Catalogue. (I wonder what happened to Mr. Roebuck?) They were either the ones that had double knees or later my mother bought "iron on patches" and heat sealed them to the knees, because shooting marbles and other on-your-knees activities soon took their toll. I also got three new shirts, usually flannel shirts of loud colors and busy plaid patterns.

The two pairs of pants went like this – Start with a clean pair on Wednesday night for church that had been washed starched and dried on pants stretchers to avoid ironing. That pair had to be changed out of the moment you got home – absolutely no playing in school clothes. Those were worn to school on Thursday and Friday and to town on Saturday. Dress clothes and play clothes on Sunday, then on Monday you got a fresh pair, expected to last through Wednesday, and the others went into that weeks wash. And so it went; when I got to high school, I graduated to three pairs of black corduroy pants – but that is another story.

So armed with new, stiff jeans – which were bound to turn your "whitey tighties" blue, and flannel shirts the colors of the rainbow, we all marched off to get an education – which no one could ever take away from you – according to our parents.

As I sit here writing it all seems as yesterday, and the thoughts and fears of that time do not seem far off at all. In my mind I can still smell the smell of chalk when the erasers are being dusted, hear the creak of the windows being opened, see the brown color of the playground dust, and feel the wonder of a life spread out ahead in seemingly unending waves of time.

Yep, "life is but a vapor that appears for a little while, and then vanishes away." Better make the most of each day so there are few regrets.

32. <u>Snow Days in Smith County</u>

It is that moment in the morning when you think you are awake but your conscious mind has not cleared to the point that you are really dead sure. I open my eyes and the light is streaming through the un-curtained windows of my upstairs room. The old fashioned wide-slat venetian blinds are open, as I left them every night. I liked the illumination of the street light on the corner, a naked large wattage bulb with a fluted piece of tin painted white on the bottom and green on the top, to shine into my room and serve as a free night light to scare the "boogers" away.

Only the top part of my face, from the nose up, was sticking out from under the covers, since there was no heat in the upstairs rooms where I slept, and I was packed down by several hand made quilts from the big wooden box in which Mama stored them. The drill was that a kid crawled under the mound of quilts and into the cold sheets on a winter night and kicked his feet, in the fashion of one riding a bicycle, until the bed warmed, then settled down on his back and drifted off to sleep, awakening in the same position in the morning since the weight of the quilts prevented tossing and turning.

(Boy, I would hate to try that now with aches in back and legs.)

I had been awakened by the smell of frying bacon, or maybe it was sausage, but it was surely some kind of salt pork. The only exception to salt pork would be if we had just killed hogs and had tenderloin or ribs that were fresh; but since it was February and hog killing time had long passed those delicacies were long gone. Adie (my great aunt, Ada, who lived with us.) would be making breakfast since Mama would be getting ready to go to work at the grocery store.

As I started to move, I noticed that the top quilt was covered with a light dusting of white powder and the light coming into the room had a grey metallic quality to it. Then it hit me – it had snowed during the night and the white stuff had drifted onto the bed through the broken window pane which Daddy had neither the time nor the money to replace. Besides, his theory was that a little fresh air never hurt anyone. "Why Son, some of the houses I lived in growing up had cracks in the walls so wide that you could throw a hound dog through them and never skin his sides." (Yeah right, and it was three miles to school, uphill both ways.)

But the conditions under which I slept were the last thing on my mind now, as I hopped out of bed, pulled on the pair of britches I had worn Monday and Tuesday. (A clean pair on Monday, wear that pair Tuesday and Wednesday, and get a clean pair for Prayer Meeting on Wednesday night – those would see you through the balance of the week.) A quick look out the window revealed about 5 or 6 inches of snow had fallen overnight. Now, five or six inches of snow in Smith County is good for about a week or two out of school. Not because, as the folks up north imagined, we didn't know how to drive in the snow. (We didn't but that wasn't the reason for closing school.)

Not because we had no snow removal equipment; which we didn't since investing in snow plows, that would only see use every couple of years or so, did not make good economic sense in a town like ours.

Rather, it was because the thawing and refreezing of the snow that would take place on the north side of hills and bluffs turned the fluffy white stuff into treacherous ice – often on the side of a bluff that dropped into a deep holler or a creek below. The penalty for leaving the road in Smith County could be disaster. Not like up north where sliding off the road meant going into someone's yard or field, only to get pulled out and maybe pay for minor damage to the vehicle. Failure here meant possible death and dismemberment of a student, and since the district collected state money based on headcount of students in attendance… Well, perhaps I had better not go there.

Usually, if you just hunkered down for a couple of days or a week, the One who put it there (the snow) would take it away as the temperature rose into the 50s again. In the meantime it meant a winter vacation for the students of the Smith County School system – thank you Mr. B. Clark Meadows!

One of life's great joys is anticipation of expected reward, and I was expecting the reward of a Snow Day at Carthage Elementary School.

These days, 55 years later, much of my joy comes from expecting the reward of a life with Him when this life is finished. We will talk more of Snow Days in the next story.

33. **Where in the World are my Overshoes**

I didn't stop to pull on the rest of my clothes in the cold upstairs bedroom, rather I grabbed my shirt and socks and dashed hurriedly to the stairs, being careful to walk on my heels, holding the flat of my feet up off the cold linoleum floor and painted steps. When I got downstairs the big old cold fired octopus of a furnace had warmed the main floor to a toasty 69 degrees or so. It had been banked with ashes the night before to keep the coal from burning up during the night and the fire from going out, then having to be restarted with kindling and coal oil in the morning. (Restarting a fire with coal oil always put one at risk of facing the next few months with no eyebrows.) I grabbed one of the hickory bark bottomed straight chairs in the kitchen and pulled it up to the old brown plastic Truetone radio and dialed the radio to WSM – "*650 on your radio dial*" and waited for the man to give the list of school closings.

"The following schools will be closed due to the snow which has blanketed the Upper Cumberland Area. Davidson County Schools, Jackson County Schools, White County Schools, Putnam County Schools, Warren County Schools, Summer County Schools, Bedford County Schools, Macon County Schools, Clay County Schools, Wilson County Schools will be delayed two hours,"

"Come on, come on, what about Smith County?"

"Now this just handed to me, Mr. B. Clark Meadows has notified us that Smith County Schools..."

(I hold my breath so I won't miss the words)..."

"will be closed."

"Rats"; Immediately a wave of regret washed over me, since I had spent a good part of prime TV watching time the night before working on a stupid book report for Miss. Young, my fourth grade teacher, and now who knows when I will really have to turn it in?

I got over it quickly however, as thoughts of how to spend the day flew through my head like so many bats catching bugs at a football game. Fisher Avenue, yes definitely, Fisher Avenue, is where everyone will be.

"Mama, where are my goulashes?" We all wore those black, five buckle Arctic type that were usually bought several sizes too big so you could "grow into them" over the next two or three years. And I, for one, hated them since they added about five pounds per leg to the load you were carrying and made you look really ridiculous. I had learned by the scars of previous battles however, that going out in the wet slushy Tennessee snow without them would only bring a ruined pair of shoes, and swift and sure retribution by Mama who was an artist with a peach tree switch. As to knowing where they were though, I had not sought their company since last year, when the last snow of 1953 had departed.

"I think they are on the end of the shelf in the basement where the fruit jars are setting – run down there and look because I don't want you going out in this mess without them – do you hear me?"

"Yes'um, I hear."

Oh no, a trip to the furnace room, the spider capital of the world. Our house had been started when we bought it, and Daddy had made some concessions to cost in the finishing of the house. Our lot fell away sharply toward the little creek that ran to the back of our house and was a perfect location for a "walk out" basement. The front foundation wall had been erected on a footing poured at the bottom of a two or three foot deep trench but the excavation to basement floor level was not finished prior to our acquisition of the house. We had dug out the front dirt making a cut and used it against the back wall to create a more or less level basement floor. Later Daddy had run a studded wall down between the front half where the furnace was and the back half, which had windows and a door, poured a concrete floor in the back half and left a dirt floor on the front side. That front half was the furnace room. It contained the monster coal fired gravity flow furnace, the big pile of chunk coal, some shelves Daddy had built to house "fruit jars" and other seasonal items and to store canned garden stuff. Since it had been left with no windows being on the upper side of the house, had a dirt floor, and a coal chute that went outside, there were all manner of critters down there, but not a sign of light. It was dark as pitch, even at noontime. I grabbed the flashlight that was at the door that divided it from other parts of the basement and assuming what I believed to be an attitude of bravery, marched in.

Just as I was about to slide through the door, Daddy called down the stairs, "As long as you are down there, you put about four big chunks of coal on that fire."

Caught, not only did I now have to find the required snow gear, I had to rummage around in that coal pile, which I was sure contained an unlimited quantity of snakes, just waiting to pounce on an unsuspecting boy. I finally located the missing overshoes inside the big five gallon pressure cooker Mama and Adie used for canning, chunked four big lumps of coal into the belly of the glowing red beast, wiped the cobwebs off my face, shivered like a dog coming in from the rain, and headed back up the stairs, two at a time. When I got almost to the top, I spied Mama's aluminum dishpan, bounded back down the stairs, opened the outside door to the basement and set the dishpan just to the left of the door. What was on my mind was not something I cared to have become the subject of parental discussion.

Having put on my best cold weather under-gear, I snatched up my blue gabardine coat with the fur collar and belt with a silver hook and eye affair which served as a buckle. I got a couple of pair of Daddy's green U.S. Army type socks out of the drawer and pulled them over my hands and tucked them inside the knitted cuffs of the coat. Put on the overshoes and I was in business – ready for a day of sledding. Well, I didn't really have a sled, but then that was where the dishpan entered the plan. There were a few kids who had actual Western Flyer sleds with steerable runners, but most of us used a coal shovel, a tub, a piece of tin (which could be wicked if not rolled in front), an inner tube, or a piece of cardboard. The days of cheap plastic disks with nylon rope handles were far in the future and we were called on to use whatever was at hand.

I tucked Mama's dishpan under my arm and started out toward Jackson Avenue where I could see a couple of kids, probably Don Taylor and Walter Booker, doing some practice runs down the hill that ran by Ben Herman Thomas' house. By the time I got out to the corner of Dogwood and Jackson, a host of sled aficionados were headed for Fisher Avenue.

By the end of the day, I had frozen ears, a big tear in my new blue coat, and a hole in Mama's dishpan. I had to buy her a new one, which I still have – after all, I paid for it. Snow days were the best!

When I hear others speak of their troubled childhood, I almost feel guilty about my own up binging. I had nothing by today's standards – yet I had everything. It had been given to me with good measure, pressed down, shaken together, and running over – Just like God gives to us. We serve a father who desires to flood us with His grace and mercy – if we will only accept His hand.

34. <u>Smoke, Smoke, Smoke that Cigarette</u>

When I was about 12 years old, my crowd at Carthage Elementary began experimenting with smoking. Carthage was a town that had as its core source of income the cash earned by farmers raising tobacco, and the numerous warehouses to which tobacco was brought and auctioned. Many years ago there was one that was owned by Dr. Sloan and his brother

Billy Sloan that opened right out on Main Street, just up from the Walton Hotel, if I remember correctly. As a result, smoking was a way of life.

In those days it was common for men to stand around outside the church building smoking until the last minute – and often after the last minute – before coming inside for worship services. It was rare indeed for anyone to hear a sermon or class in which smoking was condemned. (Political correctness is not new, only re-centered.) I remember well that when I was the janitor of the church building there in Carthage, I would weekly have to sweep up the cigarette butts crushed out just before the would-be worshiper entered the side door.

So in short, it was a town where young people learned to smoke early and smoke often. If you were big enough to plunk your quarter on the counter, you were big enough to buy cigarettes. Even my sister, who was an avowed "goody two shoes," a fact which always served to aggravate the life out of me, experimented with smoking. Yes she did! For I remember after she had a few friends over for the night, finding the cigarette butts in the old crock churn which stood as decoration in her upstairs, Pepto Bismol pink, bedroom. Apparently she and her friends, who shall remain anonymous to protect the guilty, had learned the secrets of ventilation and air control necessary for teenage smoking. It was long before the Surgeon General announced the absolute link between smoking and cancer and the only thing adults told adolescents was, "it will stunt your growth."

Halloween was coming up in a week or two, and I prepared by going to the little store, now operated by a couple by the name of Alexander, and buying a pack of Kools to increase my smoking pleasure on Halloween night. (I guess I thought I had grown enough.) Well, after puffing away on two or three and starting to feel a little woozy, I decided not to overdo this smoking thing and returned home with the rest of the pack still in my possession. Wanting to make sure I was not caught with the evidence on my person, I crept back into the attic where a big wooden quilt box sat and stuffed the cigarettes down into the bottom of the box, under a couple of old quilts.

What I did not count on was that shortly after October 31st cold weather would come and within a couple of days, Mama announced at supper that she had been back in the attic getting some quilts out for winter and the strangest thing happened. She had discovered a package of cigarettes. She paused after the announcement and looked expectantly around the table for some response. No one said a word and I became intensely interested in the exact makeup of the green beans on my plate. Finally, being unable to stand the silence, I suggested that since my Uncle Billy had been working on the roof a couple of weeks ago, perhaps he had placed them there. Never mind that there was absolutely no access to the attic from the roof without climbing down the ladder and coming through the door of the house, then going upstairs, and back into the attic. When confronted with discovery or lying, I lied – boy no easy way to put that!

"Why on earth would he have put them there?" Mama inquired with apparent wide eyed curiosity.

"Well, he was probably hot and sweaty and didn't want them to get all wet and soggy,' was the only semi-logical reply I could muster. I knew I was busted.

I knew she knew – and she knew, that I knew, that she knew – so she never said another word about it.

On at least two other occasions, when I had been smoking, she would say at the supper table, "I think I smell smoke. Does anyone else smell that?"

I generally resorted to, "I was burning some brush out in the back." Of course, I now know that burning brush and cigarette smoke do not smell anything alike, since nothing is more attuned to the smell of cigarette smoke than an ex-smoker, but she left it at that.

That's the way Big Bob and Maylean were, once they had brought you face to face with your own failings, they relied on the moral teaching they had carefully given you to convict you. They never saw a need to drive it into the ground, to embarrass you, or to call you a liar. They trusted that the conscience they and the creator had endowed you with would do its job.

I continued to smoke off and on through college and through my years in the U.S. Army, allowing it to be my vice of choice, then quit when my boys were small and the public service spot ran on TV that showed a little boy walking through the woods with his daddy, watching his dad light up, then the little boy himself pulling a cigarette from the pack and pretending to smoke. The caption, "They want to be like you," convinced me.

As a child I remember my cousin Morris teaching me this little ditty in preparation for a performance for our parents.

Tobacco is a filthy weed,
From the devil it doth proceed,
It blacks you hands and burns your clothes,
And makes a chimney of you nose.

I wish I could have been as good a parent to our boys as my parents were to Donnieta and me. I was sometimes so intent on demonstrating to the boys that they couldn't fool me, that I only succeeded in "provoking them to wrath." Rather, I should have allowed them to arrive at their own conviction, and be faced with their own moral compass.

It is a lesson we must learn when dealing with others in the church, God has given all of us free will, the right to make our own bad choices, and the right to follow our own misguided paths, and while we may bring others to the place of confronting their bad choices, they must be convicted by their own conscience.

"You can lead a horse to water, but you can't make him drink."

35. <u>Sipping Cider from a Purex Bottle</u>

I was never sure why I got the blame except that perhaps I was the oldest of the crowd and past experience had taught her that I was generally in the middle of mischief. The Rankin's had built a cabin on the river over in Horseshoe Bend on the Maggart farm (Justine Maggart) and we all liked to hang out there and spend the night. Once when we were on the farm, we discovered an apple tree in the old orchard that was hanging full of apples. For some inexplicable reason, I announced that I knew how to make apple cider and that we could let it ferment until it was "hard." Being in high school, that seemed like an activity that contained just the right amount of risk and was "anti establishment.: It was, after all, the sixties and being counter cultural was very in. I had a sausage grinder at my house and we ground the apples in the sausage grinder, wrung the juice out with a dish towel, and put the cider into a couple of old bottle neck jugs which we found in my mothers basement collection of canning equipment. We took the jugs of cider to Lindy's house and set them up in the very back of a corner kitchen cabinet to acquire the proper age. Our attention soon turned to other things and we forgot about the cider – until one morning about six in the morning when I heard the phone ring and my mother answered. "Yes? Oh hello, Yes he is here. Sure, I'll call him."

"Buddy, Justine Rankin is on the phone for you."

Oh, this can't be good when one of your friend's mother is calling you house at six in the morning and asking for you.

"Hello Mrs. Justine."

"You get yourself down to my house and do it right now."

"Yes mam, is something wrong?"

"Is something wrong?" she mocked my whiny voice, "I should say so, those jugs of cider in my cabinets just blew the doors off the cabinet and there is sticky gunk all over my kitchen. Now get your britches on and get down here because Willie Mae is not cleaning this mess up."

We were all late to school that day because glass jugs had to be picked up, and Honey's kitchen cleaned to perfection before we were allowed to leave. It was one time I was glad to get on my way to school.

One of the great things in life is Not getting what you deserve. A fellow I know told of going to the Holy Land, and when they passed the place where God was supposed to have zapped Uzzah for touching the Ark of the Covenant, he asked their Jewish guide, "Why do you suppose God was so tough on Uzzah?" He said the guide looked at him as if he were offended and said, "For the Jew, that is an inappropriate question – for us the question is, why did the rest of us get off?"

Isn't it great to know that as a Christian, you will get not what you deserve, but what God in his Mercy confers on you? How good is that?

36. <u>Pond Creatures</u>------

Some of the best days I can remember were centered on farm ponds. We had several on the Turner farm and they all had a different allure. One of them was behind our house and is down the hill from the old barn that is now visible from the highway 25 bypass. If you look to your left when traveling from Wal-Mart and going toward the MacDonald's Restaurant in town, (west bound) you will see the old barn sitting on a knob, just before the zinc mine comes into view. You will have to look in the winter because other than in January and February, the foliage will block your view and the barn won't be visible.

In the days before the bypass, or before town had pushed its way out into perfectly good pasture land, our little 4 room house sat there, just off Upper Ferry Road. The pond there was a big one, or so it seemed then, but when I recently walked over to take a look at it, it seemed pitifully small. I think it may have shrunk over the past 55 years. While we lived there Judge Turner, who owned the farm, decided to drain the pond, have it cleared of mud and silt and enlarged. Daddy worked for a week or more digging a ditch from the pond to the little creek which ran nearby, and I remember clearly when the pond finally broke through and the water gushed out in a muddy torrent.

I was watching carefully because someone had gone to Florida and brought back a baby alligator (was something people did then) and put it into the pond. I had imagined the alligator had gotten to be somewhere around ten feet long, and I was very leery about going around the pond, where I had a strong suspicion I would become a tasty morsel for the gator. I watched and watched for the next week as the pond level slowly lowered, but no gator. Only an assortment of wash tub sized mud turtles, and stunted blue gill.

When the process was eventually finished and a bulldozer brought in to clear the mud and debris, I had another interesting day watching the man clean the muddy soup out of the pond. I think it was my first view of a bulldozer, up close and personal.

Finally, the pond was refilled and stocked with a balance of fish recommended by the County Agent, and for years to come, long after we had moved from the little 4 room house, I fished in the pond. I would walk over to Ma Ma and Pa Maberry's house, catch up the old mare, crawl on her back and with no saddle or bridle she would walk over to the pond with me on her back. Hardly a process that one could call riding, but it got me there, nevertheless.

At that pond I perfected my fly fishing skills, learning the fine points of the front loop, the barrel roll, and of taking a tiny mouthed Blue Gill on a black gnat. I would go late on a summer day and often stay until dark. My parents seldom worried about my whereabouts since not much was likely to happen to you in Carthage. No one was ever kidnapped that I know of, and if there were any child molesters thereabouts, I didn't know of it. I was into catch and release before I even knew that it was a concept and I am sure some of those fish were worn out from being caught by me so many times. There was never a reason to be bored for a farm kid though.

The other pond on the place was the one on the river side of the bypass and is easily visible from the road very soon after leaving Wall Mart. I remember quite well when that pond was dug. There was little need for a pond there for many years because most of that land was either in corn, silage mix, or in Oats and Lespedeza or Alfalfa used to feed the 3 pair of mules, it took to operate the place or to feed the milk cows. As the front pasture was sold off and became 60 X 120 foot town lots on Myer's Terrace, or the north end of Jackson, or Jefferson Avenue. (Town stopped at Clyde and Margret Whites house on Jefferson, at Walter Booker's house on Jackson, and at the football field down from school house hill. The rest of what is now town was all pasture.) At any rate, as the farm contracted, the need grew greater and greater to use the land where the bypass now bisects as pasture land for beef cattle and there was only a trickle of water running from the spring where all of us on the farm got water. So in about

1955, a pond was dug and, sure enough, the spring filled it in short order, and continues to do so to this day.

That pond was the swimming pond and Jacky Woodard, Mitchell Ramsey, Foster Smith's son Jody and I utilized it for that purpose often. No, we didn't have bathing suits but the cows didn't seem to mind and we didn't either. The likelihood of traffic and prying eyes on Upper Ferry Road was just about nil.

On one day, Jody announced that his sisters were going swimming later that day and we decided to hide in the bushes on the other side of the road and satisfy our curiosity about the other sex. We likely were not even sure why they were the other sex, but after hiding for a couple of hours, we were just about to give up and go fishing when down the road they came. It was only then that it occurred to me that I was so near-sighted that I couldn't see across the road and was not likely to get much of a lesson in anatomy, but I hung in there just to be a good sport. The suspense built as they made their way down to the pond, spread their blanket on the bank of the pond, and then it happened. They simply waded into the pond wearing their blouses and cutoff jeans. Foiled again! I decided this life of debauchery was hardly worth the pain of waiting in the hot sun.

Now our farm ponds are full to overflowing, with the overflow pipes gushing water. No one looking at them now would be able to conceive of the drought a couple of years ago when the dried up to a little trickle and a patch of mud. No one looking at the sad little pond surrounded by two hundred thousand dollar homes would be able to conceive of the solitude and beauty that pond provided when I was a youngster, and no one flying by on the highway 25 bypass, in sight of Wall Mart, would be able to conceive of 4 little boys jay birding' without a care in the world in just that spot.

Life is filled with beauty and opportunity, whether you decide to let it be something that builds you up spiritually or give in to your baser nature to satisfy you prurient desires and interests is up to you.

All-in-all though, I am pretty thankful that God gave us free will and choices and we can decide to follow our animal nature or our God-like nature.

"And the Lord God made them living beings" or Nephesh Kiah (pronounced nef'ish Kai ah) which in Hebrew means Living Beings. The same word is used, not just for man, but for all of the animal creation. The difference comes when in the case of man He said, "Let us make man in Our Own Image" and it is that, that God spark, that ability to distinguish right from wrong, to act in other than our own selfish best interest that separates us from the rest of the Nephesh Kiah. Otherwise, we would be no different from the dog or the cow. God is so good.

Chapter V ⌐<del>
The Simple Life

Donnieta and I play with a Tennessee Mortgage Lifter –
Our pet pig – yep! No kidding.

37. Thank God For the Simple Life

Our family had moved to Smith County Tennessee in January of 1948 when my daddy was still a farmer by occupation. We were without land and therefore tenant farmers, working someone else's land on shares. I have sketches of memory from the little house on Upper Ferry Road, but they are only sketches that include major moments of impression like daddy setting me on the iron beam of the turning plow and letting me ride while the rich dark bottom land was turned upside down by the tremendous efforts of Kit and Lize, the pair of mules which daddy owned. Owning your own mules and live stock made you a cut above other tenant farmers and a more desirable occupant of the farm.

Nothing but the chimney brick is left of the little house on Upper Ferry Road – in fact little is left of Upper Ferry Road in that vicinity - but as I mentioned before, the barn is still standing, although hard to spot through the trees and brush which has grown up around it.

A couple of years ago, one of my sons and I climbed through the briars and weeds to look at the spot, but I found little there except sadness.

Not Sadness because of the meager circumstance in which we lived, for we hardly knew we were poor, so alike were we to those around us, rather sadness that those times are forever gone, and with them the simplicity of life that subsistence farming brought. A simplicity of life and a with it a dependence upon God that provided a peace to our little family that was pervasive throughout our lives. Sometimes one needs to thank God for what is not in our life – as well as what is.

38. <u>Drying Her Nails</u>

As I was growing up, my mother was among many women who had not learned to drive. It was considered a "man thing" and no self respecting man would be caught dead in the car with a woman driving.

Jokes were rampant about women drivers.

"If a man driving sticks his hand out the window and points up, what does that mean?" (before blinker turn signals)

"Why, it means he is turning right of course."

"What does it mean when a woman driver sticks her hand out the window and waves it up and down?"

"That she is stopping?"

"Nah, it means her nail polish isn't dry yet!!"

When Mama and Daddy sold the little grocery store and Mama started working down in the little town of Carthage, she decided that she no longer wanted to walk everywhere she went, nor did she want to be dependant on someone else. She decided she wanted to learn to drive – only she never mentioned a word of it to Daddy. Daddy had many good qualities, but patience as a teacher was not his strong suite – in fact, he was down right snappy when you did it differently than he had instructed. Mama, being the wise person she was, got her brothers, Billy and Denver, to teach her to drive.

Daddy was working for the State of Tennessee Highway Department and drove a "carryall" home each night, so the old two tone, green and white 1954 Buick sat in front of our house for the better part of the work week. While Daddy was at work, Mama would take her "driving lessons" and Daddy would come home none the wiser. But on the days she drove, she never remembered exactly where Daddy had parked the car, and when Daddy got home, he would stop, cock his head to one side, and study the location of the car. Neither of them mentioned the mysteriously moving car, but I am sure Daddy felt like the fellow he worked with who bought a Volkswagen Beetle. When he first got it, Daddy and some of his other "friends" would sneak by his house at night and put a small quantity of gas in the Bug. The fellow was measuring his gas mileage, and would come to work every week bragging about the tremendous gas mileage the Bug was getting.

"Why that thing don't hardly use no gas a'tall."

After about a month of this, they then reversed the process and began taking a quart or so out ever day or two. At first the fellow was only silent and moody, but as they continued to question him about the gas mileage, he confessed that there was, "something wrong with that thing." Finally after a couple of trips back to the dealer, they confessed to their sins and everyone had a good laugh – well, almost everyone.

Finally the big day came, and Mama went down to the Court House, took her drivers test, and passed with flying colors. That night when we had all sat down to supper, she said, "I got something today." Daddy, thinking it was probably something for him said, "Well, what did you go and do?" Out from under the table came the drivers license, which she proudly held up for all to inspect. You won't have to take me to work anymore, I can drive."

Everyone sat in silence, wondering what the reaction would be to this new found independence – but Daddy just laughed and said, "Good for you, why didn't you tell me, I would have been glad to help you." "Oh, I just wanted to surprise you," a little white lie slipped out in the interest of domestic tranquility." The rest of us breathed again, and from that moment on, Mama became the chief deliverer of kids, fetcher of groceries, and doer of errands for the household.

I don't suppose she ever drove with him in the car though – except perhaps when he was sick and she had to take him to the emergency room a few times. And, truth be told, she was always one of those drivers who looked uncomfortable at the task. A very short woman, she always stretched her neck up as far as possible, held her head high and sighted down her nose when she drove – hands at 10 and 2, knuckles slightly white. But she had learned, she had grown, she had accomplished and felt wonderful for having done so.

This is the way God expects us to be in the kingdom, to grow, to learn new skills, to accomplish with His help, what we might otherwise think we cannot. In Colossians 1:28 Paul told that church that it was his desire to present everyone mature in Christ, that they would learn and grow.

I ever hold my parents in great respect because I saw them grow, and learn, and adapt to a changing world. I saw them grow immensely in their own walk in The Kingdom and in them I found many qualities worthy of imitating.

39. <u>Backwater and the Law of Momentum</u>

When I was a child we were "River Rats." Most folks were either "River Rats" or "Ridge Runners" according to what part of the up and down landscape of Jackson County one occupied. The spring rains every year brought big water and often the Cumberland backed Roaring River up and the "backwater" stretched from hill to hill. One of my earliest memories is leaving the side porch of my house in a johnboat. The water never actually got in our house, but often flooded the barn and the stock had to be led through the flood waters to safety. Hugh and Leola Berry were a dear couple who lived down the road and their house was in lower ground and flooded almost every year. So perennial was the flooding that their refrigerator was permanently mounted on a raised platform to allow the motor to escape the backwater.

As I told this story to one of my sons he wisely asked, "Dad, why didn't they just move?" As good a question as that was, I had never really considered it before. This was where they lived. This was where they had always lived and in their current thinking, was where they would always live. After all, home is not a place one leaves lightly.

The law of physics called momentum says, "A body at rest, tends to remain at rest, and a body in motion tends to remain in motion." Not only is it true in the realm of natural science, it is also true of social science. It is the reason some of us resist change so doggedly while others of us seek out change as their friend – it is the law of momentum at work.

It is a force that impacts conservatives and liberals in politics, and affects progressives and conservatives in religion. Some churches tend to polarize into churches that seek out change while others are churches that resist change with a zealot's might – yep, the law of momentum.

When the Apostle Paul gave the direction to the church at Corinth to seek the good of others rather than self, to be dedicated to the edification of others, rather than self – he was really saying, "What I want you to do is to go against natural law."

I guess that is what Christianity often calls us to do – to transcend natural tendencies – then equips us to be able to accomplish the task.

40. Cat Head Biscuits, Sopping Molasses and Other Southern Stuff

My grandmother made pan biscuits. Now there are three distinct styles of biscuits made by Southern women. The first is what my dad called *Cat Head Biscuits*, because when done properly they are roughly the size and general shape of a cat's head. They had lots of hot fluffy dough in the middle and were perfect for sopping up sawmill gravy or chicken gravy.

The second type is Pan Biscuits, which is what Ma Ma Maberry made. She would mix up the biscuit dough with lots of lard – not shortening, not Crisco, but Lard – you know, hog fat. It was the by-product of "rendering" chunks of hog fat at hog killing time and was stored in 5 gallon containers called "Lard Stands." Now you could buy it in 5 gallon buckets but those would not have lasted "until the water got hot," as my Pa Maberry would have said. With Pan Biscuits, instead of working the dough into dry flour and then rolling it out, the still gooey dough was poured into a square bread pan that was red hot and brushed with lard to keep the concoction from sticking. When the pone of biscuit was golden brown on top – lard does that – it was cut into squares just like cornbread and they were really good with a chewy crust on top.

The third kind though was my favorite, and it was the kind my mama made. They were "country ham biscuits" or "little biscuits" or sometimes "Tea Biscuits" and they were to die for.

The biscuit dough was worked down to a thin layer — don't work it too long or the biscuits will be hard as clay clods — then cut out with a Birdseye Orange Juice can — the small size — which made them about the size of a pocket watch. You never let them touch one another on the cookie sheet on which they were baked, and each one was crusty top, bottom, and sides without much dough in the middle. Yum! I can just taste them now. The trick was to get them that thin without working them to the general consistency of a hockey puck. There was a song that went:

> Oh, the biscuits in the Army
> they say are mighty fine,
> But one rolled off the table,
> and killed a pal of mine!

Anyway, "hard as a rock" was not the effect you were trying to achieve. The were great sopping biscuits if you had honey or molasses mixed up on your plate since, unlike the other styles, there was little dough in the middle to roll out and clog up your mix of butter and molasses, which you had worked into a golden brown mixture.

My dad used to tell a story about sopping molasses (which we also either made or purchased in five gallon containers). According to him, when they were kids they had so little sweetener that when they got molasses in the fall they would sop so hard the four kids would cause their plates to fly out onto the floor and break. Eventually, my grandmother Chaffin bought them tin pie pans to eat out of but the light tin pans were even worse and flew around the room, endangering the younger children. Finally she nailed those pie tins to the table with a ten penny nail. As the story goes, the hungry children then sopped so hard they wore the heads off the nails. That is some sopping! (My son inquired whether Daddy stole the story from Jerry Clower, the truth is that a friend of Daddy's once wrote for Jerry Clower and borrowed the story from Daddy since I heard it told long before I heard Jerry Clower.)

These days my intake of biscuits is rationed by virtue of collusion between my family and my doctor, although my physique scarcely shows it, but I still sneak one now and then, and they are all as good as they ever were.

With biscuits you have a choice, Tea Biscuits, Pan Biscuits, Cat Head Biscuits, Drop Biscuits, and I am told that some folks even eat biscuits out of a can!

In a December 2008 survey published in the Nashville Tennessean, Eighty (80) percent of people who say they are "Christian" also say eternal life is not exclusively for those who accept Christ and listed at least one non-Christian group — Jews, Muslims, Hindus, atheists — who may also be saved.

But not everything in life has as many choices as biscuits even though our society wishes it to be so. Jesus said, "I am the way, the truth, and the life, and no man comes to The Father but by me.

41. <u>Working in the Tobacco Patch</u>

As I pass by the tobacco fields (patches is what we called them because they were so little, but now they are large enough to be called fields.) I noted that the color is turning that just right shade of yellow that means time to cut and spike. When I was involved 50 years ago, we cut spiked and made sure every stick got put into the barn that very day. To leave it out was to risk sunburn, or rain and ruin. Today, growers purposefully leave it in the sun to wilt down before hauling it to the barn to hang.

Old time tobacco farming was a 13 month a year job and the money from one crop was hardly settled into your bank account until the next crop was underway.

We covered the ground with brush where the plant beds were to be and set it on fire with the hope that the searing heat would destroy any weed seeds in the ground. The weed seeds would contend for the moisture and nutrients destined for the young tobacco plants and cause them to be small or even choked out in spots. Today, they simply cover the bed area with plastic and pump herbicide gas into the ground to kill the weed seeds.

We set the plants out by hand with a peg and string on a wet, steamy, May Day; or we used the old fashioned tobacco setters which had originally been meant to be pulled by mules. They were the ones where you actually picked the plant by hand and placed your hand into the ground to the rhythm of a gush of water, with the fervent hope that the two steel packing wheels following did not take your hand off. Today the setters are fed by placing plants into a set of rubber fingers which move with precision.

We dusted, hoed, plowed, suckered, topped, and wormed – all by hand and at the risk of life and limb, hoping that at the end of the process, reasonable poundage would result and that the market would be good on the day our crop auctioned. Today the risks are much less and the rewards much surer. The crops are contracted for sale prior to putting the plants in the ground and farmers insure the crops against disaster. I remember well one year when we rented a tobacco base in the hollow at Watervale, or Punch, just across highway 70N from the old McCall's Grocery in front of County House Road. (All of this is near Carthage TN for the benefit of the great unwashed masses.) When the planting, transplanting, hoeing, plowing, dusting, suckering, topping, cutting, spiking and hanging were completed, the barn caught fire and the whole year's work went up in smoke on a hot September night. No insurance, only regret. We were sad puppies!

Yes things have definitely changed and there is hardly a vestige of the old way left but for the cutting knife, the spike and the stick, and as much as I like remembering the old times, I can't say I miss the burning hot tobacco patch in August. What I do miss is the general camaraderie of the work; laughing, teasing, cutting up and the occasional tobacco worm fight, of which I will spare you the disgusting detailed description.

I remember well once when we had been cutting for days, which can seem like months in a hot tobacco patch, and had come to those last few short rows at the end of the last patch of the season. As we said it, the rows we had been looking for since the day we started cutting. Pa Maberry said, "Well boys, we got her hemmed up now," and one of the workers, I think it was Claude Armistead, said, "Mr. Edgar,

133

let's just grab a backer stick and beat the d***l out'n the rest uv it." Everyone laughed, our spirits lightened, and we finished those last few short rows with a renewed heart.

At the end of the cutting came the reward to which we had all looked forward – a couple of big watermelons out of the milk cooler and our pay. In my best days, I could earn five dollars a day cutting. Now that wasn't an eight hour day but a 10 – 12 hour day dependant upon how tired Pa Maberry was, which alone determined quitting time. Five dollars x ten days meant that I had fifty dollars to start back the school year with – an impressive sum in those days. During the cutting we had good days and bad, good moments of fun and bad moments of sweat and pain – but we had endured, we had worked early to late to receive the rewards of our labor.

Life, like those days will some be good and some bad, they will have joy and sorrow, they will have light and darkness, but Jesus told us that, "he that endures to the end, will be saved;" and thus we will received our reward.

42. Uncle Billy, The Studebaker, and Me

I visited my Uncle Billy Maberry yesterday and was distressed to see that he was feeling more than a little "poorly." Billy and I spent a lot of time together and he was a part of my growing up years that could never be replaced. He is about 12 years older than I and about 12 years, or more, younger than was his sister - my sweet mother. He was her baby brother and the darling of my grandparents. Billy was good looking, smart, hard working, innovative, and able to make a silk purse from any sow's ear – and it will no come as a surprise to you that he was spoiled, something of a big brother, and a hero figure to me.

When I can hardly remember, he already had a motor bike – not a motorcycle but a bicycle fitted with a motor with which he terrorized Carthage and the immediate vicinity.

He was probably little more than 14 when he got a special permit to drive, since Ma Ma and Pa Maberry neither were able to drive. You could get special permits through the local officials for that kind of things in the fifties.

Sometime around the year that I hit Mrs. Bridgewater's fifth grade, he went into the army. My daddy was working at Mr. Earnest Hughes' Studebaker dealership at that time and both we and Billy each had a new Studebaker. I think his was a Studebaker Champion and it was dark blue, shiny, and had white fender skirts. In my mind, it was The Car; the one everyone wanted but could not have. In retrospect, it has proven to be a product with near perfect styling and if it were still around, would undoubtedly be worth many times the original purchase price.

When Billy left for the army, he put the little Studebaker in the old wooden garage located near where the old Silo stands on the Turner Farm in Carthage, and we all sadly bid him goodbye. Before he left however, my sister and I promised to keep the little car in tip top condition until he returned. So, every few months Donnieta and I got my Uncle Denver to back the car out into the yard and we would shine it up. I suppose thinking about it now, the truth is that Denver really did all the work, or at least was responsible for all of the accomplishment, but we were allowed to be part of the general effort and to contribute in an effort to keep our promise, and it certainly brought us satisfaction.

After serving 3 years of active duty, much of it in Germany, he returned. By that time I was in the 8th grade and had grown to almost equal his size. I was about to enter high school when he came home and he was beginning a serious search for a wife. For a time, he and Billy Rankin owned and operated a portable skating rink. He was an accomplished skater, and I loved the rink. We worked together on the farm for Pa Maberry, shuttling to and from the fields in an old army surplus Willis Jeep and have chopped many a row of corn and tobacco together. He was always up for a little tussle and we spent more than a little time flinging fat green tobacco worms and dirt dabber's nests at one another. I watched in interest as he argued with Pa Maberry, his father about how to do any task we undertook. Billy always wanted to try a new way, and Pa always though that the way it had been done in the past was good enough. Billy was a "pick post" as Ma Ma colorfully put it, and Pa was, "just as independent as a hog on ice."

One love we had in common was cheese, both of us loved good old American cheese and Ma Ma made us a sandwich, slathered with Mayonnaise from the "refrigerwaitor," as she pronounced it, to have for a 10:00 a.m. break every day. Pa never wanted any; he just wanted to work as hard as he could then take off about 3:30 to have coffee with his buddies at the City Café, in its old location where the late jewelry store once resided.

After two or three false starts with lesser individuals, Billy began dating Faye Nunally from Hartsville and it quickly became a "thing." Faye was hardly older than I, and Pa worried that she would get bored (and with all of us, I suppose that was a real possibility) and take off, and was never bashful about expressing his opinion, much to the chagrin of the rest of the family. Since she was still there yesterday, faithfully caring for Billy some 50 years later, Pa's fears appear to have been somewhat premature, over blown, and unfounded.

Billy was an eternal optimist, trying to build a hay conveyor from a windmill, loading a 51 Chevy half ton truck so heavy with lumber that the front end reared up when we left the sawmill. "Oh, half ton is just what the call it, that don't have anything to do with what it will haul." Indeed! I think one of us had to sit out on the front bumper and the other turn the steering wheel to have the front wheels touch pavement so we could pull the old truck out onto the road.

We nearly drowned in a flash flood when we crawled under the jeep to keep dry in a summer down pour, were lightly struck by lightening as we tried to exit the bottom land in front of an approaching storm, and endured endless cuts, bruises, and small injuries that are a part of farm life and were mostly treated with coal oil, turpentine, and band aids.

I think the thing that most endeared Billy to me was that he treated me as if my input and effort really mattered. He, like Denver, allowed me to always be part of the general effort and feel needed and useful. I think that families today would be much better off if children were still allowed, and in fact required, to be part of the general family effort. If they felt that their contribution to the well being of the family mattered. No amount of Stuff, can replace the feeling of being needed, regarded as of value, and sought for input and accomplishment. No Wii, video game, little league accomplishment, or car presented at 16, can replace the need to be needed, to be respected, to be regarded.

It is after all, the way God approaches us. It is clear to me that He can work His will without my input, still He seeks it. He allows me to be part of the general effort through prayer – not because He needs me, but because He knows that I need Him. What a gracious and loving Father we serve.

These days Billy's son Randy and I run the farms together, and we have the same warm relationship that Billy and I enjoyed. But occasionally we still need his advice and input, and I hope we have access to it for a long time.

43. <u>The Smith County Fair</u>

The brown eyed girl and I went to the Wilson County Fair today and it truly is a great fair. The weather was unseasonably cool, it was the first weekend of the fair, and we walked through the crowd and pigged out on hot dogs, cheese nachos, and Chicken Tender (shush – don't tell my cardiologist!) We walked the crowed midway, listened to bluegrass music in Fiddler's Grove, looked to see who won the entries in the various handicrafts, and just people watched. It was a thoroughly enjoyable afternoon.

One thing we did not do however, was ride any of those glitzy, rides, with lights flashing and music blaring, nor have I ever wanted to ride those rides.

I don't think I am unreasonably fearful, it's just that I am not a risk taker by nature. We lived by the fairgrounds in Carthage, just outside the gates, no more than 100 yards from the midway. When the fair rolled into town it was a season of prosperity for our family, since they mostly bought their goods from our "little store." Cumberland Valley Shows came back year after year and Daddy and Mama got to know many of the "carneys" and in fact thought very well of many of them, despite the common perception that one had better lock their doors while the carnival was in town. (In those days most of us did not lock our doors day or night, and many of us could not have found the key to the door if we searched diligently.)

When I was very young, I was allowed to go out to the fairground when the collections of old Cadillac Cars and beat up trucks dragging sad looking trailers behind rolled in starting on a Sunday afternoon. I then observed as they erected "The Greatest Show on Earth." I watched as they parked their shoddy house trailers behind the rides and shows on the midway – out of sight once the midway was lighted and the false fronts were assembled. I watched as they assembled the tents and turned a semi trailer into the fun house, or the house of mirrors, or the girly show, as my daddy called it.

I also watched as they assembled the Ferris wheel, the tilt-awhirl, the swings, the bullet ride, and others – and I did not like what I saw. These things were snapped together in what seemed to be the flimsiest of ways, by people who obviously should not be trusted with such important work, or so it seemed to me. So I did not ride – well perhaps the merry-go-round but nothing beyond that.

All week, we watched the fair goers bounce from their cars through the entrance gates, and then drag themselves and their crying, and sometimes chunk blowing kids back at 10:30 or 11:00 p.m. We sat the old red and white metal lawn chairs in front of our house to save parking spaces for Norman and Hattie, or Hollis and June, or Roy and Francis, as a parade of relatives visited the fair and sat and talked with us under the shade of our front trees, much too long to suit the various younger cousins being delayed from the thrill of the midway. We parked cars in the vacant lot across the street to aid the cub scouts and boy scouts and we people-watched from the safety and comfort of our own front yard. Some years it rained and the misery was magnified, and on one rainy Saturday night some locals were shooting dice in the back of a tent with some of the Carney crew, when somebody accused somebody of cheating. Somebody drew a knife but was shocked to learn he had come to a gun fight armed only with a knife. Shots rang out and the crowded, muddy, midway, being doused by a summer downpour, became a nightmare of running, and fighting, and shooting. We were glad we were sitting on the porch watching the confusion and not any closer to the mud, the blood, and the beer.

Finally midnight on Saturday would bring another fair to a close, and sometime just after midnight the music from the carousel, and the cry of the barker of, "step right up and see the monkey girl, she comes from deepest Africa, part money, part girl, there is nothing else like her in the world," would be silenced. One by one, the sights and sounds would become silent and darkness would crowd into the fairground.

By the time we got home from church on Sunday the whole traveling show would be gone except for that occasional old truck or car which would not start and would have to be towed away later. The ground would be left trampled, the grass long since trodden into a muddy mess, and the whole area was littered with bottles, popcorn bags, cones from cotton candy, and other fall off from the sea of humanity that had lately been wooed by the lights, music, and excitement. Nothing was left but mud, trash, reality and ugliness. The shabbiness of the whole façade exposed once again.

I wonder sometime, if we could see the underlying shabbiness, gaze upon the frailty of that which fastens our self-dependent lives together, grasp the foolishness or relying upon the efforts of those incompetent to fasten together the needs of our life; if then we would hear the seductive music and perceive the cry of the huckster with different ears; if we would see the flashing lights, and the false fronts, and the glitz with different eyes, and be less attracted to the sin to which we are drawn like a moth to the flame. I wonder if we could see what the whole of our self-centered life would look like when played out, if we would be less inclined to roll the dice with our souls. What do you think?

44. <u>Contentment is a State of Mind</u>

I can remember in my lifetime being in almost every circumstance financially. We were tenant farmers (sharecroppers) and therefore almost always without cash money. No bathroom, no electricity, a Chevrolet pickup that all four of us squeezed into the one seat - and yet we always had plenty to eat - not fancy, but good, healthy, and well prepared.

When we lived in town, Mama worked in the grocery store at minimum wage and Daddy worked for the State of TN highway department. His yearly income was around seven thousand dollars in the good years - and yet we had a good house, which my parents made into a good home. We had dear friends and precious family who loved us, and I had a dog that I adored, and who liked me, at least marginally.

The brown eyed girl and I married as college students and had an upstairs apartment over the Collins family in Nashville - 75 dollars per month. She worked and I went to school days and worked down on second avenue nights and at the Grand Old Opry on Friday and Saturday nights. Sometimes we were down to a box of Chef Boyardee spaghetti, or a bag of the dreaded butter beans that my mother always gave and we shoved to the back of the freezer until hunger brought them to the front - But we had a pretty place to live, we able to go to church each Sunday and listen to Batsell Barrett Baxter preach, and had our little dog Shelly, who adored my wife and tolerated me. We were happy.

As the years progressed, and I was able to work my way through numerous jobs at General Motors, our financial situation progressed to a level I would never have dreamed of; GM provided me with a new car to drive, free of charge, and a tremendous discount that allowed me to buy Jan had a new car every year. Our houses became our primary source of investment and we were able to live in nice neighborhoods that were well beyond our expectations.

We moved 18 times and with each move, my sweet wife set her mind and determined that we would be happy - and then she proceeded to make that a reality. She helped the children view each new place as an adventure, and the jobs that paid the most were often not the jobs that were the most fun.

Now we are able to be retired, to linger over our morning coffee, to read the paper until we have exhausted its content, and we are happy.

The moral of course, is that happiness is not location dependant, nor financial circumstance dependant, once the basic needs of life are met. Happiness is dependant upon our view of dependence upon our maker. It is dependant upon living in the now, instead of in the future. It is dependant upon, determining with determination, that you will strive to be happy regardless of the circumstance.

I once heard a story about two men who were each journeying to the same town for a new start in life. When the first young man neared the city he encountered an old fellow, bent with age, leaning upon a stick. He ask, "Good morning friend, what kind of town is this?"

Well, replied the old man, "What kind of town did you come from?"

"Oh," the young man replied, "it was a wonderful town, the people were honest, and friendly, they reached out to strangers and were altogether pleasant to deal with."

"Well," the old man replied, "you will find this town exactly the same."

The second traveler soon neared the city and also came upon the old man, bent with age.

"Say old man," he asked, "what kind of town it this up ahead?"

"What kind of town did you come from?" the old man again asked.

"Oh it was a terrible place," the second traveler said, "the people were selfish, not friendly, and were always finding some fault with their neighbors."

"Well," the old man replied, "you will find this town exactly the same."

It is the attitude you bring in life situations, not the circumstance you find, which determines you happiness in life.

45. Our First House in Town

When our family left the farm in 1950, we had never lived in town before and Daddy was concerned about being too near other people. To make sure we had plenty of room, he bought two additional vacant lots. Now most people would have been concerned that we were buying next door to a cattle sale barn, but since our house had always been on a farm and close to a barn, we were more concerned about being close to people than close to cows.

Livestock sales at the sale barn took place on Tuesdays and Saturdays and on those days we could often not find parking in front of our own house and the bawling of calves could be heard all night. The ability for the human body to become accustomed to unbelievable circumstances is remarkable and we became acclimated to this racket, much like people who live in the big city become adapted to the noise of the city. Neither the smell of the livestock nor the bawling of the calves really often bothered our family. For the most part, we simply did not hear the racket; however when extended family from the big cities of Detroit , Dayton, or Nashville would come to visit, they would wonder aloud how we could stand to live in such a noisy place. We simply felt them to be hyper sensitive and "putting on airs".

A lot of things are forgivable in Southern culture but two things are not; getting above your raisin' and adopting a phony northern accent a few months after you have moved north.

I later lived in Michigan 35 years during my days with General Motors, and tried, really tried, not to lose my southern accent. After all, to stand out from the crowd is a good thing, even if it is only because, as a GM executive once remarked about me, "you talk like Catfish Hunter."

Daddy bought us a TV when I was in the third grade and with that event a whole era of communication and verbal entertainment, in our family as with other American families, ground to a halt. As for us, like most others around us, many of the stories and lyrics Daddy had shared with us stopped when I became addicted to the black and white Admiral Console model. Watching TV in those days was something of a challenge since in Carthage, fifty miles away from the transmitters, we had to have two antennas, one to pick up each of the two Nashville stations. Even with the two antennas, I often went out in the yard to turn one or the other right or left while my sister yelled instructions from inside. (humm, it suddenly occurs to me that I was always outside doing the work and she was always inside giving directions. Well, she always said she was smarter than me, and I suppose this proves it.) Another "fine tune adjustment" consisted of a big ball of aluminum, which we slid back and forth along the antenna wire to sharpen the reception. I also remember ordering a "Color TV Kit" from some vendor off the TV and receiving a red and green film of plastic which adhered to the front of the screen. Color true enough, but bearing no semblance of reality. It was an experience which made me leery of ordering from TV advertisements to this day.

I rushed home every afternoon to watch Howdy Doody, Clarabelle the Clown, Buffalo Bob, and Princes Summer-Fall-Winter-Spring. Cowboy Ruff-N-Ready provided a B-grade cowboy movie each afternoon with heroes like Johnnie McBrown, and other cowboy favorites. The Lone Ranger and Tonto, Hop-a-long Cassidy and Topper and Dale and Roy came to life on the giant 18 inch screen and some time about the fifth grade, I discovered the Mickey Mouse Club and Annette Funachellio, my first on-screen crush. Saturdays I got up early and watched the test pattern for at least an hour waiting for Mr. Wizard to wow all of us with practical natural science experiments and Sealtest Milk to present the Big Top where we could watch the high wire acts, jugglers and trapeze artists right in our living room.

Yes, something was gained but something was also lost by bringing TV into our living room. We had allowed into our family circle a visitor who would now occupy most of the conversation, most of the time. Rather than talking to one another, we would sit staring at the box in front of us. Perhaps worst of all was the fact that the visitor had different values than we, that while we were careful of our thoughts and language, the visitor was less concerned about the moral implications of things. Works which had never been used before in our homes began to creep into the nightly conversation, modes of dress that would have heretofore been unacceptable were slowly but steadily introduced by the visitor and we began to feel more and more comfortable with the new norm which the visitor with the one eye advocated by demonstration. Lifestyles which we would have spoken of in whispers were not flaunted as the next big thing which to which we had better get accustomed.

The scripture had warned that "evil companions corrupt good morals" and when we chose this new visitor as a constant companion, we chose this companion poorly.

46. <u>Owning the Mess We Have Made</u>

When we moved into our house in Carthage, it was a big event for our family. We had never before lived in a house with "running water," never had an indoor toilet, never been able to take a bath other than in a galvanized wash tub, never had heated water except on the stove in a tea kettle, never had electricity, other than a few wires running outside the walls, never had central heat, and certainly never had shiny varnished hardwood floors.

The floors in the house were so beautiful. It was 1950 and "wall-to-wall" carpeting had not yet become the rage. Area rugs were all that was available, or linoleum for kitchens and bath. I remember that the first time we went to check on the progress of the construction of the house and the floors had been freshly varnished, I was so excited that I ran into a room where the varnish was still wet and it had to be redone next day. Oops!

We had a living room and dining room separated by an archway, and to us it was a palace. As I look at the house now it is a rather mundane house, in a bad location, but one's view of most things in life is a matter of perspective.

Mama bought a grey wool area rug for the living room. It left about a foot or two of the hardwood showing around the edges. Mama instructed my sister and me very carefully that we were never eat or drink in the living room. It was that serious kind of forehead to forehead talk that one would be reckless to ignore.

So according to instruction, we abstained from eating or drinking in the living room, but often sat in the archway between it and the dining room with a glass of milk and a cheese sandwich. (Now that we had the store, we could have real "loaf" bread instead of all that old homemade stuff we had to eat before – how cool was that?)

For several years I wore the same style of shoes, Buster Browns with a strap that buckled over to the outside of the shoe. I have never been big on change and today have pretty much the same style of shoes and clothes I wore in college – don't fix what works for you – is my motto. Well, my Buster Browns were getting pretty scuffed up on the toes and Mama had left me instructions to polish them that day. By polish them, she meant go down to the basement, where the polish and rags were and shine and buff the shoes. That location, however, did not fit my particular schedule that day since Howdy Doody, Buffalo Bob Smith, and Princess Summer-fall-winter-spring where about to undertake a great adventure that day, and being a dedicated part of the at home peanut gallery, I felt duty bound to be present.

I decided that if I stayed in the arch of the dining room and used the old Griffin Scuff Kote liquid polish, I could make this thing work and still fulfill my obligations to Howdy and Buffalo Bob.

The clinker came when, being terribly near sighted, I began to scoot closer and closer to the T.V. and soon was sitting on the edge of the grey, wool rug. As I scooted around, somehow I hit the bottle of scuff kote and it turned over. Now this was before there were rubber tops like on a kids glue bottle and the top was open and you simply stuck a dauber down inside the bottle to glop the stuff on your shoes.

There it was, a huge reddish brown stain on Mama's beautiful grey rug. I ran and got some old rags and water, determined to get the stain out before Mama or Adie discovered it. But of course, I only succeeded in making it bigger and worse. I was frantic and began to wonder how long it might take me to work out enough money to get Mama a new rug – or better yet flee to Peru. I was desperate. My only hope lay in the fact it was a nice night and my parents might sit outside instead of turn on the T.V. tonight. Surly I would think of something by tomorrow. Maybe if I cut a piece out of another rug ….No that didn't sound right!!

At supper, I had no appetite, Mama's first clue that something was wrong. I probably also tipped her off by mentioning over and over again what a nice night it was and how good it would be if we could all set out under the trees tonight. I was the ultimate T.V. junkie and she knew that if I was suggesting other family entertainment, something must be up. Truth be told, by that time I was so nervous, worked up, and sick, I just wanted the agony over. I confessed, trying to lay as much blame on shoe polish makers, rug manufacturers and Howdy himself as I could.

She was having none of it.

She went into the living room and heaved a huge sigh ending with shoulders slumped down in that, "I just give up," position. After the few well deserved whacks and a "talking to" about doing what you are told, and owning up to things when you do them – she studied the situation and with Daddy's help rotated the rug 180 degrees which caused the stain to end up under the big heavy couch. Problem solved! There the stain stayed for the next decade, hidden from the view of company but always on my mind, and I suspect my Mama's. One thing for sure, the current furniture arrangement was not about to change.

In the meantime, I had learned a lesson about owning the mistakes we make in life. About obedience being in principle, not just in the letter of the law, and about appealing to a higher authority for help when the mess we have created is beyond our ability to clean up. (Which is most of the time.)

God's expectation of us is that we obey the principals He has laid down which provide us with the abundant life. That we come clean with him when we mess up and own the mess we have created. And that we recognize that it is only with his help that we are able to cover the stains we have caused. The more we stir in the thing alone, or the more we try hide it within, the bigger, more burdensome, and nastier the stain becomes.

47. <u>Go Getters and Red Goose Shoes</u>

In *The Adventures of Huckleberry Finn*, Mark Twain has Huck issue the following opinion,

"All the stores was along one street. They had white domestic awnings in front, and the country-people hitched their horses to the awning-posts. There was empty dry-goods boxes under the awnings, and loafers roosting on them all day long, whittling them with their Barlow knives; and chawing tobacco, and gaping and yawning and stretching - a mighty ornery lot."

In Carthage, the awnings were a color or a stripe of some description and people were parking their 49 model Chevrolet Pickup Trucks instead of their horses, when I can first remember, but otherwise the description might have been the same. Mostly the loafers and whittlers were sitting on the low concrete wall that ran around the courthouse – they were a group my daddy called "go-getters" because they had gotten their wife a job at the shirt factory and at 4:30 they would "go get her."

They had moved beyond just the Barlow and were swapping and trading Case XXX, Boker, Boker Tree, and John Primble knives, each one bragging and "blowing" as my Ma Ma Maberry called it, about the superior quality and value of their own bladed instrument.

Carmack Bradley, Roundhead Woodard, and Mose Dennis were each running a taxi from their little stands on the north/east corner of the square and you could get good eats at the Shamrock, Court Square or City Café. If it happened to be November through January, one would be lucky to get a room in the old Walton Hotel since buyers from American, Lucky Strike (LSMFT), Phillip Morris, and the other major tobacco companies had the rooms booked for weeks in advance.

The Old Shamrock Café – Now Kim's Frame and Art

Many of them stayed in private homes, often staying with the same family or widow woman year after year, sometimes getting both room and board.

The Shamrock Café was where Kim's Frame and Art is today, followed by a Goodyear Store and Draper and Darwin (an area chain with 52 stores – the building originally belonged to Mr. Chambers and is now Markum's), I particularly liked Draper and Darwin because they sold Red Goose Shoes and when your mama bought you a pair you were allowed to go over and pull the neck of the goose down, which caused it to lay a golden egg filled with some trinket or treasure, made in Japan. One of the stores in that block also sold Buster Brown Shoes which had some sort of x ray machine that when you put the shoe on you could put your foot under a fluoroscope. By 1950 the dangers of such exposure to radiation was being discovered and these miracle machines were quietly phased out by 1960.

The Western Auto (Often called, "The Western and Awe toe" and the establishment where I was to work during my high school years), was followed by Smith County Bank (the old reliable with capital of $100,000). Next came Mr. Fred Cleveland's Pharmacy (later Gene Oldham's Drug Store), The upstairs of this building had been Cordell Hull's Law Office, said to be the place the congressman was working when President Roosevelt called to offer him the position as Secretary of State. Secretary Hull did not have a phone in his office and Fred Cleveland had to send someone up to fetch the congressman down to take a call from FDR. Next to Cleveland's was Citizen's Bank (the friendly bank), A. P. Marciano Jewelry store, which was located in a small hole in the wall, and, eventually, Hire and Long Five and Dime. Finally the end of this building line was crowned by Smith County Motor Company, better known as the "Ford Garage." which was owned by Mr. John Waggoner. These all set facing the Courthouse on the East Side of the square. Today, only Markum's and Kim's Frame and Art remain as retail establishments in this entire block.

Further south and across 2nd Avenue was the Trailways Bus Station (which was eventually turned into Mr. Brice McDonald's welding shop, and later a body shop run by Mr. Melvin "Shack" Hewitt), followed by Cumberland Chevrolet Company "The Chevrolet Garage" (they were actually dealerships but everyone just called them "Garage" in those days.) The International Harvester Tractor and Implement

Company was followed by a service station that once was run by Max Long. This service station was torn down circa 1950. (When they demolished that building my dad salvaged the big flood reflectors which housed huge incandescent bulbs and put them up in our back yard. From that day on, the neighborhood children gathered there to play croquet, badminton, football, and just generally hang out.)

Finally there was the Mobil Service Station owned and operated by Harry T. Woodard (the sign of the flying red horse) which also served in later years as the Trailways Bus Station, after the real bus station was shut down. The old Trailways Bus would come across the bridge, drop off or pick up passengers, and put off packages shipped by bus.

Years later I worked for Tennessee Wholesale Drug on Second Avenue in Nashville (Now the Spaghetti Factory) packing items ordered from drugstores all over the Middle Tennessee area for shipment by bus. If one went into the drug store prior to 3:00 p.m. and asked for a specific item and the druggist was out of that particular item, the standard answer was; "I can call my wholesaler and have that for you tomorrow Mrs. Smith – and I'll have one of the boys deliver it." After the order was called to Tennessee Wholesale, we would pull, package, and ship the item that night after 5:00 p.m. and the old Trailways Bus would deliver it the next morning.

Lots of things have changed in Carthage and nearly every other small town in America. Interstate Highways, Wal-Mart stores, MacDonald's Restaurants, and other things which we wish for, sometimes turn out to bring change which we did not anticipate, or bring a metamorphosis beyond our vision.

For our forty fifth anniversary, I gave the brown eyed girl a bracelet which says, "I will never leave you, nor forsake you." It comes from Hebrews 13:5 where the Hebrew writer says, "Keep your lives free from the love of money and be content with what you have, because God has said, Never will I leave you, never will I forsake you."

Some of the things we pine for, and even pray for, turn out to be things that may be to our detriment – and a loving God keeps them from us. Other things – the simplest of things – often the best things – do not change and they are the things to which we must anchor our bark. Especially the unchanging God.

48. <u>Cherry Cokes, Chocolate Malts, and Murray Drugs</u>

If one went up the street from the town's single red light, after passing Read Brothers Drugs, The Old Walton Hotel and Hire and Jent Dry-goods; Dr. Bill Murray had a drug store, which was creatively named Murray Drugs.

Murray Drugs, like most of the stores on Carthage's Main Street has long since passed into the memory of all but a few. It was where Brenda Gregory's Mom worked, I don't know if I ever knew her name, just Brenda Gregory's Mom. She was the boss of the soda fountain and Dr. Murray (We all called Pharmacists Doctor in those days) ran the pharmacy where your prescriptions came in little brown or green tinted glass bottles, and had screw on caps that you could actually open.

North Main Street Carthage, Tennessee – circa 1950

The best part of Murray's however, was the booth section in the back, past the soda fountain. There were stools at the soda fountain of course, but Murray's had booths with high back seats with real naugahide covers (what is a nauga anyway?) and Formica topped tables with chrome edging. Across from the booths was the magazine rack, which was filled with all of the latest comics. So you could come in, order a cherry fountain coke, or chocolate malt, and read Archie, Woody, Blackhawk, or Superman comics until your hearts content. You see Dr. Murray didn't care since the comics were shipped to the store on consignment, and what were not sold simply had the cover ripped off and only the cover was returned for credit. No one ever bought the magazines or comics on the front of the rack, rather they reached to the back and drew out a fresh clean one, while the frayed used ones stayed on the front for the general use of those who did not intend to buy.

I remember that when I started to school at David Lipscomb College, the standard comparison to the girls was "remember, everyone reads the magazines on the front of the rack, but when a boy goes to buy one, he reaches to the back and pulls out a fresh new one." I'm not sure how many of the girls got the comparison, or how many were even in need of the admonition; but I'm pretty sure the boys all got it.

The thing about Murray's was that you always got more than you deserved, if not more than you expected. We are a society with high expectations, and research shows that the majority of Americans expect to go to Heaven, regardless of how we live and regardless of in whom we place our faith. But, the bible teaches that while many of us will get more than we deserve, not all of us will have our expectations met.

"I am the way, the truth, and the Life, no man comes unto the Father but by Me." If we place our faith in Him, we will surly get more than we deserve if not more than we expect.

49. <u>Of Wanderings and Wonderings</u>

I rode around Carthage a few days ago. I was waiting for the brown eyed girl to get her hair fixed and I was in a reflective mood because of the passing of my Uncle Billy, I noted how much has really changed. I know that most places have changed more, but riding down Jefferson, I wondered why there are alleys between Jefferson and Carmack and none between any other streets. I wondered if the people who lived in Mr. West's house know what a wonderful garden he once made on that spot. I wondered if anyone else remembers that Austin Cruse still lived on that street and drove a little mini sports car. I wondered if anyone else ever drove past the white building that houses the emergency response team and remembered that it once stored cheese for aging, or remembered the great baseball games that once were played in that vacant lot by Bobby Upchurch and Tyrone Pointer and that gang. I wondered who owns the old Borden's Cheese Plant and why no one has found a use for it. I wondered if anyone would walk to town from our old house on Jefferson and Dogwood anymore as we once did regularly. I wondered if I was the only person who remembered when the little church on Jackson had revivals in the summer and groups of local kids would sit outside and watch through the open windows as a source of entertainment. I wondered if anyone else remembered the night that Louis and Bob Roberts' house burned at the location of the Baptist Church on Carmack. I wondered what happened to the illegal stills that Dewitt Rollins (a revenue agent) once carried in the back of his truck.

I wondered how many people remembered the great times we all had at the portable skating rink that stood on the vacant lot across from the swimming pool.

As I rode around the square, I remembered that the west side of the square was where the Carthage Grocery and Locker, "the locker plant" was located. A sign of how dramatically the public sensibility has changed as we moved from and an agrarian society, is that today it would be hard to imagine the basement of one's grocery store is where one of Bess Blair's boys would be slaughtering cows and hogs with a sledge hammer. Farmers brought fatted calves to the back door loading chute and there they would be slaughtered, butchered, cooled, quartered, and cut into steaks, roasts, stew meat and ground into hamburger. They were then placed in your rented, partitioned, space in the giant freezer room, or locker, where those without electricity or those without a freezer (which was nearly everyone in the forties and fifties) kept the beef until ready to put it on the table. So, on Saturday, one would come to the Locker and buy groceries, sell eggs, and go back to their freezer locker to get meat for Sunday dinner and the week ahead. Unlike pork, which was generally salt cured, beef needed to be frozen to remain fresh.

Almost no farmer paid for their groceries on a weekly basis, rather they would say, "put that on the book." Then Bill Petty, Jap Hughes, Belva Hughes, or my mother, Maylene Chaffin would pull your book from the rotary rack, enter the total of your groceries and you would "settle up" when your tobacco, or a calf, was sold.

Today much is made of the new internet service which allows you to order groceries on line and have them delivered to your home. My sister got a job working at The Locker Plant when she was little more that 16 years of age, taking telephone orders on Saturday. She spent most of the day taking grocery orders which she would write in your "book." The yellow ticket was dropped into a basket and then filled either by her or some other less than minimum wage teenager. The orders were then delivered in the old blue pickup truck by a couple of boys who would take your order into the house, set it out on the kitchen, and place the refrigerator items in the refrigerator for you. Nothing new under the sun?

I have been thinking about worship a lot lately, since I am teaching a class called the wonder of worship. It seems to me that worship is a little like the Locker Plant – what you can get out of it, depends on what you put into it. And while some things may change, the elementals remain the same. Also, my sister may have liked Martha White Flour, Double Cola, bananas, and Skippy, but since she was just filling the order, she placed Gold Metal, Pepsi, peaches, and Jiff in the basket. The basket was filled according to the order of the one paying the price – and what she liked did not enter into the equation.

Oh yes, and a strict account was kept of what had been done – for one day it would be time to settle up.

50. **Guernseys on the Lawn**

I really don't remember anything of World War II since I was only eleven months old when V.E. Day (Victory in Europe) came and had only turned one year old two months prior to Victory over Japan (V. J. Day) which came on August 14, 1945 (August 15th if you were actually in Japan on the other side of the International Date Line).

The Korean War was in progress when I first became aware of events around me to the extent that they consistently imprinted themselves on my memory. Television had come to America and this war, which the government in their ongoing and still continuing quest to change reality by changing names, had dubbed a "Police Action," played out at night on the snowy, and oft times wavy, Camel News Caravan with John Cameron Swazey. Swazey, who had been picked by NBC to do a news show three nights a week because no one else wanted to do it, became a household name and went on to gain fame on several game shows. He was my first celebrity role model and I would practice saying "Ladies and Gentlemen, and good evening to you" trying to sound as much like my TV hero as possible. (Even now in my mind I can hear his voice and the way he intoned the familiar phrase.) I think that John Cameron Swazey was perhaps best known for his Timex watch commercials, "It takes a licking, and keeps on ticking," The most famous of course, was the live demonstration wherein he strapped a Timex to the propeller of an outboard motor, and started the motor. When the outboard was stopped, the Timex may have been "ticking," but if so, it was ticking somewhere else since it was conspicuous in its absence when the outboard prop was stopped. It was a segment that every American of a certain age has seen many times, and along with Candid Camera, was perhaps the forerunner of America's Funniest Home Videos, or People Are Funny.

Our family had moved to Smith County Tennessee in January of 1948 when my daddy was still a farmer by occupation. We were not landowners, and Daddy worked someone else's land "on shares." I have sketchy memory of the little house on Upper Ferry Road, but they are only sketches that include major moments. For instance, I remember coming in from the hayfield riding on the old mule and team wagon and daddy let me stand up with him in the center of the wagon, instead of having to sit flat down on the bed as it bumped and jarred along the rutted gravel road. Daddy owned his own team and farming tools which made you a cut above other sharecroppers and you were considered tenant farmers.

Nothing but the chimney brick is left of the little house on Upper Ferry Road – in fact little is left of Upper Ferry Road in that vicinity - but as I mentioned elsewhere, the barn is still standing, although hard to spot through the trees and brush which has grown up around it. A couple of years ago, one of my sons and I climbed through the briars and weeds to look at the spot, but I found little there except sadness.

Not Sadness because of the meager circumstance in which we lived, for we hardly knew we were poor, so alike were we to those around us. We had plenty to eat, albeit it plain fare, and enough money came from the tobacco to pay off what the merchants were "carrying on the books," at the end of the year. We were breaking even, and that is all one aspired to do among out people. Rather the melancholy I encounter there where the house had once stood, was a sadness that those times are gone forever, and with them the simplicity of life that subsistence farming brought.

With that simplicity of life, came a dependence upon the creator to send the rain in its season, and the harvest if the planting had been careful and the tilling of the soil diligent.

It was a simplicity of life and a childlike dependence upon God which brought a peace to our little family, and that has remained pervasive throughout our lives.

The little town of Carthage has extended its limits to the point that large and expensive homes are within a few hundred feet of where the little board and batten house stood. Chandeliers hang in their foyers, so unlike the coal oil lamps that lit our own. They have beautiful bathrooms with brass fixtures, polished granite counter tops, and marble tile, in sight of where we lived with outhouse, porcelain dishpans, and oil cloth table covers. The pasture land where our good natured and gentle Jersey and Guernsey cows once grazed, are now a part of someone's well manicured lawn.

Yet I wonder if those occupying the big homes are happier than we were. I wonder if their city water tastes sweeter than that which ran from our spring. I wonder if the brightness of the electric lights provides more warmth and glow in their hearts than the coal oil lamps did in ours.

The answer comes back, Probably not more – perhaps not less – for it is the attitude you bring, not the circumstance you find, which determines your contentment and view of the life you have been given.

⤙ **Chapter VI** ⤚
New Dogs and Old Tricks

Old Jet and Me
It was the best of days

51. <u>A Dog Named Old Jet</u>

I have never been much of a cat person, don't know why but they don't seem open to a relationship like a dog does. Now I know that some of you feel just the opposite and I am willing to honor your opinion, and hope you will honor mine. Daddy always said, "Everyone is entitled to their own misguided opinion."

I had several dogs, all of them mostly worthless in terms of actual contribution to the family welfare, but faithful friends, nevertheless. The last dog I had before Jan and I married, was a little black dog that looked like there might have been a black cocker somewhere in his family tree, but certainly there were a lot of other fine breeds mixed in there too. Perhaps he could have masqueraded as a cocker, but he had this ridiculously long tail that waved in the breeze and said, "look at me, I'm a mutt and proud of it."

People didn't have AKC pure bred dogs back then and most of them probably wouldn't have survived because almost no one allowed a dog in the house, so Old Jet had no reason not to hold his head up high.

He showed up one day at Pa Maberry's house and looked "rode hard and put up wet," as the saying goes, so we gave him some scraps of fried chicken which consisted of mostly bones. Now I know that these days you aren't supposed to give a dog any chicken bones, as they might puncture his digestive tract or some other thing, but in those days we were ignorant of that information, and what we didn't know didn't seem to hurt the dogs.

After watching the zest with which he scarffed down the scraps, Daddy suggested that if I was going to keep him, I name him "Chicken Bone." But since he was "Black as Old Jet" his name ended up being Old Jet. I don't know why but we always called a dog Old something; Old Bowser, Old Curtis, Old Lady, Old Jet, even if they were little more than pups.

Old Jet was one smart dog, not smart in that he could sit, lie down, roll over, speak or do any of those things. Oh he could do all of them, but not on anyone's command, only at his good pleasure. Old Jet was his own man, or his own dog to be more accurate, and came and went at will. To say that anyone owned Old Jet would have been a disservice to his free spirit and roving nature. He slept on the front porch, summer and winter, except on the very coldest nights when my mother would open the door and allow him to come into the house. That drill was always the same, he would look at her with some disbelief, dash into the house and scramble full speed, toenails clacking and scratching on the hardwood floors, as he rounded the corner and disappear down the stairs into the blackness of the furnace room.

The next morning, I would open the back outside door to the basement, and he would strut out looking a little like Otis when Andy lets him out of the cell after sobering up the next morning.

It was not uncommon for him to be absent from home for a week or two at the time, nor was it uncommon to pass through some less desirable part of town and see him sitting in the yard or lying on the front porch of some house as that family sat around talking. He was very social in nature and had no sense of discrimination due to race or socio economic position – ahead of his time, he was.

He had an uncanny ability to know where we were going when our family left in the car, and if it was to Pa and Ma Ma's house, he would follow, running at breakneck speeds in front of the car and sitting breathlessly panting, awaiting our arrival. It became a contest of wills between my dad and Old Jet, with Daddy starting out in the wrong direction, circling the block, or taking circuitous routes, only to always arrive to the sight of Old Jet, tongue hanging to his knees, waiting for us on their porch. Finally Daddy decided that he just ran over to Pa's every time we all left the house, and drove around the block only to find Old Jet still sitting on our porch. He just knew!

Not long after Old Jet befriended me, Daddy dispatched me to the gully between our house and the stock sale barn. He was putting me on the business end of a "Lively Lad" (For those of you who don't know, that was a weed eater without a motor.) to cut down the waist high Johnson grass that, I guess, was obstructing our clear view of the stock barn. I had made a few licks with the lively lad, using a 300 yard big Bertha driver approach, when Old Jet started to wander into the line of fire. Just as I picked him up to move him to safety, David Lollar, one of my friends showed up on his bike and to be cute for a friend, I tossed Old Jet into the middle of the patch of Johnson grass. After a considerable amount of wiggling and waving of the tall grasses he emerged from the downhill side, and immediately ran back to me. Well it looked pretty funny to a couple of 10 year olds, and David had been entertained; so, I did it again, and again, and again, with poor old Old Jet getting the worst of the deal.

Daddy had walked out to get in the big grey Buick and observed what was going on. He called me over and speaking in that low but scary tone dads can take, he let me know, in no uncertain terms, that was no way to treat Old Jet, and that if I could not appreciate him, we would simply give him to someone who could. I was fighting back tears by that time, but he went on to make it clear that to misuse or make fun of one friend, in order to impress another, was not acceptable behavior. I would rather have taken a full blown whipping than had him talk to me in that manner, mostly because I knew in my heart of hearts, he was right. It was a lesson I never forgot.

I think perhaps we do that with those closest to us sometimes, or to God himself. We act in ways that are unbecoming, to say the least, in order to show our friends that we are not "goodie-goodies" or that we are "real men," that we are clever, or perhaps sophisticated people of the world. Those that are faithful to us deserve our best, and just because they will countenance our bad behavior for a time, does not mean we should take liberties with their forbearance.

52. <u>I Love a Parade, and so did Old Jet</u>

Earlier we began talking about Old Jet, the "almost cocker spaniel" that I had from the time I was 9 or 10 until I left home for college. To me, Old Jet was smarter than your average dog, since he had not only a sixth sense for direction, but also a sixth sense for time. During the years I was in grade school, Old Jet would lie around the house all day, then at about 3:00 p.m. would get up, stretch, yawn a couple of time, and head out toward Jackson Avenue where he would sit at the corner by Mr. Lofton Fisher's house and wait for me to come into view down school house hill. Later as I was in Smith County High School, he would stroll up to the old rock house where the Apple family lived, and wait there, since he could peer through the window and see me sitting in Mrs. Kirby's sixth period English class. It was a constant source of embarrassment and I took no small amount of ribbing on his account.

When Old Jet first came to grace us with his presence, there were no paved streets in Carthage, at least not paved with hot mixed asphalt. They were either gravel or tar and chip roads, and Jefferson was mostly gravel with a little tar. We lived on the corner of Jefferson and Dogwood and a considerable hill went down beside our house. My family liked to sit in the old metal lawn chairs under the shade trees in our front yard and just talk. When we were sitting out there, and only when we were sitting out there, Old Jet would chase cars, and more than once the cars got the best end of the deal with Old Jet sliding along underneath the car and ending up in the ditch that ran along the side of Jefferson down to Mr. Homer Lewis' house. The driver was usually a neighbor who would stop and express extreme sorrow for having run over the dog, but by that time Old Jet was usually dusting himself off and walking away with that, "I meant to do that, yep, that worked out just like I planned it." strut as he disappeared around the house to pick the gravel out of himself with his teeth. I have been guilty of that exact same posture myself.

I was in the band (The Pride of the Upper Cumberland) and Old Jet liked to go to summer band practice. He was a favorite among the folks there and was not content to sit idly outside but would come into the band room and lay around near the drum section while practice was in session. (I think he had rhythm) One summer day, I noticed that Old Jet had not been around for a while but was not very worried since he was in the habit of doing "a walk about" now and then, and I just figured he would come home in a day or so.

I was the Drum Major of the band that year, the ultimate "bandit" and I had a key to the school and band room. A couple of days after I noticed Old Jet was AWOL, I went to band practice and when I opened the door, a black blur whizzed past me. Somehow, Old Jet had managed to get himself locked in the band room and had spent several days with no food and only the liquid left in a few coke cups to sustain him. He never had any enthusiasm for band practice after that.

He did however, like to perform. The band regularly played for the Christmas Parade in Carthage at Thanksgiving. Santa would arrive sitting atop the biggest shiniest fire engine in Carthage's fleet (of two engines).

Old Jet followed me to the school building and when the parade started, he simply joined in with the festivities.

My dad described the scene like this, "I looked up the street and there came the band with Buddy (his name for me) out front holding up that big baton, and wearing that fuzzy hat, looking like a big Q tip. In front of him came all of the majorettes wearing their little black outfits with white fur trim, stepping high and twirling. In front of the Majorettes was Fowler Stanton with his snap brim hat on his head, a whistle around his neck, and his little white baton stuck under his left arm. But in front of it all, marching along with tongue hanging out and a slight smile on his face came Old Jet; looking right and left at the crowd like he was acknowledging the applause he knew was for him alone. He was the hit of the parade that year."

Sometime during those years my mother became sick, Adie was already going down fast with cancer and Daddy had to do the cooking. It was during that period that Old Jet went on one of his extended absences and the joke at our house was that, "when Daddy did the cooking, the dog left home." My mother recovered, resumed the cooking duties, and Old Jet came home.

The stories of Old Jet go on and on since he was a character of the first order, but I will finish by telling you that when I went away to college at Lipscomb, Old Jet left home – and this time he never returned. Did he try to follow and find me? Did he wander away and get run over by one of the cars he liked to chase when the family was sitting out in the front yard. (He only chased them when he would embarrass all of us – I think he thought we would be impressed, a mistake all of us make occasionally.) Did he leave with a broken heart? Of course I don't know, but I like to think that he simply moved on to another young boy who needed to learn the lessons only he was able to teach.

Someone has said, "If there are no dogs in heaven, then when I die, I want to go where they went." I am not sure I subscribe to that philosophy fully, but there is some merit there somewhere.

I don't know if there will be dogs in heaven, oh I understand that they are not beings with souls like ours, but it is hard for me to imagine that a God who would provide gates of pearl, streets of gold, and a tree of life, would not want me to have the companionship of a dog like Old Jet. Of course I could have this all wrong.

Chapter VII
Southern Accents

53. Keeping an Eye on the Sky

After working in an office for 35 years, I was able to return to the home and life I loved so much, and now we raise Black Angus Cattle. This year has been a good year to be a farmer in Middle Tennessee. It is one of those years when the rains have come right on time and the grass is knee deep in the pastures. Hay is plentiful and the price of beef is decent again. Yes sir, all in all, a good time to be a farmer.

It is not always that way though; around here everyone remembers a couple of summers ago when the mercury climbed to 100 degrees and the rains did not come for weeks upon end. The ponds turned into nearly dry mud holes and the springs dried to a trickle the size of a soda straw.

At one point we had to get down on our hands and knees in the rocky bed of the stream that leads from the spring to our pond and chisel out the high spots in the rock so the water would continue to trickle into the rubber trough that now stood in the muddy slush that once was our main stock pond.

It is then that you know how dependant you are upon your maker. No matter how smart you are, and no matter how well liked in the community; you just can't make the rain come yourself.

This year though, the maker has sent the rains on time and other than the occasional trip to check on their general health and do routine maintenance, the year has come easy. No looking at the skies day after day and wondering when the rain will come. No lying awake at night and wondering what to do if the last trickle from the spring dries up.

And truth be told, not much soul searching about how dependant we are on the one who made it all - no need to, all is going well.

Isn't that a lot like we are in life? When the rains of fortune come on time, we are prone to think about everything but the one we depend upon; but when the tides turn and we are casting our eyes toward the sky in hopeful longing, we find prayer comes easy.

It is a lesson that America could do well to grasp in this trying time, and as the economic drought continues, cast our eyes toward the sky to look for the sign of relief.

54. Visiting With the Preacher

The brown eyed girl and I just got home from visiting with our preacher and his wife who had asked us to a "Christmas In July." It was a wonderful evening and as the old time newspapers would say "a good time was had by all."

I grew up close to the church building and my mother and dad would invite someone home from church with us nearly every Sunday night.

My mother was a woman of boundless energy and one who never worried about how her house looked or what we had to serve company. Not that she did not care about her home, nor that she was inhospitable to our guests, it was simply that in her view what was good enough for us, was good enough for anyone, and what we had, others were welcome to share.

"Good enough, what there is of it; and plenty of it, such as it is"; was her saying.

Sometime all we might have was cheese and crackers for a snack, coffee of course, and plenty of milk for the children - or if you didn't want that, cold water in the old refrigerator. Admittedly not fancy fare, but it always seemed to me that folks loved to come to our house, not in spite of how they were treated, but because of how the were treated. She was comfortable, and that made them comfortable. She didn't worry about whether what she served was "good enough" because what she was serving was making visitors feel like family - and they did feel like family. They felt comfortable, welcome, loved, and knew that someone was interested in them - that is a pretty powerful serving.

You were welcome to kick off your shoes, or leave them on; to sit up or slouch down; to ask for water, or look in the refrigerator and get it yourself. "Make yourself at home" was not just a saying, it was a way of life.

The result was that my sister and I grew up comfortable in almost every situation - not feeling like we had to "put on the dog" for anyone. It was a tremendous favor that our mother bestowed on us and we will forever be in her debt.

My wife once asked her if she did not get nervous having the preacher to dinner and her answer was, "honey, they put their pants on just like everyone else, no need to be nervous."

If the saying is true, "Christians are just beggars trying to help other beggars find bread," then few of us have anything of which to be especially proud nor any reason to think highly of ourselves. If we do not overly consider our own station in life, we will be less inclined to worry about how other consider our station in life.

55. <u>Shepherds Should Learn from Cowboys</u>

I don't know much about sheep, because they were the white woolly things that other people raised, but I have learned a lot about human nature from observing my old cows. I went to check on them yesterday and they were nowhere to be seen; no doubt standing in the shadows created by tree-lined Round Lick Creek. All seemed to be in order, the electric fence was clicking away, the water troughs were full and I did not see any buzzards circling in that creepy way they have of going about the job they have been assigned.

I wasn't satisfied though, because I hadn't been able to see them, to look them in the eye and feel confident that not one of them was looking sick or otherwise abnormal. So I called, just twice and waited. Now I generally do not have to call, because they know my old red truck and respond to the sight and sound of it, and come in a run when they see it at the gate or hear its bed rattling, so I knew they must be a long way away.

In about two minutes though, here they came, strung out in a long line with a couple of the old faithfuls leading the way. Of course, there were some lagging behind, taking their own sweet time, and a little calf or two running and frisking out to the sides as their mamas looked over their shoulder disapprovingly. As soon as I saw them coming, I regretted that I had not taken time to go to the barn and get a little bucket of the sweet feed they like so much, or a little of the course salt they crave. They expect something good when they are called, and I don't like to disappoint them.

We spent just a few minutes together, me walking among them talking to them as if they understood, knowing that although they did not understand my words, they certainly understood my tone. I want them to always be familiar with my voice, and smell, and even to know that when I speak in a certain tone, it really does mean "move over" or "get out of that barn."

It seems to me that shepherds could learn a lot from cattle farmers. Oh, I don't mean literal shepherds, but those who shepherd the various parts of God's flock. My cows come when I call because they know my voice and they know that when they come they will be fed. Something good will happen when they respond to my call - or, as a friend told me - at least nothing bad will happen. I invest time in them, walking among them, trying to determine if their nose is running, or their eyes look dull, if they are loosing weight, or if they have an injury of any kind. I do it because I love doing it, since as many can attest, it is not because of the money. I know them and they know me and they realize that when they gather together with me, it is to be cared for in some way.

Yes, I think shepherds could learn from cattle farmers.

56. My Crow is the Blackest

Ma Ma Maberry had a saying that went, "every fellow thinks his crow is the blackest," and I guess it is so since on our recent tour of the eastern Mediterranean, everywhere we went the guide extolled the virtues of the port we were visiting. When I looked out of the window of the big tour bus I saw ground so rocky that a bull tongue plow would wear out in a week, and the guide was talking about the richness of the volcanic soil. I saw pasture so steep that you would have to tie a goat on the side of the mountain to allow it to graze, and the guide talked about how the slopes presented themselves to the warmth of the sun and filled the grapes with sugar. I noted that the houses were small and few had glass windows, while the guide pointed out the whitewashed and blue houses that mimicked the colors of the Greek flag. I sat terrified as some driver named Pasqualie, or Nicholas, or Bruno, hurled a bus around the side of the mountain with a 500 foot drop to the sea on a road barely wide enough for two motor scooters to pass one another, while the guide pointed out that we were lucky because our driver was the best in all Italy, or Greece, or Turkey, or Croatia – I can only imagine what the bad ones might have been like. I noted that public restroom facilities were unknown unless you were willing to pay 1 Euro ($1.50) to get in (sometimes it was 1 Euro for two, which I thought took the buddy system to a whole new high.) One of our fellow travelers noted that she could have never imagined that there were so many ways to flush a toilet! Meanwhile the guide pointed out that the floor was covered with a tile mosaic two thousand years old – to me it looked as if it were perhaps covered with something else.

I think the toilet facilities in ancient Ephesus took companionship to a whole new high.

We strolled down streets so narrow that a VW Beetle would not have fit through, while the guide noted that the narrow winding streets protected one from the strong off shore winds – a fact that the ladies in our group would have disputed given that they had developed whole new hair-dos as a result of those prevailing winds.

Traffic laws are merely vague guidelines in Rome, Naples, Athens, and Dubrovnik, but the guides liked to point out the skill with which the motorcyclists, all with an apparent death wish, whisk in and out of traffic, sometime coming within a hairs breadth of another moving vehicle.

We were pointed to hundreds of churches – all of them empty except for special feast days and told with pride how the long dead body of the patron saint was trotted out five times a year and carried through the streets of the city. We could only sneak glances of horror at one another and raise our eyebrows when no one was looking.

In Venice, we were told about the beautiful architecture, only to later learn that the city has become so expensive that very few Venetians can still afford to live in the city. Most have to live far out and drive in to work for the tourists who have taken over their city.

When I saw our home and crawled in our bed after a long flight I developed a suspicion but when I went to church at Maple Hill Sunday, and our Son, Daughter-in-love, and four precious grandchildren showed up to spend some time with us, my suspicions were confirmed – my crow is definitely the blackest!

57. <u>Unexpected Endings</u>

A staple of Southern life has always been telling tall tales and spinning yarns. The best story tellers start out as if you are about to hear and actual happening, and it is not until you are well down the primrose path that you realize you have been had. They go quickly from prose that paints a truly believable and acceptable story, to the ridiculous in the literal wink of an eye.

Barney Smith, a distant cousin from the Gentry Clan occasionally is kind enough to send me a story that he particularly likes and the following is about a gentleman by the name of H.T. Miller.

"H.T. Miller was a pioneer Texas truck driver and a consummate teller of tall tales. I first knew H.T. about 40 years ago, when he was probably 60 years old and had already run up and down Texas roads for thirty five or forty years. I don't know if his stories were original but they were certainly entertaining to anyone within earshot.

Driving in those days was certainly different than now. There were no interstate highways and every trip was a slow and steady journey through big cities and small towns. Truckers were known as "knights of the road" in those days and had a valid history of assisting stranded motorists and dispensing road directions. There were no cell phones, loud and obnoxious CB radios, and only a few of us even had AM radios. You soon ran out of ear-shot of whatever you were listening to, so driving a truck could be a pretty lonesome business sometime.. But there was always a lot of camaraderie and good cheer when we took time to stop in a coffee shop, usually in the wee hours of the morning.

I recall a particular trip with H. T. and four or five other drivers hauling oilfield pipe from Houston to Kansas. We spent all day loading our trailers and finally got everybody in their rigs and headed to Kansas with H.T. in the lead. We drove several hours before we saw his tail lights turn into a small roadhouse north of Fort Worth sometime around two o'clock in the morning. We all followed him into the parking lot, grateful to be out of those trucks for awhile. The restaurant was a typically nondescript establishment and only had two or three other patrons. Nearly all restaurants had juke boxes in those days and Hank and Ernest were wailing the blues. The waitresses were glad to see some action and started bringing us coffee before we even got set down good. H. T. sipped his coffee and waited. Finally someone asked, "Where You from H.T?"

That was all it took to get him going. "I'm from so far back in the East Texas piney woods that they had to pipe sunshine to us, and I never traveled more than four or five miles away from home until I was past 18 years old. I could see the smoke from town on a cold day and I could hear a far off train whistle about once a day but that was about as close to any kind of actual civilization that I had ever seen. I got up every morning and helped Daddy milk several old cows by hand and by lantern light. After we finished milking, Daddy would send me to plow the fields and I would spend the rest of the day a'hold of the handles of a double shovel, looking at the south end of a north bound mule. I still remember those mule emissions and believe that was what caused me to take up truck driving. It wasn't all hard work though; sometimes Daddy would take me deer hunting with him. Course we lived so far out, we had to go towards town to hunt. He'd make the shot and I would run up and grab that deer by the horns and cut its throat, with it still thrashing around. I didn't find out till I was about 16 that he had been shooting blanks to save money.

I used to hunt and kill squirrels simply by hitting the with rocks but Daddy made me stop that cause he said I was tearing 'em up too bad. But one bright sunshiny day, Daddy told me he wanted me to hitch the mare up to the buggy and pick up a few things in town. Course I was tickled to death cause I was gon'na get to go somewhere. He gave me a list of the things he needed in town and helped me hook the mare to the buggy. He told me that when I got to town, I needed to be sure and unhook the mare and tie her to a rail.

"If the train comes through there, she'll get spooked and tear that buggy up."

I listened attentively and promised Daddy that I would take care of the mare and the buggy. I was a happy young'n as I started off on the first trip I had ever made anywhere by myself.

Town was about a two block affair with a train station, a hotel and a general store and as I pulled down the main drag I looked around and I was flabbergasted at the things they had that I had never seen. I pulled up to the general store and unhooked the mare and tied her to a hitching rail. I was just fixing to go in the store when Mr. Childs, the owner, appeared and asked me if I would move the buggy forward a few feet so as not to block access to the side door of the store. I decided I would leave the mare hooked to the rail and just move the buggy myself so I got between the buggy traces and was just starting to pull it pretty good when the that train came screaming through that little town doing about 60 miles per hour, sucking up leaves and papers behind it, and that whistle wailing like a tail caught wild cat. Well sir, that mare stood stock still as a rock, but I tore that buggy all to pieces."

There was much laughter and everyone knew that they couldn't top H. T, Miller when it came to telling a windy story.

Congratulations to H.T. and Barney for a great story and it occurs to me that sometimes God's solutions to our prayers and problems are like the endings to Southern Tales.

They slip up on you when you least expect them and in the most surprising ways.

Have a blessed day, and may you be pleasantly surprised by God's Grace.

58. Seeing Clearly is a Point of View

My sister is four years older than I, and has always thought she was "the boss of me." As much as I hate to admit it, on many occasions in our growing up years she was the boss of me. Mama was working, Daddy was working, and although Adie directed affairs at home, she did not drive and was not of a bent to be in charge of things outside the house. So, at the age of 11 or 12 years, it was she who accompanied me to the eye doctor to get my new glasses. I had always had to sit up front in class in order to see what was going on with the blackboard but even on the front seat, it was getting harder and harder to make heads or tails of what was written. No one took you to the doctor unless you were sick and several days of home remedy had not worked – there wasn't time nor money for that - and besides it wasn't done then. The school had through some federal or state program done one of those machine tests on our eyes – the kind they give you when you get your drivers license test – and the consensus opinion was, "this kid is blind as a bat." So Donnieta and I were taken to old Dr. Gallaher to determine if we needed glasses. She wanted them, and did not need them; I despised the thought but needed them badly. Unlike today, very few things happened in "about an hour," so the glasses had been some weeks in coming through the mail.

When they had arrived, Donnieta took me to town to get them fitted to my face and somewhat prominent ears. I was pretty offended by the thought of having to go through life with the title "four eyes" tattooed to my forehead, but it looked as if that were to be my lot in life. Looking at the charts, I was a little amazed at how well I could see the letters with the plastic rimmed affairs plopped on my face, but it was later, as we walked home that the real shock came.

Trees were no longer just big green blobs, they were a mosaic of individual leaves; grass was no longer green blur with the texture of a tennis ball; they were a massive army of individual blades – who knew? Certainly not I.

What I found out was that you don't know what you are missing if you have never experienced it. My vision seemed vaguely troubling but basically I though I got along fine. It never occurred to me that others could clearly see the preacher's tie and face on Sunday; or that others could really make out those numbers on the football players jersey. No wonder everyone else did not like to lie directly under the television set – they could see from the comfort of the couch.

Life is like that too. Sometimes we think we see clearly, when the case is that we simply do not know how "clearly" is defined. We think our life is filled with success but it only seems that way because we don't have a clear picture of success.

The Samaritan woman at the well thought she had good pure water to give Jesus, but he introduced her to the concept of "living water" that would mean she would never thirst again. She felt no thirst for such water, because she had no concept of its existence.

Maybe we don't long for the blessings Jesus is offering as we should, because we are unable or unwilling to fully visualize those blessing.

The Apostle Paul said, "For now we see in a mirror, dimly, but then face to face. Now I know in part, but then I shall know just as I am known.

By the way, my sister called from Kansas City and suggested that I put his in the blog – see - she is still the boss of me.

59. Slipping Up the Holler

There is an old song that I like called, "Dooley"

It seems Dooley was slipping up the holler, trying to make a dollar on the nectar which came from the corn. While I like the song, I have a major concern about the product sung about.

A lot has been written about the reasons for many of my ancestors choosing to make whiskey. Now not all of it was back holler moonshine, since my great granddaddy, Marlin Young, was granted a license by the federal government to run a still of a particular size. I know, because my youngest son

Patrick still has the official paper where the stilling operation was inspected before the turn of the century.

Over the years I have had occasion to council with a number of families that are in trouble one way or another, and in a surprising number of cases, alcohol is involved.

When I was a little boy I had to learn this poem to say for one program or another at school and while I may have missed a couple of words, the essence of the poem goes like this:

T'was a cold night in October, And a fellow not too sober
    was carrying home a load with manly pride
When his feet began to stutter, He lay down in the gutter
    And a pig came by and lay down by his side.
As he lay there in the gutter, with his mouth all drool and sputter
    a lady passing by did chance to say:
"you can tell a man who boozes, by the company he chooses."
    And the pig got up and slowly walked away.

Choose your companions carefully. The good book tells us that evil companions corrupt good morals.

60. <u>Evil Spirits Under the Back Seat</u>

The first car I can ever remember us having was a grey four door Chevrolet Sedan. It was one of those shaped something like a VW Beatle on steroids. We bought it when we moved to town since Daddy no longer needed a pickup truck to take a hog or a calf to the stock sale and our family of four had grown to five with Adie (my widowed great aunt) moved in with us to live. We had been able to stuff the two adults and two kids into the front of the old yellow truck, but five was more of a stretch than even we were willing to make. Some folks still rode around with straight chairs in the bed of the truck and various members of the family sitting back in the open air, but Daddy was having none of that. He bought the car at Hughes Motor Company since they had taken it in as a "trade in" on a new Studebaker, and it looked like it had a lot of good miles left on it.

The only real problem was that it was a really ugly color – primer grey and the seats were that sort of sheared mohair looking stuff Chevy used before my days with the company. It ran pretty good and seemed to have a "right smart of spunk" since it would climb the hill to my grandparent's house without putting it down into low gear. That was the test in those days of manual transmissions, how much grade and strain would the car take without downshifting. (Of course, the car was internally hemorrhaging, but it was a source of pride nonetheless.)

We kept that car for a couple of years, but when Daddy went to work for Hughes Motors, he bought a Studebaker Champion. Not the classed up model that my Uncle Billy had but a plain Jane model that everyone wanted to install a propeller on – not funny after a while.

When the fellows took the car in to detail it out and prepare it for resale, they removed the back seat, and there in plain view was a pint bottle of whiskey wrapped in newspaper. Immediately the guys at the dealership began to razz Daddy about his stash he had forgotten and left under the back seat. He was more than a little upset, being a good church of Christ guy who was a tee-totaler and member in good standing of the local church.

We had never had occasion to remove the rear seat and all of us, including prim and proper Aunt Ada, had spent a couple of years riding around sitting on a pint of "Old Crow."

That's the way life is, what you see on the surface is seldom indicative of what is underneath. We hide things away and try to forget for a time, as undoubtedly the previous owner had done with the bottle. Or we think we are pure as the driven snow, but all the time we are only inches from contact with sin and disaster.

Perhaps we are like the guys at the dealership, ready to believe the worst at the first opportunity.

We probably would be well served to spend more time casting crowns and less time casting stones

61. **I'd Ruther of Lost my Best Mule!**

While much of what I write about extols the virtues of the "Good Old Days," there are some things that are better than before. One is the way today's dads are involved in the upbringing of their children. I am amazed and gratified at the way my own sons and the young guys I know participate in family life – anything from changing diapers to giving baths at night. It has not always been that way and the old saying, "men may work from sun to sun, but woman's work is never done" did not just happen to come about.

Women of the Upper Cumberland were expected to take care of the garden, milk the cows, see after the chickens, churn and make butter, can garden fare, care for all aspects of the house, and have and care for the children, of which there was generally a large number.

It was just the way things were and old Gospel Advocate articles at the turn of the last century advised men that the way to domestic tranquility did not lie in treating wives as property and Brother Sewell advised men in at least one article that, "Women should not be treated as a prized dog or horse, rather as a partner in the home."

I suppose that one old fellow in the Peyton's Creek community of Smith County meant well when at the funeral of his lately departed wife he told consoling visitors, "She was a good-un; I'd ruther a lost my best mule."

In my own home, my dad would say to my mother, sitting on the couch beside him, "Maylene, while you'er up, get me a glass of water." She, who had been working at the shirt factory all day, would jump up with not even an eye roll, and get a glass of water,

I heard many sermons when I was growing up about the duties of women to "be subject to your own husband," but it was only as an adult that I learned that shortly before that the old Apostle had required that husbands and wives be subject to one another.

At any rate, I commend the younger generation for the more equitable division of duties in the home and have tried to learn from you.

62. A Pig in a Poke Might be a Possum

I was looking at Facebook a couple of days ago and noticed a post by a young woman with whom we are friends through church. She is from Gainesboro and all of us Jackson County folks hang to gather around here to avoid the obvious outcome of hanging separately. Tammy posted that she had done approximately $1500.00 worth of damages to her car by hitting a big fat possum crossing the road. Someone else chimed in by telling that they had torn up the radiator on their car by hitting a raccoon. It is obvious that the shortage of coon and possum hunters these days is allowing for overpopulation which is manifesting itself in increased road-kill.

Every year RBJ Farms buys a two ton bin full of feed for our cattle, which provides them with high protein content during these cold winter months. Otherwise they would be forced to subsist on hay, salt and water. It is the byproduct of processing corn to create corn oil and other corn products and contains 22% protein. They absolutely love the stuff and we must be careful when feeding, that in their exuberance to get to the feed, they do not run one of us down.

Apparently, they are not the only animals that love the stuff, for two years ago we began to notice that the bin filled with feed had begun to go down noticeably, even though we had not as yet started to feed the cattle from the bin. Upon closer inspection, we found that some type of animal had chewed its way through the plywood floor of the bin and the food was pouring down through the hole created. Randy (my partner/cousin) went to the local Farmer's Coop and bought some traps which we set nightly around the obvious runways. Over the next few weeks we sent 23 possums and raccoons to varmint heaven and put a stop to the poaching of our feed bin. Corn is too high to share with the woodland creatures just now.

Speaking of Possums reminds me of a friend's father who had some rental houses in the Detroit area and rented one of the houses to a young couple who had been raised in the city. One morning he received a distressed call from the young man who informed him that he needed to get over there right away. It seems a giant rat had invaded the garbage can in the alley behind the house. The fellow had capped the lid on the can and was calling Mr. Maberry, the landlord, to come and dispose of the critter. Mr. Maberry pulled on his coat and drove over to check out the situation straight away. There in the alley, he found a huge fat possum hunkered down in the garbage, probably somewhat ashamed of having been accused of being a rat.

Speaking of rats reminds me of a story Barney Smith shared with me about a rat.

"My son Ronnie lives in a nice new Houston neighborhood of cul-de-sac streets full of kids skateboarding, riding bicycles and is an altogether pleasant place to live. Ronnie may have a few run-of – the mill faults , but I don't believe that I ever caught Ronnie in a blatant lie. I know that sounds far-fetched but he has many good qualities, truthfulness among them. Now I do admit that he has been unduly evasive a time or two, but overall has been a most satisfactory offspring..

One bright Saturday afternoon, I pulled up in his driveway to find him sitting in a lawn chair by the garage and he motioned me to pull up a chair. He seemed excited in an agitated kind of way. "What's up" I asked him. "Well," he said, " I just killed a big rat." That sounded passably interesting so I encouraged him to tell me about it.

"I was upstairs when Toni (his wife) started hollering and I quickly went to investigate. She was in the kitchen with the door to the garage locked. "There's a filthy rodent in the garage", she screamed. I slipped into the garage and peered around but I didn't see anything. I had almost given up when I heard a rattling noise. Under a small table, there was the biggest rat I have ever seen and he was eating Boo's food. (Boudreaux the dog). I quickly shut the door and locked it, then went upstairs after my pellet gun. When I came back to the garage, I looked around until I finally, after stalking him all over the garage, cornered the nasty thing. It took only one shot and he was no more. I carried his sorry carcass to the woods.

He was a fearsome looking rat alright but he didn't look like your average Norway rat. He was awfully big and had brown & white splotches on him."

We leaned back in our lawn chairs with a glass of iced tea and were contemplating the law of the jungle when a ten year old neighbor kid from up the street walked up. He was a pleasant kid and gratefully took the coke that Ronnie offered. He stood around for a couple minutes, shifting his eyes from corner to corner in the garage. Finally he ask, "Ya ll didn't happen to see my big spotted rat scooting around here did you?

There was a long drawn out silence and finally Ronnie lowered his eyes and said with all the empathy he could muster. "No Son, I didn't."

The term we hear today from the television is "Profiling" – that is, making a determination about someone based upon the external, observable, evidence. There is much talk and lots of opinion about its appropriateness in security and police work, and obvious room for disagreement. But we are given some instruction by Jesus' brother James concerning spiritual profiling.

> " [2] Suppose a man comes into your meeting wearing a gold ring and fine clothes. And suppose a poor man in worn-out clothes also comes in. [3] Would you show special attention to the one who is wearing fine clothes? Would you say, "Here's a good seat for you"? Would you say to the poor person, "You stand there"? Or "Sit on the floor by my feet"? [4] If you would, aren't you treating some people better than others? Aren't you like judges who have evil thoughts?" NIVRV James 2:2-4

James' instructions leave little room for personal opinion for you see, we, in our fallible judgment, are often apt to confuse a possum with a rat, or a pet with a purveyor of pestilence.

63. "I never met a man I didn't like" - Will Rogers

In the years I worked at General Motors and negotiated contracts, one of the things I encouraged negotiations teams to be diligent about was managing the expectations of their management. The fact is, negotiations always look easy, and the outcome always looks like less than could have been accomplished, to those who are tourists to the deal. It's a little like the fact that everyone else's job looks easy, until you try to do it – walk in their moccasins so to speak.

It was a big surprise to me when at 20 years old, I went north to work in Detroit and found the extreme degree of prejudice against Southerners, "hillbillies" in their vernacular. Their view of the South had mostly been drawn from Life Magazine accounts of the Hatfield and McCoy feud or stories about the abject poverty in Appalachia which led with pictures of dirty faced, hollow eyed children standing in front of their board and batten shack notched into a hillside. It usually featured two or three hound dogs, an old washing machine on the front porch, and a junk car or two which had mostly been stripped for parts with the trunk lid left open.

Soon after starting work for a Chrysler Mopar Division supplier, I was asked to become foreman of the crankshaft refurbish operation. Our department would grind down the mains and throws and put oversized bearings on the newly cleaned crankshaft. It was 1964 and people in America could and did still rebuild their own cars using a chain fall in the shade of a strong limbed oak tree.

The plant superintendent came up to me and said, "We got this bunch of hillbilly boys working in the crankshaft department, and they go out every Friday night, spend all of their pay in the bars, get in a fight, and end up not being able to work on Monday morning. Besides that, they are late every other day. We think you might be able to handle them." Now, I had started work in the engine paint booth, where Chrysler engines that had failed in warranty were painted after being rebuilt. It was before the days of protection for workers or the environment, and I wore a paper mask, used a hand spray gun, and the overspray and fumes were exhausted into the atmosphere via a fifty five gallon drum through the wall with the ends cut out and an exhaust fan mounted on the inside. The heat was brutal and I spent two hours every night blowing blue paint out of my nose.

Despite the fact that the clear implication was, "you being one of them might be able to handle them," I jumped at the chance to get another job, any other job, and thus began my supervisory work in an automotive plant.

What I soon found out was, first not all of them were Southerners at all, second, of the ones that were, several were good solid Baptists who did not and would not drink. Third of the ones left, there truly were one or two who frequented bars on the east side, had been in a bar fight or two, and had showed up to work with cuts and bruises as a result. As for being late, several of them, like I, had only one car or no car that ran, so they rode to work together in Eli Smith's big old 1957 Cadillac. Eli had a tough time getting up early anyway, and any mishap anywhere in the chain resulted in the whole carload being late to work.

Since Jan and I lived on the east side, also had only one car, and she was working as well, I arranged to ride with the group. So every morning, six of us squeezed into the big blue land yacht and cruised to work to build Mopar Parts.

I learned something about life, human nature, and the danger of lumping all of the vegetables into the same bowl and calling them potatoes. It was a lesson that is always there when I am tempted to treat others according to my predetermined stereotype. It surely looks different when you are on the other side of the fence.

Will Rogers when referring to Leon Trotsky once said, "I bet if I had met him and had a chat with him, I would have found him a very interesting fellow, for I never met a man I didn't like."

Jesus told us to not look on the outside of a man to judge by his clothes or externals what we think a man might be. Unless we are able to look into his heart, we should leave the judgment of his worth to God, because men always start with expectations of behavior and worth that are based on their own limited experiences. And these limited experiences become the lens, or perhaps prism, with which we view life.

64. <u>Trying Out Old Sparky</u>

It is not something I talk about a great deal, nor am especially proud of, so most people have no idea that it even happened. I was pretty young at the time and prone to making the mistakes boys make, but the truth is that I spent some time in the Tennessee State Prison in Nashville. Oh, It has been years ago now and many of the memories of that time have left my mind, but that is the type of experience that never quite leaves you.

No, I am not a hardened criminal, nor was I actually incarcerated, but I did spend time inside the penitentiary, at least a few nights when I was a kid. You see, my Uncle U. L. Mabry had a sister named Ellie who was married to a fellow by the name of Perry Smith, and Perry was the superintendent of the Stockade on the prison farm. Uncle U.L. and Aunt Thelma would sometimes go down and spend a night or two with them while they were "home" from Detroit, and since our house was home base and my cousins Morris and Ralph, and I were inseparable when they were down in the summers, I was often allowed to go along.

They lived in a nice little white frame house in sight of the Stockade, which is where the Trustees who worked the prison farm lived. It was there that they spent the night in lockup, and were confined when not actually working under guard.

We always tried to get up early in the morning to see the trustees walking out to the fields, with one or two shotgun armed guards riding along on big horses. It looked like a scene from "Cool Hand Luke" and was pretty exciting for a 10 year old boy.

Perry and Ellie had a house boy, a trustee, who pretty much performed all of the household work, including cooking their meals. In those days the prisoners mostly wore the old black and white stripe outfits that only exist in old movies today, but the house boys all wore white coats like a porter, but prisoner stripe pants.

We were allowed to go down to the stockade and sit where the convicts ate at the long rows of stainless steel tables with welded stainless steel benches. We could drink Cool Aid from the stainless steel pitchers, and eat snacks that the convict cooks delighted in giving us. We even went to the barber shop and had a convict give us a haircut for 25 cents; did a good job too. (He offered to give me a shave, but I demurred.)

On one side of the prison farm was a rock quarry where prisoners were sent when they broke rules or refused to cooperate. There they were allowed to contemplate their sins while they made small rocks out of big ones. It was the ultimate punishment for a trustee – anything more than that and you were sent back up to "The Walls."

The Walls, was the main prison where the cell blocks were. The cell blocks were actually built into and a part of the walls which formed the prison compound. In The Walls, an inmate was either put in solitary, the worst of all places except the Death House, or you were put into a cell block. Since

"Uncle" Perry was with us, we got a pretty good tour, but at The Walls they still searched the women's purses, and patted us down before we were allowed to go through the double entrance gates. A person entering went thought one set of gates, they were locked, entrants searched and patted down, then the second set of bars were opened and one was allowed out into the courtyard. If an inmate was lucky and his behavior was exemplary, he did various kinds of machine shop work, laundry work, kitchen work, or made license plates – no really they actually did make license plates. This was prior to the days of "work release programs" but any work is better than the monotony of the cell.

The county has a law enforcement training facility beside our farm in Smith County where the trustees work around the facility and often one or more will weed-eat around our entrance gate. I once remarked to an incredibility young looking fellow in orange coveralls that he did not have to do that, but he replied, "It's no problem Mister, anything is better than sitting in that cell."

I think the memory of my days in the "pen" that sticks most in my mind however, is the visit we made to Old Sparky, the electric chair. The "Chair" was the sole method of execution used by Tennessee at the time and it was housed in the "death house." The death house was a three story building that had originally been used for hangings and Old Sparky, sat under the trap door of the gallows where the hapless victim was dropped half way to where Old Sparky then sat. It had sat there for some 90 years and claimed just fewer than 150 capital offenders.

The first floor of the death house was a medical facility of sorts that was the first stop for the body of the executed, before being prepared for burial. There the doctor made absolutely sure the job had been done. Two thousand plus volts of current was passed through the inmate's body for just over two minutes, and if he was found still alive, a second two minutes finished the job.

The condemned man was given two days in the death cell prior to execution, questioned as to his preference for burial, funeral arrangements, etc, and allowed to visit with relatives, but always under direct guard. They were fed the traditional last meal and then led in heavy shackles to their final seat of dishonor. It was a sobering place, even for a 10 year old boy.

Now abandoned cell block and Old Sparky. Although this is the original spot of the electric chair, it is not the original chair. The original Old Sparky which I saw, was retired about 1960 and subsequently purchased by Ripley's Believe it or Not Museum and has been displayed in their Gatlinburg, TN museum.

The prison stands abandoned now, having served its function from 1898 until 1992 when a class action suite resulted in an order that the State of Tennessee could never use that site to house dangerous criminals again – I suppose it was not uptown enough for the polished crowd inside. Oh my, how times have changed.

I thought of these things last night as I sat in a bible study where we talked of the scripture in Colossians 1:13,14 where Paul noted that God…"rescued us from the domain of darkness and transferred us to the kingdom of His beloved Son, in whom we have redemption, the forgiveness of sins."

And though my time "in prison" was brief and I was but a visitor, it occurred to me that in a greater sense, we all were like so many inmates of the old Tennessee State Prison, held without hope when He suddenly granted us pardon, not because we deserved it, but out of pure love. We were on death row, in the darkness and bound for a date with Old Sparky; the life was being drained out of us, when we were given pardon by the creator of the universe. What could possibly surpass that for having a good day?

65. <u>Hidden Treasures</u>

Yesterday I was looking through a drawer at Carthage and came across a little plastic box filled with treasures that our youngest son Patrick had placed there, probably when he went away to college. There was a pocket knife that his Granddaddy Lafever always carried when he was pheasant hunting, a patch from a trip we took to Standing Stone State Park years and years ago, some Canadian Money, and a squirrel's tail from his first hunting trip when he was about 7 or 8 years old.

The old black handled Barlow was one that I have seen Granddaddy Lafever break out many a time and peel an apple that he had picked from a tree in the fence line where some long forgotten Almont, Michigan orchard had once flourished. He could make the peeling stay together in one long unbroken line and touch the ground before he reached the last circle of the apple. He was the guy that Patrick got his height from – 6 foot, 3 inches, long and lean with strong legs that had done many a hard day's work in both field and factory.

The Standing Stone State Park patch is like the ones the Park Rangers have on the sleeve of their uniform. We went to Standing Stone many times with my mom and dad, along with my sister, her husband, and all of the assorted cousins. They were special times when my mom would ride in the back of a pickup truck, wade the creek, and cook endlessly good meals for us all. On one particular night we were singing together outside the old cabins, built by the CCC and WPA during the great depression, when critters started zooming out of the towering Poplar Trees and swooping down, barely missing our heads. They were flying squirrels (Google them if you don't believe they exist.) and they were catching the bugs attracted to the light of the old Coleman lantern.

One of the last great trips to Standing Stone was for the Thanksgiving just prior to Patrick and Gabie marrying, and it was her initiation into the family. Everyone had a joke of some kind to play on her, but she endured it all with good humor. We swam in the pool, climbed the trail to the old fire tower, and inspected the courts where the world championship "Rolley Hole Marbles" playoff is held. (Again, check it out if you don't believe me. The players use only locally crafted and hand fashioned marbles and the game is a dinosaur of the mountains.)

The squirrel tail came from a little red fox squirrel taken just after dawn in a little wood lot just outside Grand Rapids, Michigan. The boys and I met up with an older teenager whose family was part of our church family there. Gavin Lowe and I carried guns and the two little boys got up very early so we could be slipping into the woods as daylight came. I warned them to wear their "Moon Boots" as we called them, bulky snow boots with foam liners that protected your feet against the massive snow storms that were part of daily life in Grand Rapids. Since it was early in October or November and no snow had fallen yet, Chris decided that he would just wear his gym shoes as they were lighter and looked much cooler. What dad knew that Chris did not know was that there would be a heavy frost and as the sun began to creep over the horizon this frost would turn to very wet, very cold dew, which would almost immediately penetrate the gym shoes giving the wearer cold, wet, feet. Since he realized that he had gotten himself into real trouble by not listening, he did not say a word, even though his feet were freezing. When I finally discovered his plight, I though we were going to have to have him hospitalized for frost bite, but he recovered with nothing more than stinging, red feet, which "scaled off" in a few weeks like they had been burned.

The Canadian money, well from where we lived in New Baltimore, Michigan, one could see Canada by looking south and there were many trips to Canada, so who knows?

It is interesting what we find to cherish, and stow away in our secrete treasure places. All of us have those places, sometimes it is a drawer, sometimes a box, sometimes an old trunk, sometimes our heart - but we all hold secret treasures. Some of them have little value to anyone but ourselves, some are of incalculable and intrinsic value to the world at large.

Several times when Mary saw the evidence of who the child she bore was, and what He was to become, the bible tells us she "hid those things in her heart."

It was a treasure of incalculable value to her, and the "Marvelous Grace, greater than all our sin;" to us.

66. <u>Puttin' Enough With It</u>

There are many things that I have adopted as a credo for life, which I find are the sayings and things my daddy told me.

For instance, as I have said, he was a great and gifted story teller and always had an interesting story or joke to fit every occasion. He was against any kind of lie and believed that being truthful was important both to who one was and how one was viewed by others, but he had a theory about story telling. He would say, **"Son, if you are going to tell a story, then for goodness sake put enough with it to make it interesting."** His theory was that everyone knew that you were telling a story and that part of it was truth and part of the story was fanciful and made up. He saw it no differently than one might view writing works of fiction. The spoken word was his medium and he worked in it like an artist would water color or oils. I first noticed it by detecting that each story had small twists in plot and shades of turn in details each time I heard him tell it. The basics of the story would always be the same and were no doubt the truth that glued the tale together, but specific details that made the story interesting were changed from time to time and from audience to audience. When I ask him about it, his answer was, "If you are going to try to have people listen to you, then try to be entertaining. Life, without embellishment is dull. It is adding details that the audience will find interesting that livens up a tale and entertains people.

When it came to real honesty in day to day dealings however, his often repeated advise was, **"Be certain you keep your name worth something – the day may come when it is the only thing of value you own."**

"A good name is to be chosen rather than great riches." Proverbs 22:1

He would then go on to tell me about how his great grandfather, Abner Chaffin, went to a rich man in the area and borrowed ten dollars from him. He took the ten dollars home and laid it away in a cup on the mantel. After a few weeks, he went to the rich man again and repaid the unspent ten dollars. A little later he borrowed fifty dollars and treated it in like fashion, laying the money away on the mantel. He again took the unspent money and repaid the rich man. A few months later he was ready to bring his plan to fruition. Abner went again to the rich man and stated that he wanted to buy a farm, but needed to borrow a portion of the money. "Well," said the rich man, "you have certainly been good to repay your debts in the past, how much do you need and how could you repay the money." With that, Abner sat down with the man and worked out the terms of the loan. *"Well done, good and faithful servant; you have been faithful over a few things, I will make you ruler over many things." Matt. 25:23*

67. <u>Piling Rocks and Horse Sense</u>

He was not one for senseless and endless talking and his saying was, **"you can always tell whether a wagon is full or empty, by how much it rattles coming down the road."** He believed the Good Lord gave a man two ears and one mouth as a sign that we should spend twice as much time listening as talking. At his funeral Donald Chaffin, one of the speakers, said of their time together as elders; "When we had a meeting (the elders of the church), Bob would listen while everybody talked. Then when everyone had said their piece, everybody would listen while Bob talked." He had a double helping of common sense – horse sense, as he called it. He taught me to listen carefully to what others thought and said, (which, he rightly contended, were often two different things,) and then make a proposal based upon a workable conclusion, which, standing alone, might not represent the best answer but would bring about the best result, because consensus works. He believed that *everyone* had something of value to add, if only the world would listen. Always within that was the thought that there were certain principles that one could not, and would not, violate based upon our understanding of God's will.

Words of the wise, spoken quietly, should be heard rather than the shout of a ruler of fools. Eccl. 9:17

He was a master at helping us understand that by virtue of whom we were, the name we carried, we had certain responsibilities of conduct. He would say, **"Don't forget who you are – and remember, what you do reflects on the rest of us."**

My sister and I have often discussed how loose the discipline seemed in our home. We had very few "little" rules. We generally had no one demanding that we study, no one telling us when to go to bed at night, no one laying out what clothes to wear, or begging or threatening concerning what we ate at any meal. Instead there were a few "big" rules that you were left to extrapolate to the smaller issues. The big rules were never actually articulated, as such, but they went something like this:

We expect that you will take advantage of the opportunity for an education and do your best.

We expect that you will dress modestly, and be reasonably clean when you go out in public.

We will provide you with the best food, clothing and shelter that we are able to on our modest means. It won't be the best, but it will suffice and we expect that you will honor and respect the work we put into providing and care for what you have.

We expect you will always conduct yourself in a way that will not cause us to be ashamed of your actions.

It was by these expectations that they brought order from chaos and seemed to be comfortable that they would have children who would behave within reasonable bounds. I believe it worked.

A good work ethic was an important quality to my parents. I never heard them complaining about being treated unfairly at work, although I know that those times must have been part of their working life. Instead, they always took pride in being singled out as being a hard worker, or being trusted with greater and greater responsibility, even when they often were not given additional pay commensurate with the responsibility.

As a result, my sister and I did not start our working life expecting an unpleasant experience nor expecting to be taken advantage of by the boss. Our parents demonstrated the ultimate object lesson in, "The boss may not always be right, but he is always the boss."

Daddy's way of saying that was; **"If someone hires you and wants you to pile rocks on one side of the fence, then make sure the pile is straight – if he wants you to move them back to the other side – then move them, and do your best – after all he is the boss."**

He would go on to explain that the boss might have information that you did not have that he was unable to share with you, or which you might be unable to grasp. *"And whatever you do, do it heartily, as to the Lord and not to men." Col. 3:23*

What a favor they did for us having us march off into the work-a-day world with this philosophy of lending our hand to the general effort. If only we could all grasp these things in corporations of the world or congregations of the church, how pleasant life would be.

68. <u>Cider Mills, Orchards, and Million Dollar Days</u>

Friday afternoon our youngest son, Patrick, called and asked what we were going to do on Saturday. Now we occasionally have some event that is so locked in that we are unable to change, but more often we know that, "what are you

all doing tomorrow?" means there is a chance we might get to spend the day with he and his family. We don't see any of them nearly as much as we would like, but we take what we can get and try not to be complainers, knowing that they have busy lives to live, just as we did when we were at their stage of   life.
As it turns out, he wanted to know if we would be interested in going apple picking. Interested – why it was just the thing we were anxious to do – at least after he mentioned it. We have a long history with apple picking in the fall having lived in Michigan for 35 years, where the cold weather makes the apples grow crisp and juicy and keeps the insect population to a minimum; and where the overcast skies prevent frost from forming and killing the flower when it is in bloom.

The first place we fell in love with was a cider mill near where we lived in Rochester, MI which was only a sleepy little town thirty two miles north of Detroit 43 years ago when I went to work for General Motors. The water powered mill had been in operation since 1863 as a grist mill, but in 1873 the Yates family installed a cider press into the existing water-

powered process and began producing delicious Michigan cider. It then became known as Yates Cider Mill. Local farmers, orchard owners and landowners would bring their apples to Yates for custom apple pressing. We loved going there on a crisp fall afternoon and getting a jug of the real stuff, and with a box of donuts picked up at the local Dunkin store, have a feast at the little park across the road. The smell alone was worth the trip.

There was also a favorite orchard or two out by Romeo, MI where the folks would load the family onto an old farm wagon and let the John Deer pull you out to the section they were picking. They were actually commercial operations, but were beginning to discover that allowing families to "pick you own" was a lucrative side business.

At our last home in Michigan, we were only a bike ride away from the Paint Creek Cider Mill which had originally been located on the old Detroit and Bay City Railway, now defunct and converted to a walking trail and bike path. Paint Creek Cider Mill had the best sugar donuts in the state – hands down.

Of all the apple orchards to which I have ever been, Robinette's, just north of Grand Rapids, MI, is my favorite. The family for whom it is named bought the orchard in 1911 and it has continued as a family run operation for nearly 100 years. If the season is very good and the apple crop abundant, the crew will hand-thin the apples to make sure there are plenty of "big reds" ready for families to pick come September.

When we left Tucker's Crossroads and the orchard this morning we all scurried back for a delicious lunch at Cracker Barrel and then spent plenty of time sitting on the big front porch; rocking, talking and playing checkers – why is it grandparents never win when playing grandchildren?

As we sat and rocked, Patrick told John Patrick about the many times we spent in the back yard, under the big trees at my parent's home in Franklin, KY. We talked and talked, and swung in the big porch swing mounted on the frame from a child's gym set. We helped Grandmommie shell butter beans and green peas, we shucked corn for the freezer, and pulled tomatoes from the vines next to Granddaddy's little red barn that sheltered the see-through bee hive. Each one was a "million dollar day" as my cousin Jo Norton would say, and today was of no less value.

It is a continual source of amazement to me that The One who made us is so aware of our needs. He has provided for us by providing family, friends, and fellow believers who form a network of love and support in spite of the trials of this life. It is a significant source of comfort that at 65, very few but good memories remain, and those provide a constant stream of amusing pictures to contemplate. Not only do I say, "Life is Good," I would be remise if I did not add, "God is Good."

69. <u>Crossing Over the River</u>

One of the real joys of doing a book or a blog is the response you get from others who wish to share their stories with you. In the case of Tom Brokaw and the Greatest Generation, the responses from readers became the source for a whole new book.

My friend, Marie, commented on one of my stories that she remembered taking her first long ride in their very first car. She had never been far away from home before and the others in the car began telling how exciting it was going to be to take this trip, because they were going to go "over the river."

"I did not say a word," she said, "but I was terrified. How could this big car go over a river? Surly we would all sink into the muddy water and be drowned." After all, little girls were reminded regularly about the dangers of the rivers and streams around, and how they could drown if they got to close and slipped in. No mother wanted their children to go near the water until they learned to swim???

Well of course, when Marie's family came to the big bridge, one of those old ones where the planks rattled thunderously as you drove across, she began to understand that "over the river" actually meant "over" the river. "I didn't even the mind the clattering of the boards," she said, "I was just so relieved the tires were not touching that water."

Our fears are often unfounded and we spend many sleepless nights and anxious moments dreading events that unfold entirely different than the dark image our imagination paints.

I remember once starting s small grass fire in the vacant lot behind the little store my parents ran. I put it out quickly, but later that night as I lay in my bed, I began to worry that I had somehow not completely extinguished the blaze – that a spark had remained. Soon my imagination had painted a picture of the store being consumed by a mighty roaring fire. My stomach, always troubled, soon began to churn from the worry of the unknown and I called out in the night that plaintive cry, "Mama, I'm goanna be sick!" Mama came running and soon began to sense that there was more wrong than gastric distress. Finally, I confessed my transgression, and Daddy got up out of bed and drove me to the store so I could see for myself that the blaze in my mind was non existent in reality.

My stomach trouble immediately went away, and we all went home and crawled back into the bed. I would add that the incident was hardly finished, and there was some payment the next morning, but for that moment, it was "well with my soul."

In both Marie's story and in mine, the fear of the unknown was much worse than actually confronting the situation; and in my case, confession brought help from one who had the means to provide aid and comfort.

There is an old song about "Living by Faith" that goes like this:

"I care not today what tomorrow may bring, if shadow or sunshine or rain, The Lord I know ruleth ore every thing, and all of my worry is vain."

The situations we imagine in life are seldom as terrible as our fears lead us to believe, and our honest confession and trust in one who can bring a clearer view of the problem, may set our churning stomachs at ease.

70. **The Leader of the Band**

When growing up in Carthage, I was the ultimate band kid. I had no particular musical ability, either vocally or instrumentally, but when Mr. Fowler Stanton, the new Band Director, asked my 8th grade teacher to send me over to the band room to speak with him, I was glad to go, if only to get out of regular classes for awhile. I had taken the required 5th grade music class and learned to play the flutophone but only with marginal ability. Flutophones cost money, and my sister had an old black tonette which she had used four years prior, so my parents saw no reason to purchase the newer model. If there is anything you hate in the fifth grade it is to be different from everyone else, but there I was with an old black tonette while everyone else used a new white flutaphone.

Nevertheless, I found the class enjoyable once I got past the initial embarrassment of not being like everyone else.

I didn't know much about Mr. Stanton but the eighth grade was in the old grammar school building and so was the band room so I could hear the high school band playing every afternoon, and noticed that they often got to go outside to practice on the football field, or march on the streets around the school building.

With not a little fear and trepidation, I went over to the band room at the prescribed time and met Fowler Stanton, a person who would in time become a major influence on my life. Mr. Stanton, who was then probably in his early to mid thirties, explained that he wanted to give me a unique opportunity, to be able to be in the high school band while still in elementary school. I could not understand why this offer was being made to me, particularly given my inability to play an instrument, but he said I should let him worry about that problem. He explained, that he was looking for young people who were good kids and wanted to learn and was willing to make a lot of exceptions and do a lot of special teaching for the right kind of kid. He told me he had noticed me around the school and had spoken to a number of the teachers about me and that he believed I could fit in with the high school kids.

No one had ever talked to me like that before and I have to admit that it felt pretty good. Now that I look back, it may be that he only wanted to fill the holes in his marching band, or that he felt that if he cast a broad net he would catch some keepers, but regardless, I agreed and the following week I was excused from the afternoon study period and started to be a band–it.

True to his word, Mr. Stanton found a place that fit me perfectly. He brought me in, gave me a pair of really big cymbals and explained how to use them. Joan Thomas, the other cymbal player helped me and I soon learned how to twirl them and since I had a decent sense of rhythm, I picked up the nuances of cymbal playing pretty quickly.

I learned that trips on the band bus are the reward for all of the work, that they were really fun, and by the end of marching season, I had graduated to snare drum.

My real expertise however, lay in organization and administration and Mr. Stanton soon found a number of extra jobs filing and organizing music, repairing instruments, and keeping up with uniforms, which gave me additional responsibility, not to mention additions excuses to get out of regular classes.

Now my plan had always been to play high school football, but when August rolled around and I came out for practice, I found that playing football for an extremely nearsighted kid was less than exciting. When you can neither see a receiver down field, nor a ball coming at you, you are not likely to be a star. I struggled through the August practice, in the heat, having spent the day in the tobacco field pretty well though until the band started to practice on the adjoining field a week later. Mr. Stanton had done it. He had hooked me and I could not enjoy one minute of football for wanting to be with the band. Finally, much to the disgust of everyone but Mr. Stanton, I dropped football and showed up for band practice.

It was sometime during my freshman year that he began to put in my mind that I could be Drum Major of the Band and wrote a note to that effect in my annual. I took it seriously and began to work on my playing (I was now playing tuba and reading real music.) and began to work toward being a leader. In the meantime Mr. Stanton gave me more and more responsibility, giving me access to the yellow station wagon, his personal car, and sending me on missions all over town. I began to have responsibility for writing the band show and concert scripts and enjoyed a relationship with him that I never enjoyed with another teacher.

By my senior year, I was indeed elected Drum Major of the Pride of the Upper Cumberland. I had found my place. I had found my people.

There is probably no greater need in this life than having a sense of belonging, of fitting in, of being one of the group and Sports, Music, and Academic endeavors such as debate club, and other groups fill that need in high school.

Isn't it wonderful that our creator realized this need and provided an opportunity for us to belong, to fit in, to be accepted, in our church family? He, like Mr. Stanton, provides encouragement that we can do, can achieve, can play above our game, and that He will be there to mentor, tutor, and pick us up, if needed.

I am sure that Fowler Stanton changed my life by his interest in me personally, by his ability to steer me in the right direction. I am confident that many of the things I achieved were because he believed in me and convinced me to always be the best I could be in everything I do.

How much more my Heavenly Father has believed in me and given me confidence, not just in my ability, but in His Love.

71. <u>Call Me Johnny Boy</u>

Fourth man from the right, fourth row from the bottom, Charlie Rogers Chaffin – Daddy's brother for whom I am named. WWII veteran of Iwo Jima and other major battles for the Pacific Islands.

Call Me Johnny Boy was written for a Veteran's Day Program at Maple Hill Church of Christ, 2008.

You know me, I first made my appearance at the Battle of Lexington and Concord in 1775 and they called us the minutemen. It took a few years to wrap up that little scuffle with King George's regulars - them in their shinny red coats, but we kept at it and had that job wrapped up by 1782 – a free country at last – or so we thought.

But those pesky Brits popped back up again in 1812, and we had to convince them all over again that we weren't joking – All men had indeed been created equal and these United States are and of rights ought to be free and independent States.

Then there was that little misunderstanding with Mexico concerning Texas in 1846, and we demonstrated to our neighbors down south that the lone star really was going to be "one among many" other stars, on that field of blue on the old Stars and Stripes. We do like to do a job up right though, and we ended up not only with Texas, but with California and the whole southwest thrown in for good measure.

Our next job came in 1861 and it might have been the saddest and hardest of all. They called us Johnny Reb or Billy Yank, and we had to fight brother against brother and brave men on both sides sacrificed and died for hearth and home. Five Aprils that job dragged on – from 1861 to 1865 and no war has ever been more costly. The first battle was just off Charleston Harbor at a place called Fort Sumter and the Last one – Well, it was right here, over in Nashville.

Some say that as many as 700,000 of us didn't come home from that one and a lot of those that did would never be the same. But the Union – it lived on.

For our next little frickkas they hung the name of Rough Riders on us and we sailed off to Cuba in 1898 with old Teddy Roosevelt himself. It wasn't much of a war unless you were one of he ones there. But to the soldiers who are there, every war is the biggest war – the only war – To them it was the war in which they gave the last full measure of their devotion.

By 1917, we were called on to go help our friends in Europe as German aggression threatened freedom all around this old world. Doughboys – that's what they called us for this one, and we fought and suffered in a whole new way as our enemies gassed us in the mud filled trenches where we huddled. Between the Hun's 88s, the wretched trenches, and the Spanish flu – we suffered terribly, but we Yanks went over the top on command. We didn't start it, but we sure ended it, and by 1918 it was over, over there. In fact it was over 90 years ago this very day. On the eleventh month, the eleventh day, and at the eleventh hour, those big guns stopped, there was silence, and a new wreath of freedom was laid at the feet of the Statue of Liberty.

That last one had been the war to end all wars, the Great War, we called it, but Hitler and His Nazi cronies didn't play by our rules and by 1941 we were called on again. This time the Japanese had attacked our fleet in Pearl. Dog Faces, Leathernecks, fly boys and swabbies, we were, and we were on the move around the globe. On Normandy Beach, and on the sands of Iwo Jima; we fought for the things we held dear, and for the loved ones we left back home. Finally it was over when President Truman dropped the big one and convinced Emperor Hiro Hito to stand down..

In 1950 we had a little job over in places like Wiejombu, Pusan, and at the Chosan Resovior, and even

219

though thousands of us never came home – the politicians didn't want to call it a war, so they said it was a police action. 169 Thousand Casualties – some police action.

In 1962 we got involved in a little country in Southeast Asia none of us had ever heard of, and most of us couldn't pronounce – Vietnam they called it – that one was the big winner as far as time goes because it drug on for 13 years. We didn't have any pet names for that one – in fact most people stateside didn't seem to like us for the job we had to do. But like always, we just went and did what we had to do, then came home and quietly went back to work in the world – just thankful we were not one of the 58,000 that got shipped home in a bag.

Now we have a whole new part of the world to worry about – a place called Iraq and we are in the middle of our second war, where sunglasses and desert battle fatigues are the uniform of the day. Oh, and by the way there is a little side job in Afghanistan thrown in just for good measure. I guess we don't have all of the outcome pegged on this one yet, but we have always done the job before – even when the politicians didn't exactly cooperate. You see, a soldier's job has never been to consider the politics of the matter, just to do what we were sent to do, and let the politicians, the professors and the civilians ponder the right of it.

We are American soldiers, sailors, airmen and marines, and we have fought, suffered, sacrificed, and died for your freedom. Our families have waited with dread, fear, and loneliness for our return – sometimes waited in vain. It is the price of freedom and we are proud to have served –

I guess it doesn't much matter what you called us, because whatever you called us, we always answered the call.

↦ **Chapter VIII** ↤
Not All Liars are Politicians

"Little Crump"

72. The Price of Strawberries

My home town is Carthage, Tennessee and it has long been known for its numerous politicians which included, a governor, a secretary of state, an attorney general or two, numerous power brokers of the local, state, and national scene. It made the town an interesting place in which to live and the locals told numerous stories about the various actors on the political stage. Mr. Albert Gore was a United States Senator and lived across the road from us when we lived in the big white house on the south side of Cookeville Highway, just before you crossed the Benton McMillan Bridge. The Benton McMillan Bridge was narrow to the extreme and it was not unusual for trucks to lose their west cost mirrors while crossing this bridge. "Little Al," as he was know locally, later to become Vice President, but had just seen the light of day and was spending most of his waking hours in Mrs. Pauline's arms when we moved to Carthage in 1948. My first memory of the Gore family was that they bought their groceries from us when we owned the Community Grocery. (Better known as "the little store") They spent much of their life in a hotel in Washington, D.C. but in 1952 still lived in a house in Carthage, I think it was on Fisher Avenue, as the house on the farm was not yet completed at that time. When they returned from Washington after an extended stay in Washington, Mrs. Pauline would call the store as they neared Carthage and order groceries so there would be food in the house. At about eight years old, I remember taking groceries up to their house, walking in the back door, (Most people in Carthage did not even lock their doors at all in those days – even when away for an extended time.) and placing the items ordered on the kitchen table or in the refrigerator, if required. This was standard procedure for grocery stores in the 1950s.

Senator Gore, was fast developing a long term friendship with Estes Kefauver, also of Tennessee and four years Albert's senior in the senate, and was sometime know to use Estes as a sounding board to deal with the frustration of a freshman senator.

The story, as told locally, is that a group of strawberry growers from Portland, Tennessee barged into Mr. Albert's Washington office complaining about the collapse of the strawberry market and the meager prices they were faced with in the current season.

"You ain't got no idea how much a flat of strawberries is bringing, now do you?" one of the disgruntled constituents asked.

"Well do you know or not," another said, "or don't you even care?"

After much fluster and bluster, Mr. Albert calmed the group down and herded them out of his office, then straightway barged into Senator Kefauver's office to complain about the flogging he had just endured.

He stuck his mouth out, as he was want to do and with his voice dripping with indignation said, "Can you imagine, then expectin' me to know what a quart of strawberries sells for in Portland, TN. – why I can't be worried about that. I got important things to worry about. I got to worry about Russia and Red Chiney and them places."

Estes leaned back, propped his feet up on the desk where the famed coon skin cap lay and said, "Albert, how many votes you reckon you goanna get from Russia, or Red China, or any them places?"

"Why none, I reckon." said Mr. Albert.

"Well then, I suggest you keep up with how much a quart of strawberries are going for in Portland, Tennessee." said Estes with a grin on his face. A lesson that would serve any politician well.

Taking care of our own business is an important but difficult lesson to learn, since what looks like our business, often is not – and what does not, often is. The Apostle Paul wrote to his young protégé Timothy about dealing with widows and made this statement, "Besides, they get into the habit of being idle and going about from house to house. And not only do the become idlers, but also gossips and busybodies, saying thing they ought not to." I reckon this is good advice, not only for widows, and widowers, but also for married and unmarried – old and young alike. Easy to say, but hard to do – but obviously we are called on to make our best effort.

73. The Yankee Clipper in the South

I've had some pretty incredible opportunities in my life, mostly in the line of my job. I had dinner with two presidents, one Democrat and one Republican, and eaten in the room with a First Lady (it was a big room). I have a picture somewhere with Howard Cosell and me, he with his arm around me like we were best of friends; (we were not). I sat and talked to Tommy Lasorda and met most of the Cleveland Browns, back when they were the real Cleveland Browns. I sat in the bleachers at Tiger Stadium in 1960 before it was Tiger Stadium and watched Mickey Mantel play center field. The Tigers whomped them, but Mantel hit a ball that looked like the launch of Sputnik. I watched John F. Kennedy pass so close in an open car on Franklin Road in Nashville that it seemed I could have reached out and touched him. A few days later he was dead. Probably the greatest thrill however, was when old Senator Albert Gore had a cattle sale at his farm in Carthage and Daddy and I went to the sale. Senator Gore caught Daddy by the arm and said, "Bring that boy over here; I've got someone I want him to meet." I walked up and a tall man with the biggest hands I had ever seen in my life reached out, shook my hand, and said, "Hello son, I'm Joe DiMaggio." And there he stood, the Yankee Clipper, Joltin' Joe, The Man himself. It was a moment that a boy dreams of and can still picture clearly as an old man. That day, I vowed to never wash that hand again, and did my best to keep that promise until Mama interfered in a significant way.

I have stood on the stage as Peter, Paul, and Mary sang, held Loretta Lynn's purse while she performed, and seen Paul Newman drive a race car – still, nothing compares with the experience I had this weekend. I was in the presence of Royalty – The King of Kings, and the Lord of Lords. "For where two or three are gathered together in My name, I am there in the midst of them." Matthew 18:20

74. <u>Redemption's Old Sweet Song</u>

Today the news is filled with the death of Edward (Teddy) Kennedy who has been a U.S. Senator since I was a freshman in college. I never saw Ted Kennedy but one time, and that in a hotel in Grand Rapids, Michigan. We lived in Grand Rapids from 1978 to 1983, during the time I worked for Fisher Body and it was a pleasant time for all of us. Patrick had just started to school and Chris was in the fourth grade when we moved there. Jimmy Carter had replaced President Gerald Ford (I'm a Ford, not a Lincoln) as president and during the years we lived there built his presidential museum on the banks of the Grand River, where the boys and I fished for salmon. President Ford was a native of Grand Rapids and had a true fondness for the town.

A fellow by the name of Will Jones and his family moved to Grand Rapids to direct the building of the presidential museum. Will worked for the Smithsonian, which oversees presidential museums, and he was a faithful member of the church we attended. We owned a sailboat at the time and Will took to sailing like the proverbial duck to water. He and I spent a lot of happy hours on the sailboat at Reeds Lake in East Grand Rapids.

When the museum was finished, a great celebration was planned and dignitaries from everywhere flew into Grand Rapids for the big day, Including President Regan, Vice President Bush, Former President Carter and a host of Senators and Congressmen, including Ted Kennedy. It was my first view of the unloading and loading of Air Force One and the accompanying entourage.

General Motors who had a considerable presence in the town at that time, was asked to provide the transportation for the affair and I, being the 35 year old budding executive and resident "hey boy," was tagged to coordinate. I remember that one of my young accountants who had volunteered as a driver was assigned to drive Bob Hope around, and since it was the time of the Muhammad Ali and Leon Spinks rematch – Hope, being a boxing fan, was looking for a satellite TV set-up where he could view the fight. Satellite TV as a rarity in those days but one was finally located just out of town and a 25 year old accountant by the name of David Jones spent the evening in the company of Bob Hope watching Muhammad Ali regain his world title.

We who are of the baby boomer generation are now watching a whole generation of news makers pass from the scene. Walter Cronkite, Maude, Barnaby Jones, Paul Harvey,

William F. Buckley, Paul Newman, and on and on the list goes of those who have been the "movers and shakers" of our era, but who will soon become but a faint memory; and with the death of Eunice Kennedy Shriver and now Senator Kennedy, an era of U.S. politics and the brilliant reminder of "Camelot" comes to a close.

I think that perhaps the story of Ted Kennedy is best described as one of redemption; struggling to redeem himself following the scandal of Chappaquiddick by relentlessly working on the agenda in which he believed. He was the very caricature of a political liberal, yet one known for being able to bring compromise to the table to reach agreement on legislation. I, for one, do not have to believe in every cause that another embraces to be able to appreciate their passion and dedication, nor to value them as a human being.

Redemption, bought back at a price, is what we all struggle with in one way or another, for each of us has things in our past which they would erase if we but could – a mean word to a colleague, a snap at a loving and supportive spouse, a compromise of integrity, a failure to appreciate a loving parent, dissention brought where unity should have existed. It is easy to believe that ultimate redemption is within our grasp and within our power, that we can somehow do enough good deeds to strike the balance with the mistakes, but true redemption only comes by the deeds of another who was willing to pay the price in our stead – "For you have been bought with a price, therefore glorify God with your body." The Apostle Paul

75. **I Don't Care if It's I. D. Beasley.**

There are a lot of stories around Carthage about I.D. Beasley, a State Representative, and a storied politician of some note in and around Smith County and on Capitol Hill in Nashville. I. D. was the boss in there were many in Carthage and surrounding areas who had jobs that were a direct result of I.D. Beasley intervening on their part with some business man, or government official. My dad, who worked for the State Highway Department, or TDOT is it is known today, used to tell the story of his early days on the highway department when a rock slide on highway 70 had closed the road. Crews were out clearing the rocks from the highway and one of the County Road Crew was acting as "flag man" stopping traffic until the loose material could be scooped up by a front end loader and hauled away. The slide had occurred in front of the old Cordell Hull Bridge across the Cumberland into Carthage, and there was little choice but to wait while the grizzled, tobacco chewing, flagman waited to get the flag from the other end of the line of cars, signaling it was clear to allow traffic to proceed in the opposite direction.

As it happened, Frank Clement, who was then Governor of Tennessee, was on his way to Cookeville for a meeting at TPI (or TTU if you prefer) and was, as usual running late. The trooper driving Frank G. tried to be patient for a while, then at the Governor's urging, jumped out and told the flagman, "Say buddy, I've got to get through here. The man I am driving is going to be late for a very important meeting in Cookeville."

"Well, he'll just have to set tight for a while, till this truck is loaded with them rocks."

"Say man, do you know who I've got in that car?' the trooper shot back, "that's "Frank G. Clement in that car."

"Well, I don't give a hang, if it's I.D. Beasley," the flagman replied, "He ain't gettin' through till that there loader fills that truck."

I guess that just goes to show how distorted our view of whom or what is important can become. Frank Clement probably expressed it best when he noted in a speech once that the longest road might be a thousand miles away, the widest road might be a hundred miles away, but the most important road is the one that runs by my front door.

I hope your day is a good one and that you are able to sort out the things which are important from those things that seem urgent. They are most likely not the same list of priorities.

76. <u>Little Crump and the Coffee Club</u>-----

My grandfather – Pa Maberry – was essentially without formal education although strangely enough his father was a school teacher. Being without education did not keep him from fancying himself a great politician and he never failed to take sides in whatever political race caught his interest – which was generally every one in the county. Generally political interest only centered around the Democratic Primary in Smith County, since in the 1950s it was a foregone conclusion that the winner of the Democratic Primary was The Winner. It was prior to the days of Lyndon Johnson signing the Civil Rights and Voting Act of 1964, when he had stated aloud that he had, "handed the South to the Republicans for decades to come."

In our family, we were Democrats – FDR Democrats, who spoke in reverential tones about how Roosevelt had saved the country from destruction and saved us from starvation during the great depression. Our view of Republicans were that they were a bunch of rich guys in three piece suits sitting around in the exclusive clubs up north, thinking of ways to take advantage of folks like us. Of course with Richard Nixon's first term victory leveraging the sentiments of the "solid south" to his advantage, the "solid south" swept "you won't have Nixon to kick around anymore" to a stunning landslide 70% victory over liberal Democrat, George McGovern, The Southern political world changed forever. If Pa Maberry had not already been dead, that would have killed him.

He liked to spend some part of each day visiting with his buddies at the City Café, drinking coffee and "politickin." He was so wrapped up in politics that the locals, particularly those of the other wing of the Smith County Democratic Party, dubbed him "Little Crump." E. H. "Boss" Crump had been the father of the political machine run from Memphis in the early part of the century, and Boss controlled the Tennessee political scene from his position as Mayor of Memphis. In the years he did not serve as Mayor of Memphis, he effectively appointed the mayor. No one could get elected or get a state job with the approval of Boss Crump.

Pa was, as I have said, essentially without formal education, but not without political ability. He worked daily at obtaining and distributing political favors. If you wanted your road graveled or your daughter working at the shirt factory, you needed to see "little Crump."

Delicacy was never one of his strong points and he was prone to talk when listening would have been more appropriate. On one particular occasion, he had been taking sides strongly in an upcoming county election and was engaged in telling more than what he knew about the candidate whom he did not favor. As a result, he had gotten up the ire of the other side and they had decided to just settle it by direct confrontation. They encountered him at the City Café and the conversation became heated to the point of loud and abusive language, a trait which seems to especially lend itself to the political forum. Finally one of the loyal opposition voiced the opinion that they were just going to get a local tough to "whip the fool" out of Pa.

Pa, uneducated but certainly no fool, decided that strategic withdrawal was the order of the day and beat it home. When he came through the kitchen door it was 10:30 in the morning; he did not stop, but went directly to the bedroom pulled off his shoes and shirt and climbed into bed. "Lola, if any of them fellows come looking for me, you tell them I am sick." Pa stayed in bed for a day or two until things cooled down and then was miraculously cured of the illness that had so quickly beset him and emerged a wiser man.

It is amazing to me that we think that a lack of civility is ok when politics is involved and I am astounded by the things I see printed in newspapers, and on the internet. Last night we were studying Colossians in our Bible Study Class and came across the instruction that the Apostle Paul gives concerning slavery. His instruction is a little amazing to the current mindset as it was in essence, your position and influence as a Christian supersedes your other rights – even your right to freedom from slavery. Undoubtedly, Paul knew that slavery was an offense to all that is right and decent. Undoubtedly, he knew that the practice in no way fit with God's Mercy and Grace. But his instruction was: Slaves be good slaves, masters be good masters, for you have a Master who is over all and He expects behavior in the model of His Son.

As I see the country heading into a period of deep division that is reminiscent of the days of student protests, counter establishment hippies, and civil (and even criminal) disobedience, it occurs to me that we who profess Christianity have a higher calling. Don't let yourself become part of the howling mob, nor caught up in behavior that is not Christ-like in tone and in fact. Be willing to surrender your rights for His cause.

77. <u>Some of the Biggest Wins are Losses</u>

In 1952 Frank G. Clement from Dickson, Tennessee began his run for governor of Tennessee against Gordon Browning. Browning considered the 32 year old Clement a "pipsqueak" but Frank was a man of considerable oratorical skills and Pa Maberry was quickly and easily persuaded to be a Clement man. Soon we all became involved and were traveling around the state in motorcades lending support wherever he was to speak. I remember quite well sitting on a platform in front of the old Wilson County courthouse and looking out over the square at the large crowd that had gathered. On the stage with me was Bob Clement who was also 8 years old and we amused ourselves making faces at one another while his daddy spoke.

Since we lived next to the stock sale barn in Carthage, I was out each week working the crowd of farmers in the auction arena, handing out bumper stickers and giving a eight year old's version of a Frank Clement speech. Sometime during the campaign, my fervor for the candidate came to the attention of the campaign and I received a letter from Buford Ellington, then campaign manager for Clement. Disappointed that the letter had not come from the man himself, I failed to hang on to it, not knowing that a few years later Ellington would also run for governor and be elected. Frank was elected, primarily as a result of his revival meeting style of speech making and my daddy was rewarded with a job on the State Department of Transportation, now the TDOT. It is the way things were done then.

When the 1956 Democratic Convention rolled around, Tennessee had not one, not two, but three contenders in the race for nomination – if not for President, then at least for Vice President and Governor Clement was tapped to give the keynote address for the convention. Our family was of course, glued to our Television Set as two relatively unknown men by the names of Chet Huntley and David Brinkley broadcast from the floor of the convention in a new ping pong, back and forth style. The whole thing had not yet been staged for TV as it is now, and the convention is memorable for the "free vote" for Vice President in which Carthage's own Albert Gore Sr. was placed in nomination. Mrs. Pauline Gore, Albert's wife, is said to have remarked, "I spent all summer picking vice presidential lice off Albert – I must have missed one." As it turned out Estes Kefauver actually won the nomination for Vice President, beating our a young senator from the east named John F. Kennedy, to become the running mate of the ill fated race by Adlai Stevenson against President Dwight D. Eisenhower. Loosing to Kefauver may have been one of

Kennedy's better political moves. Sometimes it is what you fail to win that brings the greater victory.

78. <u>Chicken Today and Feathers Tomorrow</u>

When I retired at the end of 2000 and moved back to Carthage, my Stepmother, Lovell Wilson Chaffin, asked the brown eyed girl and me if we would come to a reception being held to welcome the recently defeated Al Gore Jr. back to Tennessee. Having grown up in and around Carthage and having known Al fairly well, we said we would love to attend. Lovell was a major figure in the Women's Democratic Organization and she and Mrs. Pauline were friends and at the reception Mrs. Pauline was sitting right in front of us. I tapped her on the shoulder, told her who I was, and said, "Mrs. Pauline, I sure did use to like to come to your house." Quick as a wink she shot back, "You must not like to come any more, I don't ever see you." She was a very sharp lady and a pleasure to know.

Al introduced himself that night as, "the former next President of the United States," and told how he and Tipper had rented a plain Jane Ford Taurus that had somehow acquired a banged up fender, to drive up to Carthage. They were enjoying their new found freedom from Secret Service escorts and limo drivers and decided on their way up to stop and eat at the Shoney's in Lebanon. Al said he noticed two of the waitresses watching out the window as he parked the banged up rental car, walked in and ordered from the food bar. One of the waitresses came over and asked if he was not the former Vice President and he of course said he was. The waitress then shook her head and walked back to her

234

companion and said in a stage whisper, "ain't that a shame, driving a beat up old Ford and eatin at Shoney's. That's the way it goes in politics – you'er eatin chicken one day and feathers the next!"

While all of us may never experience as sudden a change in circumstances as the Gores, we will all have our ups and downs in life. Some days will be mountain tops and others will be the depths of the valley. If our sense of self worth and accomplishment comes from circumstance, we are sure to find our dreams smashed from time to time.

If however, our sense of worth comes from knowing that we are created in His image, and if our sense of safety and security comes from knowing that neither height nor depth, nor things present, nor things to come, can separate us from the love of God, then the valleys will seem less deep and the shadows less long.

Chapter IX
Holidays in the Country

79. Hog's Jaw and Black-eyed Peas

New Years Eve in the Country changed dramatically when TV came on the scene. Prior to TV, New Year's Eve had been about having the folks down the road come over and play Rook (Christian folks did not play with "gambling" cards back then), or later play a late night game of Monopoly while the kids played blind man's bluff or Thimble, Thimble in the back bedroom. On the old Zenith Radio, the strains of Guy Lombardo and The Royal Canadians filled the airways; first from the Roosevelt Grille, then in 1959 the "sweetest music this side of heaven" moved to the ballroom of the Waldorf Astoria. As midnight neared and the new year was about to begin, the band broke into Auld Lang Sine (a phrase literally translated Old Long Since and meaning, more familiar to us, Long Long Ago). The song was thought to be from an old Scottish poem, which many believe was written by Robert Burns, but made famous by Lombardo in his New Years Eve broadcasts. Even in years to come, it is likely to be the first song played in Times Square upon the arrival of the new year. Lombardo is said to have quipped when questioned about his life, "When I go, I am taking New Year's Eve with me;" but since his death in 1977, it appears that rather, he has lingered in his music.

Fifty years ago in the Upper Cumberland, when the New Year actually arrived, the man of the house typically went outside and discharged his old 12 gauge shotgun into the air several times, then listened for answering shots from neighboring farms up and down the road. With that the host would generally say something like, "If you folks are sittin' up with me, I'm better, so you can go on home." Or, "Come on, Lilly, let's go to bed so these folks can go home." And with that, the party was over. Folks gathered their hats (every man wore one winter or summer) and coats from the bed in the corner of the "front room," started the old Ford or Chevy, and exchanged from yard to front porch;

"Y'all better stay the night."

"Can't do it, y'all go with us."

"Better stay around here, I guess."

"Well, y'all come then."

"We'll do her, y'all come back."

And with that customary back and forth, they rattled off into the night two or three miles down the road, made sure the fire was banked for the night, crawled under the quilts, and got up the next morning before dark to feed and milk, and eat black-eyed peas and hog's jaw in a new year.

When TV made its way into nearly every living room – or by the 1970s the *family room* – in America, the tradition changed to a New Year's Eve party where chips and dip, cheese balls, and hot wings, were served to a crowd playing more sophisticated games. Children were now typically left with babysitters, who were to see to the children's New Year's Eve entertainment.

The center of attention had shifted from the Old Roosevelt Grille to Dick Clark in Times Square where crowds had waited for the ball to descend 77 feet, arriving at the bottom at exactly midnight, since 1907. At midnight, families in the south would customarily shoot the remaining complement of Christmas fireworks, Now parties tended to run later since the only activity people were likely to engage in on the morrow was arising to catch the color TV version of the Rose Parade from Pasadena, or watch in one of a number of "bowl games." (I'm surprised someone has not started The Toilet Bowl game yet.)

This New Year's Eve we are at a cabin in the Smokey Mountains, sitting by the fire while the kids (and sometimes adults) engage in golf, baseball, bowling, and race car driving, all courtesy of the Christmas Wii game. Tomorrow we will each start our separate ways traveling several hundred miles to our respective homes, ready to start the day-to-day rigors of life in a new year. No one has made any resolutions, at least not ones they have shared (although, by tapping into the cabins wireless internet I saw that one Facebook friend shared their resolution was not to make a resolution), and we will probably celebrate by having lunch at Krystal and eat chicken from the deli at Kroger, and likely not stay up until midnight at all – even though we are in the eastern time zone and would be cheating the clock.

The common thread running through the years seems to be gathering with friends and family and underlying it all, a thankfulness that we have made it through another year in this old world. Tomorrow we will begin another decade, dependant upon the generosity of others and the Grace of Almighty God. Let us resolve to remain in the sprit of thankfulness that today finds us.

80. **Bow Ties and Bare Feet**

Easter had another meaning for me other than just Easter Eggs. It meant a fresh new start to the year ahead and a time to get a new set of Sunday-go-to-meeting clothes. Sometimes it was a new shirt, sometimes a new Sunday pair of pants – no wool please, it scratches. Sometimes it was obviously a bow tie, which I thought was very dapper.

We were all decked out on a fine Easter Morning ready to go to church wearing suits, and my cousin Ralph was a double breasted model, no less. The date on the side of the picture is May 1955, which would mean I was eleven years old. I don't know what the occasion was that caused my cousins Morris and Ralph Mabry to be in Tennessee at Easter, but it was likely someone in the family had passed away since they generally only came "home" in the summer when U.S. Rubber was in shut down, occasioned by the model change of the automotive companies. (The little guy in front is Tommy Kittrell, now a lawyer in Nashville and bigger and taller than any of us by nearly a foot.)

One thing I know for sure, a few hours from the taking of this picture, this gang looked nothing like they do now, for

Easter was a big day for me. Not only were there egg hunts, sweet potatoes and ham, and buttercups blooming a startling yellow contrast to the green grass, more importantly it was the time when little boys could begin to go barefoot. I would be willing to bet that in two and one half hours from the taking of this picture, the guy in the middle was wiggling his toes in the scattered new grass of spring. The ground would still be a little cold, but not so cold that it didn't feel like your toes were ten friends who had just been let out of prison.

Of course with the freedom came some perils. There were the pies that the cows made and left for you in the pasture, which would turn you toes a pretty bright green this time of year, and the pieces of old fruit jar which lurked below the surface of the grass ready to slice a big smiley face on your foot. Some Lava soap coupled with elbow grease would take of the first problem and coal oil and sugar would take care of the second one. There were stone bruises, stubbed toes, stinging nettles, and honey bees in the clover. There were yellow jackets, prickly pear cactus, and rusty nails sticking up through old barn boards – all of them ready to pounce on you at a moments notice. Oh yes, there was a price to pay for the freedom of the lately liberated toes and the dangers would befall you at the least expected time. All a part of the price of freedom.

It is a little like the way God has treated us; He has given us freedom to make our own choices – bad or good – but there is a price to be paid for the freedom, dangers which may befall us and bring us pain, just as surly as the stinging nettles or honey bees bring pain to our liberated feet. And as with my feet, over time we learn to be immune to some of them as we toughen up, but other dangers remain ready to

241

waylay us when least expected – regardless of how tough and resistant we become. Then only a little coal oil, or Watkins Liniment, or Clover Salve can bring relief to the feet – as to relief for the injured soul, "there is a balm in Gilead."

81. <u>Dick the Bruiser and A Dozen Eggs</u>

I always looked forward to the coming of Easter every year, not because the day was particularly a religious thing, since being Church of Christ, we believed that each Sunday was as special as the one before and did not observe Jesus' resurrection on that day, at least not above any other. We did have fun with Easter eggs on that Sunday, although the Easter Bunny had not chosen to make his appearance yet – at least not in our neck of the woods – and every man liked to brag that he had eaten a dozen eggs for breakfast on that day. "Oh, the humanity."

Sometime about the time that I got too old for them, candy eggs made their appearance. They were not wrapped in cellophane like today since the theory then was "every kid has to eat his pound of dirt," but other than being a little larger, they were pretty much like the sugar loaded eggs one can buy today. Every color in the rainbow, and then some, was available and pretty cheap. Of course, we always hard boiled at least a dozen or so "hen eggs" the day before and used cake color to color them, under Adie's watchful supervision. I can remember having an Easter Egg Hunt in almost every conceivable location, usually with assorted cousins and church friends who would be invited to join us on that day. We have had the hunts in the backyard, in my grandparent's yard, in the basement at our house, in the living room at our house, and once or twice at a park or field where a community hunt was taking place. That usually meant there was a Golden Egg that had a half dollar inside – listen, don't make fun, that was a lot of money to kids who had to work all day to make fifty cents.

One such hunt was somewhere just outside Cookeville and for some reason, then unknown to me, Daddy saw fit to take me. I was probably eight years old and being only a couple of years off the farm, was pretty shy of strangers. But, as kids do, I went along and tried to pretend I was having the time of my life, for Daddy's benefit. He had driven so far, and seemed so excited about giving me this opportunity – how could I tell him I would have just rather been at home.

Everyone lined up in a general mob at the starting line and some local official blew a whistle and away we all went, running at breakneck speed toward where they had told us the eggs were hidden. Being possessed of poor eyesight from birth, which had not yet been diagnosed, I was not having much luck. By the time I spotted an egg, some other kid swooped down and scooped it up, and I began that nearsighted squint in another direction, trying by some miracle or internal radar to spot another. Not that I really cared about the eggs, I just wanted so bad not to disappoint Daddy, who would feel terrible if I came back to the starting line with no eggs.

Finally I spotted one in the fork of an old tree, put radar lock on it and headed in that direction. About the time I arrived there and laid hands on it, a tough looking kid (at least he looked tough to me) and a couple of his ruffian friends surrounded me and the tough said, "Hey kid, that's my egg." "Yeah," one of his bloodthirsty looking toadies parroted, "That's his egg."

"No it ain't, I saw it first and I got here first." I said with my perpetually queasy stomach beginning to churn.

"Say, where you from anyway? You don't talk right." (It was the River Rat vs. Ridge Runner thing again.)

"I'm from Carthage, and my Daddy's standing right back there with his eye on me."

Obviously not one skilled in the fine points of debate nor properly fearful of parental authority, the tough kid grabbed me in a headlock that was reminiscent of Gorgeous George's treatment of Dick the Bruiser on T.V. wrestling, and threw me headlong into the dirt while hanging onto the front of my shirt. The first button popped off my shirt and the button hole ripped open, my pants knees were dirty and there was a dirt burn on the side of my face. Now he had done it, I would have to deal with Mama over this, and worse yet, I would have to confess to Daddy what had happened – and I hated so bad to disappoint him, because he was sure I was going to have a good time.

Now was the time for action, and I was ready – I knew if I didn't do something I was going to cry, and that was not an acceptable alternative. So, I turned on heel and ran like a yellow dog – headed for the big grey Buick, with the hole in the wall gang in hot pursuit. I jumped inside and locked all four doors just as the murderous crowd clamoring for my hide arrived. They circled the car for awhile, like a pack of Blue Ticks with a raccoon up a tree, then lost interest and with a few nasty remarks and a warning never to come into that part of the country again, they wandered away. Never much of a risk taker, I stayed in the car until a very worried Daddy showed up looking for me. He did that thing that parents do;

the minute he got over being worried sick, he was mad as a wet hen.

"What are you doing sitting in the car? I've been looking all over for you."

"Some kids, a whole bunch of 'em jumped on me and tore my shirt, and got my pants dirty, and skinned my face."

"Didn't you do anything?"

"Yeah, I run right back here to the car and locked 'em out – and they was mad too."

He sighed, "Well, did you get any eggs?"

"Naw, they took the only one I could see away."

"Well, I thought you would have a good time," he said his voice dripping with disappointment. Now I had done it, I had made his day rotten, and he had such high hopes.

"Okay," he said, "don't worry about it, Uncle Claude's place is not far from here and we are going to ride over there, Aunt Nancy asked us to come over to have watermelon."

When we arrived at Uncle Claude Maberry's house he came ambling out in his tall angular way and welcomed us in. He was Pa Maberry's brother and we only saw them every year or two at family gatherings at my grandparent's house after Pappy Maberry died. As we came around the corner of the house, I came face to face with, you guessed it, the tough kid.

"Buddy, you remember Floyd don't you?" Uncle Claude asked. Now, I hadn't seen his son Floyd for a couple of years – an eternity in kid time, but I remembered him alright because I had been looking him in the eye only a short time before. Things changed immediately, and neither of us ever mentioned the altercation to our parents or to one another. We were always cautiously friendly after that, after all we were cousins, but I kept one eye out for trouble and stayed within seeing distance of Daddy when we were together. In retrospect, I suppose he was just grateful that I kept silent and didn't snitch – the biggest violation of kid etiquette of all – and the fact was, I was grateful that he never mentioned it either. There are times when our actions – even among the best of friends or relatives – are not things that we wish exposed to the bright light of public inspection. Floyd is gone now, and he kept my secret and I his, which in some strange way made us confidants.

There are lots of things in our lives most of us would prefer be kept hidden, but Jesus said, "For there is nothing hidden which will not be revealed, nor has anything been kept secret but that it should come to light." We need to live our lives accordingly, doing our best but trusting in God's redeeming grace.

Perhaps the most amusing thing is that when I think back now I realize that Floyd was actually a small, quiet boy but in my mind, he was a giant that day.

82. <u>Poaching Pumpkins</u>

Although I often hear people say that Carthage has not changed, it is a far different town than the Carthage of my youth. The newest residential section was out in our neighborhood on Jackson, Jefferson, and Carmack. Jefferson came to an end at the old oak at Clyde White's house, while Carmack was little more than a private drive for Hollis Petty beyond the Stock Sale Barn. Jackson continued to the big white house the Booker family built, but each of the streets were interrupted by a number of vacant lots and little creek bottoms that snaked their way through the housing.

Highway 25 came right through the middle of town, and was a main route for northerners headed for the warm weather in Florida. On some Saturdays, when northern snowbirds were contending with local farmers for space on Main Street, the traffic back-ups could stretch from the Cordell Hull Bridge back to the edge of town by the old hospital. Drivers' tempers would often flair, especially when the whittlers and "loafer'ers" on the square sat laughing at the "Yankees" sweltering in their hot cars, long before cars were air-conditioned.

Highway 25 itself wound its way through Beulah Land, around Devils Elbow, past Turkey Creek, and hooked back up through Peyton's Creek and Monoville entering back into the current highway near Riddleton. The thought of bringing the highway through the enormous cut that now exists in sight of a MacDonald's and chiseling a shelf for the road on the steep bluff above the river where David Lollar and I hunted squirrels was unthinkable.

Many people on Carmack, and other places on the edge of town, still had back lots in which they kept chickens, and in some cases a cow. After all, many of the homes had been built when horses were kept in town and small barns were not an oddity. We had a large garden beside our house as did many others, and kept chickens and rabbits for personal consumption. Mr. Homer Lewis kept a cow out at the barn just beyond the fairground and taught eighth grade. It was a town that was less than a generation from an agrarian society, and many of the folks who lived in our neighborhood had been born, and raised on farms, and a few still kept farms that they "worked" in addition to their "public works" jobs. My Uncle Billy lived on Jefferson but always made a tobacco crop and raised cattle on the farm now owned by his son Randy and me. Very few people worked but a single job and almost none did not either make a garden, farm, or work some kind of part-time work in what would now be "free time." As a consequence people did not have an on-going quest to determine what hobby or activity would occupy their free time – they simply rested in what little time to rest existed.

The creek bottoms behind our house were cultivated by Pa Hensley, and his son Zee, who lived a little back from Carmack just before one got to the Fair Grounds. He kept mules and raised corn in the little rich creek bottoms that regularly flooded when Cumberland River backwater crept into them from time to time and were some of the last land to have houses constructed on them. Dogwood Street was gravel from Jefferson north on around the Stock Sale Barn, which was the section lying in front of our house. This was years and years prior to the street being closed off as it is today.

To each side of that Carmack extension up to Hollis Petty's house, Pa Hensley planted corn in the little bottoms and often "hog pumpkins" amidst the corn. No one I knew raised the bright orange pumpkins you see for sale today to carve Jack-o-lanterns, rather they were squatty and pale, although often very large. We regularly used an axe and "busted" them up to feed to the hogs.

One afternoon as I was tramping back down off the hill side where I spent as much time as possible, I cut through Pa Hensley's corn field and, on impulse, "harvested" a large pumpkin and lugged it home. Thinking little about it, I sat it down beside the front porch making a mental note that the jack-o-lantern requirement had been met.

When Daddy got home, he stopped and contemplated the pumpkin with his weight shifted to one hip. When he came in, he asked, "Where did the pumpkin come from?"

I replied, "I found it over in the cornfield up the creek."

"Do you know whether anyone planted that cornfield?"

"Sure, Pa Hensley," I knew he knew the answer to that question and was starting to feel a little uncomfortable.

"Do you suppose he planted those pumpkins among the corn, or was that the only one?"

Feeling a little better, I replied, "Oh no, there was a bunch of them and I don't think Pa Hensley would miss this one."

"Well, you see, the problem here is not whether Pa Hensley will know, it's whether you and I know. You are going to have to take that pumpkin home."

I felt a little bead of sweat trickle down my back – just kill me now.

Well, as the saying goes, to make a short story long, as soon as supper was over I hefted the pumpkin and hiked over to Pa Hensley's house.

I knocked on the door and Pa came out on the porch and I explained my transgression. He inspected the toe of his work shoes for a while, then said, "Well, I suppose the place I really wanted it was in that cornfield, but I guess you can leave it right here on the porch." As I started to leave he said, "Tell your daddy I said howdy."

"Yes sir, I will."

"And tell him I said much obliged."

"Yes sir, I will."

In retrospect, I am thankful for a parent who cared enough to have me tote that pumpkin all the way "home." I am thankful for the lesson it taught me. I am thankful for mistakes it helped me avoid. And, I am thankful it helped me understand my relationship with a father whose expectations for me were beyond my own, and with a Heavenly Father who still has high expectations of me.

83. **Reflecting on Halloween at Christmas**-----

We were away in Europe when Halloween came around this year and I missed my opportunity to reflect on Halloween Past. It was of course radically different than Halloween today, in terms of what kids did to celebrate. It was much more about tricks and less about treats in those days and no one worried about razor blades in candy or kids being abducted in our little town of Carthage, Tennessee.

Farmers' wagons were disassembled and re-assembled in barn lofts, and bags filled with animal droppings were lighted on the front porches of those who refused to participate in the general spirit of the night. Watching the grouch stamp out the flame was, of course, the diversion this provided.

One of the best stories came to me today by way of a distant cousin of the Texas sort; One of those who comes from the branch of the clan that continued the western migration to Oklahoma and then on down to Texas in the early 1900s.

Barney writes.

"Halloween 1952---

If you were a kid in Pampa, Texas in 1952, Halloween was a big deal. Not many stores carried Halloween costumes at that time, and even if they had not many of us could have afforded such luxuries. We made our own "costumes" from cast-off clothing that we would find lying about, and pirates (a patch over the eye) and bums were plentiful. Our masks were bought at the dime store, but we called them "false faces" and picked them with care. They were made out of some flimsy material that had been starched to make them moderately stiff. The eye-holes were hard to see out of and, as we later learned, dangerous since we couldn't see on-coming cars – but since there were few cars, who cared. The hole for our mouth soon became soggy from all the candy we were stuffing through it, but our expectations were low since a mask only cost about twenty nine cents.

When the big day arrived, I volunteered to take my little brother, Moe and my little sister, Susie, trick-or-treating with me. After all, I was eleven years old, (nearly grown in my eyes), Moe was about eight, and Susie was about three and cute as she could be in her home-made costume. Moe couldn't wait to get started and carried two bags just to hold his anticipated loot. Susie stayed close to me and it was fun to hear her tiny voice cry out "Tricks or treats...money or eats".

We went around the neighborhood houses about an hour before we decided to work an apartment building a couple blocks from our home. There was no air-conditioning for folks like us in those days, and all the apartments in the building had screen doors. We went up to the first apartment, knocked on the door, and were greeted by a man of considerable girth who yelled, "what do you want," through the screen door. He was sitting behind a small kitchen table playing dominoes with three other men. The rotund guy got up from behind the table with a big, fake looking smile. His eyes were pig eyes - small and mean looking. His teeth looked like they had never made acquaintance with a tooth brush and vaguely reminded me of candy corn. "I have a wonderful treat for you", he said, with a spider talking to a fly kind of voice. He moved toward the door and we stepped back as he squeezed out of the door. Once outside, he stood us in a line next to a balcony and told us to "wait right there until your treat arrives."

By then I had gotten uncomfortable and was suspicious something was up; then I spotted it – a pan of water balanced on the edge of the second level. I grabbed Susie, and pushed Moe, just as the big creep tipped the water and missed us. He was disappointed and swore roundly at us. We beat it out of there and Moe and I took Susie home.

Moe and I had not quite grasped the concept of "vengeance is mine, sayeth the Lord, and both knew that we had to avenge this attempted assault and immediately laid plans. Moe said, "Let's tell the old man. He'll kick that guy's backside to the middle of next week". Now this was true but when that whirlwind started, it carried certain unnamed risks that Moe didn't understand, and I certainly didn't want to wind the old man up without knowing the consequences. After considerable discussion, we abandoned our "costumes," looked around the house, and found a 32 ounce tin can, that we filled with water, then we headed out.

When we got to the apartment complex, we went up to the big man's door. Since we were not "costumed" any longer, the object of our adventure did not recognize us when we knocked on his door. He and his three friends were still sitting behind the table, playing dominoes.

"Trick or Treats... money or eats"

"I have a fine treat for you", he said and started to struggle to get his fat frame from behind the table. As he was in the process, half up and half down, I opened the screen door myself and flung the water across the room and it landed squarely on him. He was furious and in his haste to catch us, he knocked over the table and dominoes & chairs went flying. His domino buddies were rolling on the floor laughing at the turn of events, but Moe and I didn't stay to enjoy the sight, we had it in high gear by then.

I was certainly surprised at how fast a fat man could run but he only lasted about a block and Moe and I went home and ate our candy with the satisfaction of a job well done, and by ourselves.

Barney Smith"

Thanks to Barney for a really good story; and I find in it a parallel to ourselves in our everyday struggles. While it is ok to want of "fix" everything yourself at 10 years old, and to be careful about "winding up the old man," some of us continue to think that everything is on our shoulders when we are grown; that we are dependant only upon ourselves and that God either would not, or does not care to, be our constant aid and comfort. "Where does my help come from? My help comes from the Lord, maker of Heaven and Earth."

84. <u>Refugees in Copley Square</u>

Like thousands of other Americans I was traveling on 9/11/2001.

I had taken an American Airlines flight from Nashville to Boston's Logan Airport on the night of the 10th for a company meeting the next day. I grabbed a taxi and headed for the Westin Hotel in Boston's Copley Square.

Shortly after the meeting began, someone rushed into the conference room and informed us that a plane had hit a tower of the World Trade Center.

Since several of the people in the room were from New York City, and our company currently had a team of employees working at the trade center, we broke the meeting to allow folks to check on the safety and whereabouts of friends and family.

Just as the rest of us regained order and restarted the meeting the 2nd plane struck and the horrible truth dawned on our group that this was an attack – a planned event.

Trying to be good corporate citizens, we soldiered on with the planned agenda of the meeting, while a number of administrative personnel traced the whereabouts of our team is

New York as they escaped by water taxi to New Jersey and began a long grueling drive back to Huston, TX.

The next morning the FBI, accompanied by a SWAT team of Boston's finest, surrounded our hotel, detained three people on the floor below me, and then evacuated all of us into the square as my wife watched the events unfold on CNN. The bomb sniffing dogs that the police had brought in had gotten a "hit" and without any warning we were standing outside wondering what came next.

The account from the Boston Globe read like this:

> "In Boston this afternoon, heavily armed law enforcement officers stormed the Westin Hotel in Copley Square and took three people into custody for questioning. The three were not immediately identified, Hotel workers said the F.B.I. had faxed them a list of names connected to the credit card account, and one of the names matched that of a man who had rented two rooms on the 16th floor of the hotel. The man and two companions were later led out of the hotel, surrounded by armed agents with plastic shields, and whisked away for questioning."

When we returned to the hotel, hours later, the decision had been finalized to not restart the meeting and let folks make their way home the best they could. Rental car companies had closed their doors, but I was lucky enough to make contact with someone who had rented a car on the 10th, and at about 5:00 p.m. three other refugees and I began the drive, away from Boston, toward North Carolina, Florida, Tennessee, and Alabama, our respective places of residence.

The brown eyed girl was kind enough to pick me up at the I 40 Gordonsville exit at 2:00 p.m. the next afternoon.

During the entire ordeal and the days it took to get back to Tennessee, I was most struck with how priorities had changed in such a short period of time.

Safety of friends and family and getting home seemed to be all that was on anyone's mind now. Believe me no-one cared one whit about sales numbers, business strategy or Financial Forecasts.

I wonder if we don't often have our priorities messed up. I suspect a time will come, more suddenly even than 9/11 when all priorities will change for eternity.

"51 Behold, I tell you a mystery: We shall not all sleep, but we shall all be changed— 52 in a moment, in the twinkling of an eye, at the last trumpet. For the trumpet will sound, and the dead will be raised incorruptible, and we shall be changed. 53 For this corruptible must put on incorruption, and this mortal must put on immortality." I Corinthians 15: 51

Have a blessed day, and may God bless the United States of America.

85. **The Theory of Relativity – Carthage Style**

Here it is Thanksgiving again and I have hardly finished celebrating the 4th of July. I was shocked when the brown eyed girl told me I needed to start changing the pictures. We have a few winter scenes that we get out just prior to Christmas and replace with spring and summer scenes when the weather turns warm and the buttercups start to bloom, but it can't be time to get them out again, I just pushed them under the bed a few weeks ago – or was it longer?

I remember when I was a child and summer seemed like one long endless string of golden days when you could spend your time lying on you back at the bank of the pond with not a care in the world. The time from late May, when we no longer had to pull up school house hill, until the start of school again after Labor Day seemed eternally long and one could easily imagine that homework might never again be a part of you daily irritants. Once school started though, then time really slowed down and you sweated through those eternally long last days of hot weather in the pre-air-conditioned climate of Carthage Elementary School.

There were no vacation or holiday days between school starting in September and finally arriving at the blessed relief of Thanksgiving Day, when teachers with an ounce of decency did not give you a bit of homework for the four day weekend.

At our house Thanksgiving Day was not focused around football games, parades, or even Turkey Dinners, it was something much more important. It marked the opening of rabbit and quail hunting season, and Thanksgiving was Opening Day to us.

Mama and Adie would fix a big dinner, not turkey usually, but a hen, or fried chicken, and lots of lately canned summer vegetables, and Daddy and I would be out hunting early, along with who ever wanted to join us. Many times dinner was at Ma Ma Maberry's house and Mama's uncle, Fred Montgomery and Aunt Gladys, would join us along with his sons and son-in-law or my Uncle Billy might come along. Everyone liked to go hunting with us because we raised Beagle Hounds and trained them to hunt rabbits and few things in life are more like poetry than watching a really good beagle trail a cooperative rabbit. Two or three beagles sound as if a pack of wild dogs are headed toward one at breakneck speed yapping and bawling and howling like they were chasing old scratch himself; but when they come in sight they are walking along slowly, working every inch of the trail making sure Brer-rabbit not get away in the briar patch. It is especially beautiful when you are on one hillside and the rabbit and dogs are on the opposite hillside and you can watch the drama unfold in full. The rabbit doubling back on his own

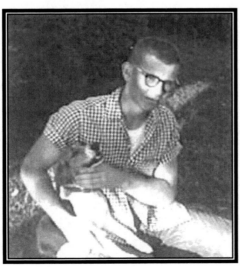

trail and circling and crossing his trail while the dogs work slowly and methodically the same ground covered by the rabbit. It gives you a view to the whole other world that a dog must experience where the sense of smell is so acute and the world is filled with sensory perception that simply escapes mere humans.

The biggest thought in the mind of children was the hope that the weather stayed mild for thanksgiving and not bring "hog killin weather" in the middle of the holiday. If the cold weather had not arrived in earnest, hogs would not be killed until after Thanksgiving Day and a little boy would get that day off from school too. Hog Killing meant everyone in the family was involved from the early morning hours, way before daylight, when the old scalding pan would be snaked up to the fire hole and put in position over the hole that had been filled with dry wood the night before. It would be positioned next to the wooden platform where the potential bacon and sausage bearer would be placed before being rolled in the water for scalding, after Daddy had dispatched him to swine heaven with a single shot from the 22 rifle placed just so between his eyes. "They don't even feel it son," he would say, but it still looked pretty daunting to me. But being a farm kid meant that you knew where ham, bacon, and sausage came from as well as steaks, eggs, and fried chicken. It was much more real than the sanitized process of going to the Kroger and picking up packages neatly cut and wrapped with shrink wrap to keep you from having too much to do with the reality of fresh meat. Someone said that, "if slaughter houses had glass walls we all would be vegetarians." Today that might be true, but those ribs still tasted pretty good the next morning to me.

The thing that surprises me the most however, is the speed with which time moves at 65 years old compared with the movement of time at 12 years old. It is only a flash now between Thanksgiving and Christmas, while it once seemed an eternity. Time and its passage truly is relative, although I am not sure that is the way Mr. Einstein meant his theory to be applied – because in my experience it is relative to our age.

All of that being said, it seems we ought to take the admonition to "Remember now your Creator in the days of your youth, Before the difficult days come, And the years draw near when you say, " I have no pleasure in them." (Eccl. 12:1)

The difficult days will come soon enough as you draw older and time moves at "warp speed."

86. **When Opportunity Comes Knocking**

When I was a boy of nine or ten, one of my favorite games was playing "army." My Uncle Charlie Chaffin had brought a 31 caliber Japanese military weapon home with him, complete with bayonet and had given one to my dad for me to keep. As incredible as it might seem today, I was allowed to play with it day in and day out and carried it all over Carthage and through the pastures and hills of the farm shooting imaginary "Japs" as they darted from tree to tree in the forest on Iwo Jima, or Okinawa, but the best place of all was the old gun emplacement, on a knob in the pasture not far from where the elementary school near Smith County Memorial Gardens is today. I can call it a gun emplacement today, but then it was a "foxhole" to me and the friends I sometimes drug there to play with me.

The "foxhole" had been dug by soldiers taking part in the 2n Army maneuvers held by the War department from the autumn of 1942 until March of 1944. In 1941 General George Patton had held Third Armor maneuvers at Camp Forrest, near Tullahoma, and perfected the armored tactics that were to become his claim to fame at the Battle of the Bulge.

Nearly a million soldiers took part in the maneuvers which were headquartered in Lebanon with highway 231 and US 70 N as the crosshairs of the operation. The troops were divided into red and blue armies and the Cumberland played the part of the Rhine, as it was crisscrossed by pontoon bridges. Flour sack bombs and mock "problems" were used to prepare the troops for the Normandy invasion which would come on the occasion of my birth, 6 June 1944.

I had grown up on stories of Pontoon bridges across the Cumberland and the young soldier boys, barely old enough to shave, who had been fed chicken dinners while lying "dead" in one relative or another's yard. Some became fast friends of families in the area, and a few found girls to marry or returned after the war, having fallen in love with the grandeur of Middle Tennessee. I ran into a number of old timers in the factories of Detroit who would perk up when I told them I was from Tennessee and tell the story of their time in the "War Games." It was almost without fail, a time filled with fond memories of folks who provided a little bit of home to boys so far away from their own hearth. Often in the confusion of mock battle, individual soldiers were forgotten and left for days with no provisions except those provided by the genial local citizens of the Upper Cumberland.

At noon on Friday or Saturday a light plane would fly over the "battlefields" sounding a siren which would signal end to activities for that week and the "combatants" would rise from the dead and surge into Lebanon, Carthage, Cookeville, Lafayette, or best of all, Nashville, if located close enough. Some would spend the weekend with families they had grown close too, in search of the solace of home.

Churches opened their doors and set up canteens for the comfort of the soldiers and schools opened their gyms for recreation and weekend dances. The Grand Old Opry was flooded every Saturday night with soldiers seeking relief from the oppressive boredom of war games.

On D Day the preparation and training paid off, and the Allied Forces won the day on Omaha, Utah and other beach names that suddenly became standard fare in every conversation in America.

As for me, I would take my little tin of food commandeered from Mama's kitchen up to the "foxhole" where I built a fire to cook bacon and scramble eggs, accompanied by crackers, while I defended the hill top in the pasture and dreamed of glory which might one day come. Fifteen years later I was to learn that there is very little glory, a plenteous supply of boredom, and not a little fear associated with the real thing.

For the soldier boys, it was a chance to practice the skills that would soon become central to their survival, while for the citizens it was an opportunity to practice the skills expected of them by their King.

Matthew 25:40 "The King will answer and say to them, Truly I say to you, to the extent that you did it to one of these brothers of mine, even the least of them, you did it to Me.

87. <u>Veteran's Day on Freedom's Frontier</u>

I remember the day well, it was October, 1966 and I had come home for lunch while working at the General Motors Technical Center in Warren, Michigan. When I pulled in the driveway and got out of the car I noticed that the brown eyed girl was standing at the door with a piece of paper in her hand, and as I got closer I saw there were tears in her eyes.

I had finished college at Lipscomb on June 6, 1966, my 22nd birthday, and when I went to the mail box that afternoon there was a letter in the box from Elizabeth Key, Secretary of the Smith County Tennessee Draft Board. It was to notify me that my college deferment was being cancelled as of that day, and that I had been reclassified 1A.

Since we were at the height of the Vietnam War, my expectations of remaining a civilian for very long were low, and sure enough, only three months later the letter in Jan's hand read; "Greetings from the President of the United States," I was instructed to report for induction at Fort Wayne processing center on 17 October, 1966.

Within a short period of time the brown eyed girl and I were required to make arrangements for such things as; where would she live? How would we pay the bills, since I was going from my GM salary to the standard $92.00/month? What about my job with GM since I had only been there 3 months? How about the money we still owed from school, car payments and apartment leases?

When I showed up at the induction station, it was with my best friend, Richard Maberry who had received similar treatment from his draft board. They informed me at the induction station that I was eligible to request a 30 day deferment, since the time of induction was less than thirty days from receipt of my induction letter, but I could see no point in that and forged ahead.

After shaking us down for knives, guns, brass knuckles, and other weapons, (of which there was a plenteous supply) we left from the old Fort Street Train Terminal in downtown Detroit. Richard and I spent too much time smooching with and clinging to our respective wives and the train was moving when we jumped on board. The troop train pulled out on the night of October 17th and we found that although there were two of us, there was only one sleeping birth left on the train. So, our first night in the army, Richard and I shared a single birth on the southbound train. The girls had decided to live together and share expenses and it did not escape our notice that we were sharing a bed while our wives did the same – what is wrong with this picture?

With typical troop train speed, twenty four hours later we arrived at the Fort Knox reception station and fell into a temporary bunk. That night someone lifted my wallet, and relieved me of what little money I had taken with me – less than forty dollars. Welcome to the Army!

The next morning, we were ordered to fall out into a common company area and following the old axiom, I was standing in the middle and keeping my mouth shut when a cadre of Drill Instructors walked out to the raised platform in the middle of the mob. One of them stepped forward, raised his bullhorn and said in a booming voice, "Which one of you %$%&*#@s is Chaffin? I felt my knees go weak and my mouth go dry, what had I done? What had I done that they had found out about? I called out, "here" and was corrected "here drill sergeant." When I got up to the platform, a short stocky guy with a Joe Palooka face put his nose one inch from mine and the brim of his Yogi Bear hat against my forehead and said, "My name is Sergeant Tommy. They say you got a college education, that right?"

"Yes drill sergeant."

"Well, they say you got some potential so I am making you my Platoon Guide – don't you mess up." (His words have been cleansed to protect the innocent.)

"No drill sergeant."

"Then form this mob up and march them over to the company area – that white building with a 5 on it yonder – you got it?"

"Yes drill sergeant."

And so began my military career.

When we finished basic training – which had been reduced to seven weeks in order to provide more replacement stock (cannon fodder) to Vietnam, Richard and I were assigned to the Reconnaissance Scouts Training Area in Disney Barracks to become 11D10 Scouts. The barracks were the newest and best at Fort Knox but that meant little to us since we seldom were not out in the field. Almost all of our company was college graduates and the training was outstanding for the time. We qualified on five weapons, M14 rifle, M60 machine gun, 45 Caliber automatic side arm, 50 Caliber machine gun, and M69 grenade launcher. We learned to build pontoon bridges, call in air support and artillery fire, work with compound C explosives (which makes an acceptable substitute for Sterno gel with which to heat you coffee.) We drove jeeps with 50 Calibers mounted in the center and were known to the rest of Fort Knox as "The Rat Patrol." It was tough, it was cold, it was hard and physical, but we loved being the elite group. We looked down on Tankers, Gravel Crunchers, National Guardsmen, Reserves, and especially those in clerk school – esprit de corps was high. We marched and sang to "I want to be an airborne ranger, I want to go to Vietnam," and "Ain't no use in going home, Jody's got your girl and gone."

After training both Richard and I spent several months at Fort Knox as permanent party cadre for the Training Brigade, then both Richard and I were shipped to Korea in August of 1967. The DMZ there was a boiling pot, as the North Koreans took advantage of the distraction of the Americans with Vietnam.

When we arrived in country with an 11D10 MOS (Recon Scout) our expectation was to be sent to patrol the DMZ, but while waiting in the reassignment station an announcement came over the PA asking for anyone with a college degree, some aptitude or training in writing, and 60 words or greater typing skills to report to the First Sergeant's Office. That sounded like a good deal to me and I met the qualifications, so I beat it up to the Top's office and was assigned to a special team of career army and DOA civilians doing a combat readiness audit for the Commanding General of USARPAC. My job was to edit and type the final drafts of the report for Admiral Sharp back in Hawaii. So for five months I traveled with the team based out of UN Headquarters in Seoul Korea – It was what is called "good duty" in the army.

Unfortunately, The Tet Offensive in Vietnam threw a monkey wrench in the works when all available combat units were pulled from Korea, including the famous White Horse Marine Division of the Republic of Korea (South Korea), and sent in as reinforcements for the beleaguered forces in Vietnam. With that move came the reassignment of all available personnel with a Combat MOS (Military Occupational Specialty) to Reactionary Force Duty and they took away my typewriter and handed me back my M14. (M16s were in use but the supply was limited and 100% were being diverted to Vietnam.)

While I was on this tour of duty, both Robert Kennedy and Martin Luther King were assassinated and student riots wracked the United States. Somewhere I still have the cartoon I carried that showed two GI's hiding behind an overturned jeep, receiving hostile fire, while tanks rumbled by. The caption was one of the soldiers saying to the other, "Well, at least we are not overseas." It was a trying time for America.

Shortly after my reassignment, the North Korean Navy took possession of an American spy ship called the Pueblo and the US and ROK forces went on red alert. This provided an excuse for the army to extend all of us one month, which did nothing to improve the general moral. There are few things worse than having your plane leave the country with you not on it.

On January 21, 1968 a suicide squad of North Koreans slipped across the border and executed a raid on the Blue House (Korean equivalent of our Whitehouse) trying to execute the President of South Korea. In the ensuing fire fight 131 casualties resulted. The DMZ was leaking like a shot up water bucket and the border patrols seemed totally ineffective. Finally it was discovered that the North Koreans had sunk a shaft far north of the border, tunneled under the DMZ and come up in a wooded area far south of the border. Creative if nothing else! The captain and crew of the Pueblo would be held as POWs for 11 months.

Finally the day came and I got on a plane, flew back to Fort Lewis Washington, out-processed after 35 hours with no sleep, took a taxi to SeaTac Airport and within another 24 hours was meeting the brown eyed girl as I walked off the plane in Detroit. It was a time when returning soldiers were not treated with any fanfare and oft times not even with civility. America was tired of that war and somehow it had become the soldiers' fault. A one hour ride from the airport and into civilian clothes and one was supposed to continue with your life as if nothing had happened. But something had happened, something that would alter our lives forever. I was struck with how much everyone had gone on with their life and seemed unaware that my own life had been profoundly changed by what I had experience in the last two years. The closest I can come to drawing a parallel is the feeling one gets when loosing a loved one to death. Your world is profoundly changed, yet all around you the world goes on as if nothing had happened.

I used the GI bill to buy our first house, get a masters degree and the mental toughness and ability to adapt to a hostile environment that I learned in my time in service became a giant plus factor in my life. I have never regretted having had the experience and feel that I benefited greatly from my time as a citizen soldier, but I was definitely ready to put it behind me and get on with my life – which I gratefully did. Some of my companions were not so lucky, either they did not return, or if the did they were never able to re-acclimate themselves to civilian life. Some had now passed from this life.

Faith in God and a good wife with faith in me, were what sustained me – I owe everything to the former and much to the latter.

88. <u>A Birthday in the Park and Managed Expectations</u>

Well, it is almost time for the brown eyed girl's birthday to roll around again and I have been reflecting on the difference in the expectations of birthdays now and birthdays "in the olden days" as my grandchildren would say.

Today children expect a really big to-do about their birthday with lots of money being spent by parents and grandparents on their behalf. The minimum expectation is that each year there will be some sort of "event" planned by their parents which might include a trip to Chucky Cheese (whatever that is) or a Tea Party (no political ramifications) if a little girl is involved. I have attended a number of these events and loved each one and enjoy seeing the joy on the face of my grandchildren, but can't help drawing the comparison between this, and the experience you and I had growing up. My daughter-in-law/love even recounted to me a party which she lately took my five year old grandson to which included a back lawn filled which wood cutouts which filled the back yard and were shaped and painted to represent Gotham City – obviously a Batman theme.

For me and probably most of you, your birthday was mostly another day when you might be allowed to choose your favorite dinner which mom would make in your honor. At our house, we usually received a small gift of some description which would be lying on your plate when you came down for breakfast. I remember that once there was a Roy Rogers watch on my plate when I came down. It was a very good day indeed. I have been trying to remember if I was ever invited to a birthday party for one of my friends, but can't seem to remember one. I am not sure if that is because they did not have one or if I simply was not on the A list for invitation. Usually it was more about family and no one expected more than a single gift and certainly not one from grandparents, siblings, or friends.

My sister did have one birthday party that I can remember, but it was after she had gone away to Lipscomb for school and it was primarily engineered by her college friends and her then boyfriend, now my brother-in-law. Guess the party thing worked for him! It was designed by the college group but executed by my mother and Adie at our house and I thought it was really a grand occasion. It was the first store bought birthday cake I can really remember.

I had one birthday party too, and although there were no other children present, it remains in my mind as a highlight of my childhood. It was planned by my Aunt Gene Kittrell, who lived near the Vanderbilt Stadium in Nashville, and was at Centennial Park in the shadow of the Parthenon. The picture which accompanies the story shows from right to left: Mama, the birthday boy, my sister Donnieta, Tommy Kittrell, sweet Aunt Gene, Daddy, and Adie (who always lived with us).

It was good having a birthday in June because the spring chickens would sometimes be at a size that Mama could put fried chicken (always my favorite) on the table. I was amused to note the straight chair over my right shoulder, which was our country version of lawn chairs. Also the "picnic basket" sitting in the foreground was undoubtedly a box from Carthage Grocery and Locker.

I guess it is ok that things have changed and that expectations have grown. My own children did not have elaborate birthday parties, but did have a pretty special day where they got several presents and sometimes got to go to Ferrell's Ice-cream Parlor, where the group could order "a Zoo" (it's a Detroit thing) or perhaps to Burger King where the paper crown was placed on their head.

It seems to me that our expectations of "worship service" have grown in the same way where we now believe that each assembly must be perfectly choreographed and the song-leader (now often called a worship-leader) must be of professional quality, the preacher be entertaining and funny, speaking in flawless grammar, and the Lord's supper be carried off with NFL play precision and a minimum of interruption to the singing and preaching, now considered the "main events." It is expected to be a multi-media event with PowerPoint, appropriate pictures, and songs displayed on the big screen and, of course, must be flawlessly timed not to exceed the magical one hour, which is now the maximum acceptable time for "worship service."

I expect that like the birthday celebration, it is ok for things to have morphed, as long as we do not loose the central meaning; to celebrate our arrival on the earth in the one instance and to celebrate our purpose for having been put on the earth in the other. Things change, and that is ok, but the heart of the matter – that which is of first importance – does not; and that is the principal to which we must cling.

89. <u>Gravel Bar Swimming</u>

For many of my growing up years, we spent every Fourth of July with our cousins on Roaring River. We would drive the 18 miles up to Roger and Gwen Lynn's house on the river. It was the old Abner Chaffin Place, The Home Place, and in that house I had been born on the 6th of June, 1944. While American boys were fighting and dying on Omaha Beach I was making my entrance into a world for which they were giving "the last full measure of their devotion," Something about that chance alignment of fates has, I think, instilled in me a special measure of patriotism.

I always looked forward to this holiday in mid summer which followed so closely behind my birthday for many reasons. The first was that I got to be with my cousins on the river. I hung out with Geraldine and Velma Jo Chaffin, and with Betty Jo Lynn, who was my same age, "six months difference, to the day" her mother always said. Geraldine was a year older than I, pretty, dark haired and dark eyed, a bit quiet and seemed more serious than she was. Her sister Jo was a year younger and was a little bit of a girl, full of exuberance, laughs and smiles, with a good word for everything and everybody. They were two of five girls who belonged to Daddy's cousin Norman Chaffin and they lived in Tally's Hollow, just around the bluff from the Home Place. Betty Jo, same age as me, was Roger and Gwen Lynn's daughter and was full of fun, always talking, had a big idea every minute or two about what we should all do, and Bobby, her little brother, was the smallest of that passel of cousins. With his red hair, friendly manner, and country boy talk, he was always ready for any challenge that the older kids undertook. We played town ball (like baseball only different), blind man's bluff, Whoop and Hide (hide and seek to you), 1 – 2 – 3 Red light, Thimble – thimble, Mother May I, and ran and played until our hearts were content.

Donnieta hung out with the other big girls, Matilda (Tildy), Jamie, (two more of Norman's girls) and Barbara Lynn. Barbara was James Lynn, Rogers brother's daughter and lived "up in the holler" beyond Aunt Eva's house. They were allowed to wear shorts on this outing and each of them was pretty dedicated to showing off their legs – or at least so it seemed to me. They sat in the shade, away from the grown-ups and talked about boys, or whatever girls of that age talk about, but they were old enough to have to do duty helping with the dinner, even on this special occasion.

The second reason I loved the Fourth was the Food. Roger would pull the big rubber tired farm wagon up into the front yard (we all had yards, not lawns then) and the wagon would be filled to overflowing with fried chicken, Adie's potato salad, cheese sandwiches, fresh green beans, slabs of cornbread, sweet potatoes, sliced and fried Irish (as we called them) potatoes, pickles, kraut, tomatoes, and corn on the cob. Somewhere there was sure to be two or three watermelons sitting on a block of ice gotten from the ice house, gallons of lemon aid, and oceans of sweet tea.

A Fourth of July gathering, Some present (left to right) are: Roger Lynn leaning on Truck, Maylene Chaffin, Barbara Lynn, Jamie Chaffin, Hattie Chaffin, Bobby Lynn, Matilda Chaffin, Donnieta Chaffin, Betty Jo Lynn, Mary Rachel Lynn, Ada Sue Hawkins, Geraldine Chaffin, Ada Berry, Janice Hawkins, Jo Chaffin, (the shadowy figure behind Jo with the big ears is yours truly), and Aunt Eva Lynn (I'm sure Harold Hawkins, Kermith Lynn, James Lynn, Norman Chaffin and my daddy are the men in the background but the light is too bad to tell with the hats shading their faces.)

But most of all, I liked the Fourth because we were allowed to go down to the gravel bar and go swimming. Not right after dinner though, for you had to wait two hours after you ate or you would get cramps and drown. I don't know if that was a valid fear, but it was surly a steadfast rule and there was no getting around it. Now, I don't suppose that any one of us was actually able to swim, but we had collected every inner tube we could get our hands on and when inflated they filled the back of Rogers old farm truck as we and them were driven down to the gravel bar where the TWRA has now build a dam to control the migration of rough fish up Roaring River. There was a big gravel bar there and a swift rapids of narrow water on the north side of the river which had once been the site of my Great Granddaddy Marlin Young's water mill. Some of us had bathing suits, mostly the older girls, but most of us younger kids just wore shirts and cut-off jeans, boys and girls alike. Every year the standing joke was about Gwen telling Betty Jo and Bobby that she didn't want them going to the river until they learned to swim – Gwen took the teasing in her usual good nature.

We generally started out in the shallow water above the swift rapids and floated around in two or three feet of water warmed by the July sun, but eventually one or the other of us, often little Velma Jo, would venture into the swift water and shoot down the rapid race. Then every one of the kids would follow experiencing the thrill of the swift rolling water and the knowledge that the depth was considerably over our heads. Of course, you had to pull out at the end of the rapids and walk over the blazing hot gravels back to the water above the rapids. By July, we had been going barefoot for a couple of months and the skin on the bottoms of our feet was so tough that we could probably have walked on a stove, still we did not linger on the hot rocks.

As the afternoon passed and our fingertips and the bottoms of our feet became wrinkled, and our lips became a tale – tale blue hue, we were ordered out of the river and back up to Roger's where we would linger until long after dark. If there was a new male married into the family, he was likely to be taken snipe hunting and if anyone had firecrackers we would all shoot them off. Most of us had plenty to eat and a warm house to live in but we did not have money for fireworks to simply blow up, but Bobby or I might have come up with a pack of firecrackers or two we had hoarded for months.

Finally it would be time to go home, and we would pile into the car, Daddy driving, Mama riding shotgun, Donnieta and Adie in the backseat, and me between Mama and Daddy. I would usually be awake until the lights of Roger's house had disappeared in the rearview mirror, but not much longer. That day being ended, it was likely to be another year before we were all together again like that and a sense of sadness would come over us all.

If anyone had passed while we were there in the front yard, enjoying one another's company, laughing, joking and playing, there would have been little doubt in anyone's mind that we were family. Little doubt that we loved one another. Little doubt that it was a joy for us to be together.

Jesus said, "By this shall all men know that you are my disciples, that you love one another."

If someone drove by on the road and could observe us as we are assembled together, do you think it would be as obvious to them that we are family? Would it, like that Fourth of July gathering, be obvious that we love one another, that we enjoy being together? If not, why do you suppose not?

90. <u>My Christmas Wish</u>

We have been away caring for grandchildren this week, since Patrick and Gabie had a chance to go to NYC in connection with his work; a little work and a little sightseeing in the big city at Christmas time. The three of them that stayed with us were good and we enjoyed being able to be with them, but I was struck by how different their life is than my own growing up. Maggie is a fourth grader, John Patrick a kindergarten student, Ryan is three and baby Cameron will soon be eight months; and while the world they live in is only 60 or 70 miles from the world I was born into, it might as well be a million miles away.

None of them will ever be able to imagine a life where middle income farm families did not have electricity, or central heat, or indoor plumbing. Where TV had not even been invented and the main family recreation was sitting around the fire talking and telling stories which confirmed who our family was. It was by oral story telling and the talk of our elders that we learned who we were, what made our family our family and about the incidental odd character or two who made us interesting. In the same light, I could have never imagined a time when in the bonus room through the miracle of the Wii, one could drive race cars, play golf or tennis, snowboard (what is a bonus room, a snowboard, or for that matter golf, or tennis?) or do just about any other sport without going outside at all. In fact, I would never have been able to imagine the point of the whole thing – if you're not going to get out of the house, why do it?

They will never know a time when their food will be identified closely with its source other than in the class room. They will never experience "taking a turn of corn to mill, grabbling new potatoes, drying apples, or hog killin." They will miss the pre-holiday season when Mama would begin baking just before Thanksgiving and wrap jam cakes, fruit cakes, and various candies in tea towels and put them in the cold of the upstairs rooms to keep for the season between Christmas and New Year's Day. They will not know that chicken strips were once part of a real live animal who sacrificed themselves so that we could have a delicacy on the table, or that tomatoes, watermelons, and cantaloupe ripened to near spoiling on the vine are the sweetest and best of all. They will wonder what kind of plant or animal produces a corn dog, a cereal bar, or a McNugget.

They won't know what it is like to sleep in the bed with so many quilts that the position you go to sleep in, is the position you wake up in, nor what it might be like to find that a light dusting of snow had drifted through the broken "window light" beside your bed, or to find that the water bucket had frozen during the night because it was sitting too far from the "fireplace." When we reminisce about bringing wood in for the fireplace, they will wonder why someone didn't just think to turn the gas burner on. They won't wonder if the moon is made of green cheese, or how many people will come to church in wagons rather than cars this Sunday.

When their dad takes out the pre-lighted Christmas tree, it will be hard for them to imagine walking miles through the pasture as your older sister hunts for just the right cedar tree, which you will then have to chop down and drag back to the house. They will see bubble lights in antique shops and wonder if granddaddy might have had some like that when he was a boy (yes) and they will make a list of their heart's desires, which will mostly be filled. The list itself will have been prompted by slick marketing techniques utilized by toy manufacturers and spread liberally around the cartoon and Disney networks. It will be beyond their ability to comprehend focusing upon one item for Christmas which you picked out by wearing thin the Sears Roebuck Catalogue.

It will be hard for them to think of Santa leaving a bow tie on the Christmas tree for your present and being neither surprised nor disappointed by his practicality.

And yet some things do not change; they will be looking forward to the season when parents, grandparents, uncles, aunts, and cousins get together, eat too much, and are noisy, loud, and generally all talk at one time. They will look forward with great anticipation to Santa coming on Christmas morning (didn't he once come on Christmas Eve?) and will still put out a snack for the fat man in the red suit. They will want to stay in their pajamas (who wore pajamas?) and play with the things they received all Christmas day.

Most importantly, they will still have a sense of what our family is about, that our lives are not our own, but that they belong to The One who is the reason for the season. They will still understand that the worship of our life is more important than worship in our life, and that both have a place that can never be taken away by the changing world around us. They will still assemble with others on Sunday mornings and use the vehicles of worship that have been part of the Lord's church since New Testament times and the will reflect on the marvelous gifts that have been provided to us by The Creator. They will realize that nothing on TV, even HD TV, nothing on the Wii, or any DVD will ever be as real, or as compelling as that story of the trip to Bethlehem when The Baby was born.

Someday, one of them may sit at a device not yet invented and record his or her thoughts about the changes in the world which I cannot yet imagine, but above all, it is my prayer that their priorities will not have changed, although circumstances and environment will likely be far different. That is my Christmas wish.

91. **God deliver us from Bad Choices**

I have just returned from delivering 21 Thanksgiving meals to needy families. It is something we do at Maple Hill Church and this year we delivered 2300. One house in a questionable neighborhood, had a big sign in the window "BEWARE OF DOG" and standing there with eight meal boxes in my arms I wondered if this would go well? When I knocked on the door, the dog I was to beware of was making his considerable presence known - loudly.

Then someone yelled from inside "Who is at that DOOR?

While I was considering if this was my invitation to introduce myself, the blinds were swept aside by a little girl of about nine who replied, "Don't know, some guy with some boxes in his arms."

"Where, outside this door?"

"Yeah, he right outside."

The door opened and I was nose to nose with a big African American guy of about 300 lbs who said, "Hey"

I said, "I'm Bob Chaffin and I have meals for you from Maple Hill Church - Happy Thanksgiving."

Big Smile from the other side of the doorway and the big guy said. :"Boy we sure do thank you folks."

We exchanged Happy Thanksgivings, I invited them to visit us at Maple Hill Church, and went on my way, feeling warm inside.

When I returned to the church building, one of the other deliverers shared that when he arrived at the destination on his delivery sheet for nine meals, he was shocked to see a Hummer and two skidoos in the driveway.

"Un huh," he thought to himself – but when he rang the bell and asked for the family on the sheet, he was told that a few of he kids were there but the mother had returned to the shelter to pick up the rest; her car was not big enough to transport all of them at once. They were a homeless family, perhaps the victim of circumstances and bad choices, who sometimes spent time with the family that lived at the address, who was trying to give them some relief.

"Boy, you couldn't have provided a meal for a more needy or better family than this one," said the person who answered the door. "They are really struggling."

The deliverers point was how quickly he jumped to the wrong conclusion about the status of the family, and how wrong he turned out to be.

How many of us have been delivered from our own bad choices by the grace of God and courtesy and love of others?

May God Bless the several hundred people who were involved in preparing, furnishing, and delivering 2300 meals and may God bless all those who received a meal.

May we never be so timid or so judgmental that we miss an opportunity when it comes knocking. As Daddy would have said, "Let's just be seed sowers, not soil inspectors."

92. Christmas on the Road -1929

In the winter of 1929 – 1930 my wife's father was one of thousands of young men riding the rails across America looking for work. He often told this story of Christmas on the Road in 1929 when he was trying to get home to Cherry Hill Tennessee, but had ridden the rail 150 miles in the wrong direction, being the butt of a joke by older and more road savvy hobos.

"By the twenty third of December, he had managed to make his way to Evansville, Indiana and across the river into Kentucky. He wasn't home but at least the weather was a little milder and his old coat didn't feel quite so thin and threadbare.

By Christmas Eve he was in a little town just south of Owensboro, Kentucky, cold and hungry. He went to the backdoor of a little store and asked if they had any bologna ends or other things that he might have since store owners sometimes gave away scrap ends or overripe fruit just to get rid of what they could not sell. The man said no but that he had heard a rumor that some of the local merchants downtown had made arrangements for a meal and a warm bed for those unfortunate souls on the road at the Christmas season. George followed the directions offered by the storekeeper and soon came to the business district in a run down section of town. As he made his way down the street, he had a tiny house on the edge of town. It was just getting dusk, the lights were already lit in the house, but the shades had not yet been drawn. Through the front window, he could see a Christmas tree already standing in the corner of the room. Inside, a little boy and girl were sitting on their legs, Indian style, looking at the tree and the few presents scattered underneath. Few or not, the homey scene looked pretty good from where he stood. George felt a hot tear trickle down his cold face and immediately wiped it off with the back of his hand. He vowed never to be in a situation like this again at Christmas time. If he ever had his own home and family, he would make sure Christmas was a special time for all of them.

He finally arrived at the building the old storekeeper had told him about, sure enough there were a few other grimy faced men in tattered clothes standing outside the front door. George got in the line and stood shivering, trying to strike up a conversation with some of the un-kept men standing outside. When the group was finally ushered through a plain grey door, a fellow asked them to take a seat on one of the benches around the walls. In a few minutes a constable entered the room and ordered them to hold out their hands. He roughly placed handcuffs on each of them and herded them out the back door and into a waiting paddy wagon for transport to the local jail.

They were ushered into a large common cell with bunks having wire mesh "springs", a dirty mattress, and a hole in the floor that served as a toilet. Each of them was given a metal pie tin and served a "Christmas Dinner" of fatback, bitter turnips, white beans, cornbread, raw apples and water. The bed in the dimly lit cell seemed to be moving and there was little doubt in George's mind that a large number of grey backs (body lice) made it their home. The other characters that shared the cell were so rough looking that George was afraid to go to sleep after the incident in the boxcar. It never occurred to him that he must have looked as rough to them as they to him, nor did it come to his mind that he really had nothing anyone would want to steal, having been robbed a few days prior.

George, along with dozens of other road warriors spent Christmas Eve and Christmas Day of 1929 in jail and appeared before a Justice of the Peace early the following morning, charged with vagrancy. Each of them was sentenced to one day of hard labor working on the county roads or they could each pay a fine of two dollars to reimburse the county for their accommodations. Since few, if any of them had two dollars, and since most of them had more time than anything else, the bulk of the men spent the following day on the business end of a "short handle shovel." They were released early in the morning on the 27th of December with an admonition to find somewhere else to call home. They needed little encouragement to leave a town so obviously devoid of the Christmas Spirit.

In this season let us experience God's Rich Blessings on each of us and remember as we look around, "There but for the grace of God, go I."

∘⇒ Chapter X ⇐∘
The Brown Eyed Girl

93. <u>The Brown Eyed Girl</u>

When I first saw her it was 1958, and she was sitting in the passenger seat of a baby blue 1958 Thunderbird Convertible, with some guy driving. She had a brown ponytail done up with a little pastel blue ribbon, and the biggest brown eyes I had ever seen in my life. She was wearing a pastel blue cardigan sweater with what looked like a ribbon sewed up the front where the button holes were worked, and a full skirt that made her waist look like I could span it with my hands. I don't know for sure, but I think she had on a pair of little red shoes, the kind the girls called "flats." Petite would hardly have been the word for her, since she might have weighted 98 lbs, provided she had a ten pound weight in each hand. She appeared to be about 15 or 16 and I couldn't help staring as only a 14 year old boy can. I am suspicious that my mouth was hanging open because the T Bird alone was enough to make a teenage boy's mouth water, but the girl – a piece of art.

Down east, as the local New Englanders like to call it, the conversation goes like this, "Where did you summer this year?" And the answer will come back, "Oh, we summered in the Hamptons," or the Catskills, on The Vineyard, or some other spot where they could escape the summer heat of Long Island, or Boston, or Providence. I used to tell everyone that "I 'summered' in Detroit"! My dad's sister lived in East Detroit, Michigan which has now had its name officially changed to East Point, so no one thinks any of them actually live in or near the city of Detroit – but we all know better – only Eight Mile Road separates them. Aunt Thelma was a tall, soft spoken woman with light red hair. She was Daddy's oldest sister and she and my Uncle U.L. Mabry had gone north for him to work in the U.S. Rubber tire "shop" on Jefferson Avenue, near Belle Isle. U.L. was not the initials for some other name, that was his name U-L, and when he entered the Navy in World War II, the navy was at a lost to know how to pigeon hole such an oddity as his name, so they kept trying to change his name to Ewell – but that is not part of the story.

Uncle U. L. and Aunt Thelma were the parents of three of our favorite cousins, Marva Jean, Morris, and Ralph.

Marva was a little younger than Donnieta, Morris one year older than I, and Ralph, one year younger. What a mob we all made when thrown together.

Every year Aunt Thelma and Uncle U. L. "came home," as southerners stuck in the north do, and "home" was our house. Aunt Thelma and Daddy had become the heads of their household when, while only in their teens, they were thrust into that position by the death of their sole remaining parent, their mother. The other three children had all struck out into the big cities to make their fortune, but Daddy and Mama stayed close to their place of birth, and where Mama and Daddy lived was considered home base by the others.

By the late fifties, Donnieta and I would also go north to stay with the cousins a week or two, thereby lengthening the time we were all able to spend together. We would ride with someone going north to see relatives, or on at least two occasions, rode a Greyhound all the way to Detroit. It was pretty exciting stuff for a kid from Carthage, Tennessee, since we got to go to stock car races, drag races, Boblo Island Amusement Park, Tiger baseball games, and once or twice to the horserace track (oh, wait, strike that last comment, I don't think we were supposed to be there.)

My cousins went to church at the East Town Church of Christ, down in the city and that is where I spied HER. I asked one of my cousins about her and was informed that the good news was that the boy driving was her brother, Gwan; and the bad news was, she was a little older than she looked; and the information giver strongly implied that she was, "way out of my class."

But hope springs eternal in the mind of a 14 year old and a week later, when the teenagers from church went horseback riding, she went along. No one had church busses, rather travel was by private vehicle, and the brown eyed girl's brother had swapped the T Bird for a brand new 1959 Chevy hardtop coupe – black with red and black interior. How cool was that?

I stayed a respectful distance, but kept a watchful eye on her. Sure enough my big chance came when her horse started to run away – well actually it began to walk away and return to the barn, instinctively knowing it had a rider that was not likely to jump of and whale the stuffing out of it. Sensing a big moment in the making, I immediately sprang into action and rode to the rescue, since I actually had a horse of my own back in Tennessee and knew which end was to be pointed in which direction. She thanked me politely in the prettiest voice I had ever heard, then smiled a smile that made me go instantly weak in the knees – thankfully I was on the horse and not required to actually stand on those legs. I stopped just short of saying, "Ah, shucks mam, twern't nothing."

When time for school came, I came back to Tennessee and went on about my life composed primarily of football games (band) in the fall, basketball games (pep band) in the winter, Spring Festival in the Spring (how convenient) and farm work in the Summer (along with summer band practice). I saw the brown eyed girl a number of times on subsequent trips to Detroit, but generally just admired her from afar. I liked girls but had not yet begun to date or be very comfortable around girls. (When does that come? I'm still waiting.) She sure was pretty though, and even a bashful 14 year old can appreciate "easy on the eye."

In 1962 I started to college at David Lipscomb and when my cousin Morris, an upper classman who had come to school early to check out the freshman "talent" ran into me for the first time in the Student Center during Freshman Week, said, "Guess who is down here as a freshman this year? Jan Lafever."

Well the rest of this story is a long and bumpy road which we will talk more of later, but for the moment, I was just surprised, happily surprised, to see the brown eyed girl from the baby blue T Bird, standing in the middle of the Student Center, looking very alone and slightly homesick. Hmm, Now, I was just a country boy, but it seemed like an opportunity to present a familiar face, given that wide eyed look.

A number of the Michigan kids were headed for the movies at Melrose, I think Elvis Presley in Kid Galahad was playing, and I tagged along, and by some miracle ended up squeezed between someone, I don't remember who, and the brown eyed girl.

I guess the moral of this story is how our lives twist and turn and but for a moment earlier or later, things would be entirely different and outcomes would be more or perhaps less filled with triumph or tragedy – or would they? Would they somehow turn out much the same no matter how we raced forward or lagged behind?

Although I ruminate about such things, all I really know for sure is that "All things work together for good for them that love the Lord." How blessed we are to be able to face the daily ravages of the unknown and unforeseen with those words wrapped around our heart like a parka sheltering us against the cold. How fortunate we are to serve a God who controls history, and works His own ends, with man's cooperation, or in spite of man's blunderings. How fortune we are!

94. <u>A Bonding Experience</u>

Last night the Brown Eyed Girl and I were reminiscing with our son and daughter-in-law, telling those irritating stories older people tell of how things once were, how little we paid for our first house, how small our pay checks were, and how tough travel was before the days of the Interstate Highway. In the course of the conversation, Jan remembered what my dad always said about the first time he ever saw her. With a slight grin and a gleam in his eye he would start, "I looked around the corner of Fanning Hall, and there was this little girl with big brown eyes peeking through the bushes at me." Now the truth was that the "bushes" were actually the shrubbery outside Lipscomb's Fanning Hall, and he was much too far away to know what color her eyes were, but he was able to turn a good phrase and tell a good story.

My sister, Donnieta, and her husband, Bob White, were living in East Detroit, Michigan at the time and Jan did not have a way home for Thanksgiving break, so I had offered for her and Judy Thomas, a college friend, to ride with us. The Brown Eyed Girl and I were not yet an item, but were friends and I had done considerable maneuvering to ensure that she would ride with my family for the 600 odd miles of the trip.

Daddy owned a 1960, white, Chevrolet Bellaire and It was pretty new for us being only 3 years old. It had belonged to Mr. Hugh West of Carthage, and everyone knew that if you could get his recent trade-in you had gotten yourself a good car. I'm not sure if Daddy had laid in wait or if Mr. James Clay had called him, but he had snapped up the trade-in as soon as he saw a newer model in Mr. West's driveway.

The Chevrolet did not have a lot of miles on it but it was in the days prior to radial tires and 25 thousand miles was a significant amount of miles on a set of tires in those day.

Since the tires were beginning to show some wear, daddy had gotten them recapped, not being able to afford a new set. A local entrepreneur, Sam Hughes I think, had opened a recapping business in Carthage, and daddy had availed himself of the services of the newly opened shop. Now in case you don't know, recapping was the process whereby the original worn tread was ground off the tires and a new tread vulcanized onto the body of the tire. As Ralphie said in *A Christmas Story*, "Now my father's tires were only tires in the sense that they had once been made of rubber and were reasonably round in shape."

We started out for Detroit on the Wednesday Night before Thanksgiving at about 4:00 p.m. since both Mama and Daddy worked and would not have considered taking off one minute early. They had driven from Carthage to pick us up from Lipscomb and we were on our way, winding up old 31W through Franklin, Kentucky, Bowling Green, and finally coming to the premier piece of highway on the whole trip – the Kentucky Turnpike. It was the only piece of limited access, four lane, high speed, road on the trip and ran the 35 or 40 miles from Elizabethtown, KY. to Louisville.

When we hit the turn pike, paid our toll and stretched the 60 Chevy out to run, we began to discover that the bugs had not all been worked out of the recapping process of the new business. We had only gone about 7 miles when the first recap went – flying loose, flapping the fender, and loosing itself to become one more "road alligator" on the turnpike. A fluke, we said, and began to change the tire.

The brown eyed girl, wanting to seem a good sport and much more hearty than her ninety eight pounds would have one believe, volunteered to hold the flashlight while the work was done. "Oh, I do this for daddy all the time," she said, "sounding something like one of the pit crew of the Indy 500."

The weather was foul, coming one of those fine driving rains that made it impossible to determine if the windshield wipers should be on or off in the days before pulse wipers, and here she stood, holding the flashlight while Daddy and I struggled with the driver-side rear tire as 18 wheelers passed us five feet away doing 70 miles per hour and creating gale force winds and a sheet of blowing mist. One after another the big rigs passed and when we got back in we were all soaked and my future girlfriend had a hair style that looked like it had been created on a roller coaster.

Once was bad enough but a scarce 5 miles up the road a second recap gave way. Fortunately, Daddy had stopped at a station in the center of the turnpike and paid an unthinkable sum for a spare – being unwilling to travel without one.

So the process began all over again, tire changed, driving rain, passing semis and new spare purchased. Brown Eyed Girl held the flashlight again and was quickly becoming endeared to my daddy.

Another 15 miles and a third and final recap gives way setting the process in motion a third time. To say that my plan to impress this girl was not going well would have been the understatement of 1963.

Finally, we got off the turnpike, a third spare tire was purchased and we wound our way up old highway 42 from Louisville to Cincinnati, then across the Ohio River and onto the flat farm land of the Buckeye State.

The trip became uneventful until we reached Monroe, Michigan where the flashing idiot light signaled that the car was HOT, HOT, and HOT. We pulled over just as the sun was peeking above the flat Ohio landscape. 5:30 a.m. on a country two lane blacktop, on Thanksgiving morning with a broken fan belt, 25 degrees outside, and no way to run the engine to keep the car's occupants warm.

I got out of the car, tucked the broken fan belt in my pocket, and stuck out my thumb. Before too long, a nice gentleman stopped who introduced himself as the superintendent of schools for Monroe County, Michigan. He was on his way to the J. L. Hudson's Christmas Parade in downtown Detroit where the Monroe County High School band was scheduled to perform. He carried me up the road until we came to one of those gas stations with a cover sticking out from the front, looking like Goober from Maberry might show up to open up at any minute. Miracle of miracles, it was already open with a sleepy-eyed, already greasy, attendant making a pot of coffee on the old oil burning stove. I showed him the broken belt; he rummaged around in a pile of v belts and came up with a farm implement belt of the same or near same size. He and I loaded in the old 1952 wrecker parked out front and drove back until we found the stranded travelers – a potential Donner Party.

The belt fit, Goober fixed it, and we were on our way, arriving in Detroit about 16 hours after our departure from Nashville; hardly record time, but certainly a memorable trip. It was a bonding experience for all involved and the story was good for many telling and re-tellings at various family gatherings.

When I listen to people telling how they prayed and God suddenly provided them with a parking space, I often wonder at the thinking that turns God into some sort of cosmic bellboy in our mind, and gives us the audacity to believe that the creator of the universe has nothing better to do than pander to our every whim. It seems to me from a 65 year perspective that rather than keeping us from life's experiences or the winds of tempest blowing on us, he provides us with an anchor to which we can lash our bark. All of us will experience flying recaps and broken fan belts in life, and much more serious difficulties, but as the Apostle Paul said, "Neither death, nor life, nor angles, nor principalities, nor powers, nor things present, nor things to come, nor height nor depth, nor any other creature shall be able to separate us from the Love of God."

95. Laughing All the Way

Just after the 1963 Christmas break from David Lipscomb College, the Brown Eyed Girl, Dottie Crow (Warren), Lavern Winters (Williams), and I all caught a ride back from Detroit with Billy Nettles, who was making his first trip to Lipscomb, having enrolled for the Winter Quarter after his discharge from the U.S. Army. I had gone north to visit my cousins (and chase after the Brown Eyed Girl who had invited me home to meet her parents) and it began to snow in Detroit while we were all at church that Sunday morning. By the agreed upon time to leave for Nashville, about 2:00 p.m., it was coming down heavy and the weather man was talking about 8 to 9 inches by the following morning. Being young and not good at waiting things out, we decided that it would probably "let up" as we traveled south, and since it was before the days of The Weather Channel and CNN, we had little actual information about conditions south of Toledo, Ohio.

When Bill arrived to pick us up, he was driving a brand spanking new Plymouth with a slant six engine, a pretty new innovation for the time. He had already picked up his cousin Dottie and her luggage, which included a trunk of massive size which was occupying nearly half of the back seat and reached to the roof; but somehow the remaining three of us fit ourselves into the unoccupied space and headed west on I 94 which was slushy but still in passably good condition. We caught old U.S. 10 at Telegraph Road and turned south toward Toledo and as we slid southward the trip became a little more intense. For the next 60 to 70 miles we wedged ourselves in behind a car carrier hauling new Chevrolets south and with the big eighteen wheeler breaking a trail for us, we moved slowly but steadily toward Lima Ohio. By the time we reached Dayton there was 18 inches of snow on the ground and the cars we passed parked on the sides of the city streets were just huge mounds of snow. Luckily the plows had been working the main highways and we were able to continue with but 3 or 4 inches of slush on the actual roadway. Eventually, we decided to stop for gas, a nature break, and snacks and it was then we realized that the conditions off the main highways were pretty bad. Finding a station open at all was the first challenge; getting to the station through the deep snow was a second concern. We would have been stuck beyond hope several times except for the 4 able bodies who would jump out and push. By this cooperative technique, we managed to muscle the car out of each drift.

Sometime around 6:00 a.m. we had reached Bowling Green, KY., slipping and sliding and "laughing all the way" and trying desperately to avoid the "drifting banks."

We stopped to get a bite of breakfast at a little Mom and Pop café in Bowling Green and while drinking coffee and congratulating ourselves on getting this far, we heard the local radio, tuned to WSM, announce that David Lipscomb College was closed and that dorms would not be opened that Monday as previously planned.

Well, now what, was the question of the hour. Since the others were from Michigan and I was from Carthage, I decided it was my place to find lodging for the pitiful group, and played the one ace I always had in the hole. I picked up the phone, made a "collect" call to my mom and told her of our plight. She said, "Listen, if you think you all can make it, just head on down Highway 25, and I'll have a good breakfast when you get here and the beds will be ready for everyone to crawl into. To my mom's way of thinking, there were few problems that could not be fixed by a good breakfast and a good nights sleep – a remedy to which I also subscribe.

Given that this was not only the best offer we had, but also the only offer, and was the only alternative we could think of, we headed out down the two lane back roads, through Scottsville, down to Four-Way-In, and through Hartsville, giving the girls the thrill of a life time as we navigated old highway 25 passing on the high bluffs just above the Cumberland. It was snow covered and treacherous but Bill was an experience snow driver with new tires and two hours or so later we arrived at Carthage. It was about nine o'clock in the morning by the time we sat down to breakfast, - some 20 hours after we had left Detroit City.

When everyone had eaten generous helpings of Country Ham and Biscuit, had gotten some much needed sleep, and had sunk our teeth into Mama's "to die for" fried chicken for supper, the group began work on a 750 piece puzzle with the obligatory red barn in the middle. Not wanting to waste 8 inches of snow, I hunted up my old Western Flyer Sled and tried to get up some interest in sledding down the hill on Jefferson which ran beside our house; but there was little response from anyone but the Brown Eyed Girl, and I am suspicious that she was merely humoring me. Finally, my mother, ever the good sport, said she would go out with us and the three of us bundled up in all the clothes we could find and braved the elements. I took one trial run down the hill that ran by Homer Lewis' house and as I was about to begin the second decent my mother said to our visitor, "Lay down on his back and both of you can slide down." Now we were wearing so many layers of clothes that anything that might have been improper about this would have been wrapped, bundled, and swaddled, so completely that we might have as well been shaking hands, but the brown eyed girl looked at my Mom as if she had suggested entering a life of sin. Finally, with something of a deer-in-the-headlights look she said, "Ok?" and Mama helped her climb on the sled; although, it was clear to me that the brown eyed girl had some rather serious reservations about the strange barbaric customs of Carthage,

TN. We were after all, proper Lipscomb students at a time when even holding hands on campus was considered too much PDA (public display of affection) and those in authority were apt to admonish a couple sitting too snuggled up to, "leave room for the Holy Spirit" between them. As a Resident Assistant, Jan had been counseled by Miss Gleaves (resident dorm-mother of Fanning Hall) about engaging in what the students referred to as "Premarital, Co-sexual, Inter-digitation. (or holding hands), thereby setting a bad example for other students.

After one more day of fun at my parent's home, the girls (Jan and Lavern) made the mistake of calling Miss Gleaves to inform her of our whereabouts, since both girls were R.A.s in Fanning Hall. They received terse instructions from "Mother Gleaves" to come to school immediately – obviously there was a reason she had remained <u>Miss</u> Gleaves. It was years later that my new bride confessed she had been less than comfortable with the sledding arrangement, but did not want to seem like a prude, especially in front of my mother, so she made one or two trips down the hill but then decided she was pretty much caught-up on sledding and went into the house.

We all have decisions to make every day which may become pivotal decisions in our life, and we can seldom know for sure if we made the right decision or the wrong decision. What if we had waited and left a day or two later – what truck might have slammed into the car? Suppose we had not stopped at the café in Bowling Green, would our lives have been permanently altered by so simple a decision? If the girls had not called Miss Gleaves would the outcome have been simply more fun in Carthage, or some more sinister path not expected?

My father often said that if he had the chance to do things over again, he would probably do everything just as he had the first time. His point was not that he believed he was infallible the first time, rather that God had blessed him and his family in such a way that he would not want to take a chance on messing up the way things had turned out. My parents had a simplistic trust that God would provide, and that church, family, fiends, and health were more important than wealth or fortune.

May you be blessed with a loving family, good friends, and a church where you can share "like precious faith."

96. They Don't Build Them Like They Used To.

When the brown eyed girl and I first married we were poor as church mice and I still had two years of college to finish and could not work full time. A good salary in 1964 was 100 dollars per week and we were renting a "furnished" apartment above "fessor" Boyce's brother's house on Granny White Pike for 65 dollars per month. They were really sweet people but the place was a musty dark converted attic with a kitchen stove that, honest to goodness, stood up on high legs and served an imaginary function. All of the furniture was early "grandma's attic" and was also dark. I think all of those things would have been bearable for the brown eyed girl, had she not been informed by the Mr. Boyce that his lately departed mother had lived up there, and it was from there that she had lately departed.

So, being young, optimistic, and energetic, she made it her business to find another palace. She found one on Grandview Drive which ran between Granny White and Belmont. It was located above the Harmon Collins family, a cousin of Willard, and was light, airy, had beautiful hardwood floors, a stove that looked like it was from this century and could be had for 75 dollars per month. Well the extra 10 dollars per month was a challenge, but that was minor when measured against the fact that it was an <u>unfurnished</u> apartment. We did not have a single stick of furniture, having moved all of our worldly goods from Michigan to Tennessee in a homemade, plywood, car-top carrier that looked like it should have been made from Gopher Wood.

Mama and Daddy had promised us that they would have a cherry bedroom set made for us by the Bain Boys, Johnny Bain's uncles who ran a woodworking shop where eventually Johnny Bain would reign as Sheriff of Smith County. We talked about the possibility of getting the more desirable location and decided to approach Mama and Daddy about getting the money that would have been used for the cherry wood bedroom suite, and using it to get the bare necessities of furniture for the apartment.

Following their usual good nature, they agreed and gave us $300.00, which is what the bedroom suite would have cost, and in the bargain threw in an old veneer bed, dresser, and chest of drawers that they no longer used, and a magazine rack with spool legs. We took the 300 bucks and scoured the unclaimed freight stores on 2nd and 3rd avenues and out Nolensville Road, and came up with a brown colonial style couch and chair of very light construction, a Boston style rocker (Jack Kennedy was president and Boston Rockers were very in.) a five foot round green rug and then paid 13 dollars for a very used black and white Admiral TV – a cabinet model. It worked !

What we did not have was a table to eat on and chairs to sit on when we ate, so we approached Raymond Upchurch, at Smith County Hardware, and asked if he had any used furniture he had taken in trade. He had none at Carthage, but he also had an interest in the furniture store in Gainesboro that was where the Dusty Rose Antique Store was before it also went out of business. At the Gainesboro store, he had a Formica dinette set that he had been forced to repossess. In the fifties and sixties, stores often "carried their own paper" or "we tote the note," that is, they self financed and people came into the store every Saturday and made a payment on major purchases. Bank Cards had not yet been thought of and if people had a plastic card at all, it generally was for a major gasoline company or large department store.

Daddy drove us to Gainesboro and we there first laid eyes on the most beautiful charcoal grey and chrome dinette set we had ever seen. It had six chairs, and two leaves which made it big enough to get our parents around when they visited for a meal. It was perfect – at least to us – because it could be purchased for 35 dollars. We loaded that baby up and took it to Nashville in the back of Daddy's 1957 Chevrolet pickup truck, which we then had to drive back to Carthage to pick up our car. A minor inconvenience considering that we now had a fully furnished apartment which might have appeared shoddy to some but was shabby chic to us.

We had completely furnished our home for 300 dollars and the goodwill of our parents. And it felt great.

The apartment proved to be all that we had hoped it would be and the Collins were wonderful landlords. Mr. Collins was an elder at the old Hillsboro Church of Christ where Batsell Barrett Baxter preached and we attended and the Collins treated us like children of their very own. I went to school from 8:00 a.m. until 1:00 p.m. then worked at Tennessee Wholesale Drugs on Second Avenue, now the Spaghetti Factory, from 2:00 until 8:00, caught the late bus to Green Hills and walked to our house by Granny White. (By the way I had occasion to walk that same walk a month or so ago and was shocked to learn they had moved Granny White much further away from Green Hills.) Jan got a good job working for insurance brokers, Carson and Armistead on Hardin by Bell Meade and loved the job. Our cup was filled to overflowing and we had learned a valuable lesson about being stewards of a little.

We continued to live there until I took my job with GM and we moved to Michigan in 1966, and when I graduated, we sold the bedroom suite, on Daddy's instruction, and got something like 25 dollars for it from a used furniture dealer. Following my graduation, Daddy took us all out to eat and we "ate up the bedroom suite." The gray Formica table however, we kept for many years, doing duty in the basement of several homes as the utility table, and sometime to host a big family gathering. I am suspicious that it is still serving some family. They just don't build them like they used to.

God fills life with lessons if we will only seek to learn them. Sometimes our learnings came hard and we were unwilling students, but looking back it is easy to see how all things do truly work together for good for them that love the Lord.

97. <u>Push Button Drive and Lay Back Seats</u>

The first car I ever owned was purchased the summer before I married the Brown Eyed Girl. I had gone to Detroit to work and been able to get a job with a remanufacturer for the Mopar Division of Chrysler. I knew that it was going to be pretty hard to find someone who was willing to double date with us on our honeymoon and that Jan might just take exception to that, so I began to look around for a used car that was within my price range. Now my price range was pretty small, since I had spent every dime I had in school the year before and had zero when I started the summer. I looked around and found a 1961 Chevy that looked to be in pretty good shape, and called my dad for consultation. He said it sounded like a pretty good buy and that he would lend me the $800.00 needed for the purchase (which was of course the real reason for the call.)

While I was waiting for the money to arrive by mail from Tennessee, the lady who owned the Chevy, and had promised to hold it for me, found a buyer with cash and when I showed up the car was gone.

I began to look up and down Gratiot Avenue for a car and stumbled across a real buy – a 1962 Nash Rambler. Not only did it have pushbutton drive, it also had seats that let back into beds, which I though given our apparent financial future, might come in handy. So when the check came, I spent the $800.00 on my first car – what a lemon.

If you are not familiar with the 1962 Nash, it had an engine with a cast iron head and an aluminum block, which meant that the difference between the heat dissipation of the two metals twisted head gaskets loose and required a redo about every 10 – 15k miles.

We managed to drive the thing to Mackinaw Island for our honeymoon and back without incident – thankfully, but within a few weeks it began to over heat and I discovered a suspicious grey milky color to the oil which indicated the presence of water in the crankcase. Long story short – first head gasket.

Fix it up – drive 10,000 miles – another head gasket.

When Jan was working at Corson and Armistedt in Nashville, it began to have white smoke billowing out of the tailpipe as water mixed with gasoline and the concoction burned and sputtered. When she pulled out onto Harding Road, headed for Woodmont Blvd. and home, traffic behind her would come to a halt until the smoke cleared enough for navigable vision again.

The whole thing was a nightmare of ongoing effort to keep the clap trap mess doing that which it was intended to do.

Don't you suppose that this is the way God feels about some of us now and then. That keeping us doing what we are supposed to do, is a nightmare of ongoing effort on his part. Operate for a few miles at semi-peak efficiency and then it's into sick bay again for a major overhaul. Others are a little more like the old Chevy might have been, not too showy, no frills, a little more noisy that most would like, a few oil leaks that make them messy to deal with, but they keep on clacking year after year, mile after mile.

I wonder which God would rather deal with? I know what my choice would be.

98, __Just a Bowl of Butterbeans__

There aren't many things that I don't like to eat, as is witnessed by my waist size; but I really don't like butterbeans. You know the kind, those old brown ones that make your thumb so sore when you shell a bunch that it feels like it's going to rise and fall off. To me, butterbeans have a taste that is somewhere between a slice of corrugated box and a MacDonald's hamburger – which, now that I think of it, is roughly the same.

When the Brown Eyed Girl and I were students at the late David Lipscomb College, our total monthly earnings amounted to about $375.00 and that allowed us to allot $10.00 per week for food. As the saying goes, a lot of times we ran out of money before we ran out of month, Mama's freezer in the basement at 901 Dogwood was often the sole safety net between us and deplorable destiny.

Mama and Daddy raised a big garden in those days and Mama seemed to have a knack for raising butterbeans and the little creek bottom behind the house on the corner of Dogwood and Jefferson seemed to have the perfect soil mix and nutrients for growing bumper crops of butterbeans. Before I started working at the Grand Old Opry, we would go up to Carthage on Friday nights, get a free meal, and then help shell and freeze butterbeans the next day. By Sunday nights we would be on our way back to Grandview Avenue in Nashville with sore thumbs and a box full of frozen packages of butterbeans. I would lug them up the wrought iron, fire escape type stairs and carefully pack them to the back of the small freezer compartment in our little Frigidaire Refrigerator. The freezer was small but adequate for the things we got from Mama's garden.

In some ways, the Brown Eyed Girl and I were about as opposite as two people could be when we married. I was the grasshopper and she was the ant. I didn't understand why having fun all the time wasn't a good idea and she thought work was the sole aim in life. I remember once accusing, "You worry about something all the time."

"Well, somebody has to worry about things," was her reply, which absolutely baffled me because I didn't understand why anyone needed to worry. Over time we each grew more like the other, and I think struck a pretty good balance of shared healthy concern without constant worry.

I remember that one night she was fixing supper, boiling our last box of Chef Boyardee Spaghetti, when I nagged her about going up to Hutcherson's Drugs, across Granny White from Lipscomb, to look for a notebook I needed for school the next day.

"Come on, I'll buy you an ice cream," I begged, "We won't stay but a minute and you can just turn the spaghetti down on low. It will be all done when we get home."

She finally relented, and once out of the house and at the drugstore, we ran into friends we knew, looked in the window at the jewelry store, perused the furniture store looking at things we would never be able to afford and became lost in a world of our own.

Finally she gasp, "The Spaghetti!"

"It will be fine," I said with more conviction than I felt and when we opened the door to our little upstairs apartment, we knew – things weren't fine. The smell of burnt and stuck spaghetti almost knocked us down.

There was not another thing in the house but the butterbeans in the back of the freezer, so there was nothing to do but pull them out and thaw them out with me all the while saying, "Oh the butterbeans will be fine. We'll put some ketchup on them for taste and they will do us just great – I hate butterbeans.

Well, we did not starve, thanks in part at least to Mama's butterbeans, and we learned to balance work with play, but pulling the butterbeans from the back of the freezer always provided a valuable object lesson.

It is not mandatory for me to like every circumstance in life, and, as the signature line in Steel Magnolias goes, "That which does not kill us, makes us stronger."

I think sometimes we feel that God owes it to us to make sure our expectations are met, no matter how ridiculous those expectations might be. That He might be some sort of cosmic bellboy standing by just to attend to the strong desires of our heart – even if the strong desires of our heart are a Happy Meal. I am thankful for the lessons of life that remind us that while, "all things work together for them that love the Lord," that is explained in the next verse as things that conform us to the image of Jesus. (Romans 8:28,29) So I am thankful that through life God teaches us that sometimes we eat steak and sometimes we eat butterbeans, but He has provided all things.

Have a blessed day, and I hope you don't get butterbeans today.

99. <u>Whose Girl Are You?</u>

My wife, who grew up on the east side of Detroit, has fond memories of their family trips "down home" several times each year. Down home, meant going to Silver Point, TN where her grandfather and family anxiously awaited each visit. One of the things she remembers is that wherever they went someone would ask, "Now, whose girl are you"? It was not a casual question in the rural Upper Cumberland, rather it was an attempt to quantify and place her in the context of the local family which was so important in this rural area.

There was little dependence upon social institutions other than church and family in that era. In fact, few interactions with other social institutions existed. Churches themselves, often consisted of extended families, or patchworks of extended families, and young people tended not to marry outside their own religious group. Church of Christ boys married Church of Christ girls, Baptist girls only courted Baptist boys, and so it went with the Presbyterians and Methodists.

To know "whose boy" you were was to place you in the local culture with great probability. Knowing whose child you are, was to know your socio-economic status, your political affiliation, your religious preference, and to be able to discern a great deal of information about you with statistical probabilities running high. It was, I suppose, a bit of "family profiling" which would be politically incorrect today, but was part of everyday life in that time.

The family provided a safety net against old age, sickness, and disaster in the time preceding the concept of government responsibility for such events. The church provided the next level of defense against being hungry and homeless, and these things all worked well until the Great Depression, in which whole family clans and regions found themselves in similar circumstance.

So our question today is whose person are you? Knowing to whom you belong is still to know a great deal about a person. What family are you part of? What name do you carry?

If you belong to Christ, one ought to be able to assume a great deal about you – provided you live up to the promise of the name you profess.

My father often told my sister and I, "Be careful to protect your good name, for the time may come that it is the only thing of value you possess." What he meant was, live up to the promise of the name you profess – meet the expectations of the name you carry.

100. The Toils of the Road

When I came to Detroit in the spring of 1966, I was looking for a job. I was a married college student about to graduate in June with no full time employment yet in sight. Oh, I was working part-time as a janitor, a packer at Tennessee Wholesale Drug, and general "hey boy" at The Grand Old Opry. The brown eyed girl and I did not have a car that would make the trip to Detroit and back, since we were the proud owners of a 1962 Nash Rambler which was almost always broken down. Instead we caught a ride with others that were coming north from Nashville and stayed with her parents, who lived over near the old Hudson Motor Car Company near Jefferson Avenue and Chalmers.

I got up early in the morning of the first day we were there and announced I was going job hunting. Having no other means of transportation, I caught a city bus downtown and having no knowledge of how to find the General Motors Building, enlisted the aid of the bus driver to notify me when I needed to get off the bus.

I had no appointment with anyone but surveyed the marquee which once hung in the rotunda and decided that the Director of Salary Personnel was perhaps the correct place to start. When I got to the eighth floor and found the large mahogany paneled office, I announced to the secretary that I was there to see Mr. Turner, whose name had been on the board downstairs.. She asked my name, checked the appointment book, and let me know that I had no appointment – which of course I already knew, but after contacting Mr. Turner on the intercom, she said with some surprise, "He will see you but says you will have to wait about an hour." That was no problem for me since time was the only thing I had plenty of and certainly more time than money.

When the secretary finally let me know that I could go in, Mr. Turner was sitting behind an imposing desk and asked, "Who are you and why are you here?"

I told him my name and let him know that I had a dream of working for General Motors (actually just a dream of working) and after some conversation he smiled, leaned back in his chair, and put his foot up against the edge of his desk. "I have a job," I thought to myself, but it was not quite that easy.

The Personnel Director arranged an interview at the Ternstedt Central Office, which was located at the General Motor's Technical Center in Warren, Michigan. I had a full day of interview and when I arrived back in Nashville, there was a job offer waiting for me. I was to start on 13 June, 1966 and was to be making $500.00/month, which truly sounded like a fortune to me.

I began work for Mr. Walter Bee pricing invoices in the centralized accounting function. My job was best described by a fellow work who said, "A moderately trained monkey with a stamp could do my job." But, It was a job.

I began my employment in June, and by October I was drafted into the U.S., Army. The folks at Ternstedt were kind enough to interview and then hire the brown eyed girl. They had informed me that they would try to find her a job, but had a policy against hiring husband and wife into the same division. After testing her secretarial skills, they called me down and asked if I thought we would be able to work in the same building. I replied that it would not be a problem, but questioned the policy to which they had referred. "Well," the Personal Director said hesitantly, "when they score as high as she did on the skills test, we treat the policy as a flexible guideline." So she worked as a secretary to the Director of Packaging and Material Handling while I was away for two years and then continued to work down the hall from me for a period of time until she was forced to quit in anticipation of the birth of our first child.

Shortly after my return from military service in late 1968, Fisher Body reacquired the Ternstedt Division and made the decision to decentralize accounting, and I volunteered to go to the Fort Street Plant to work in the plant accounting department. I guess I was tired of being the "monkey with a stamp." I remember that Mr. E. J. Wray was the Resident Comptroller and shortly after I arrived, GM was struck by the UAW Union for 67 days, one of the longest strikes in history. It was so damaging to the national economy that the GNP actually fell 4%. As for me, salaried employees continued to work and I personally rearranged files and burned obsolete documents all the way to the sub basement. My primary job daily though, was taking the Comptroller's car out to be washed.

The Fort Street Plant, which had been the original location of Alva Ternstedt's 1910 manufacturing facility, was a wonderful place to work, if somewhat located in a changing neighborhood. Certainly it was a culture shock for a boy from Carthage, Tennessee. The plant, located at Fort Street and Livernois was only a short distance from 12th Avenue where the 1967 riots had been centered. It was an intercity plant, a ghetto plant that was an important link in the "Hard Core Unemployed" program which had been much discussed during President Johnson's Great Society efforts in the 1960s and we had many people working who had been unemployed for years and had long ago quit searching for work. We hired them, issued them alarm clocks, and had special training programs designed to retain the hardcore unemployed. The saying was that they came out of Jackson Prison one day and we put them to work the next.

As a result, many undesirable individuals were put to work, with the outcome that fights, knifings, and prostitution was extant, if not common, within the plant. I can remember such incidents as a supervisor being stabbed while I was working in the area, a robbery in which two men held up the

Brinks guard as he was removing the cafeteria receipts. The perps then wrested his gun from him and shot and killed him on the stairwell. Violence was common, and when you left work after dark it was standard procedure to head for your car in a dead run. On at least one occasion I can remember, the car would not start and when we opened the hood, the battery was missing, the cables cut and he battery lifted right out of the engine compartment.

The plant had high speed presses doing heavy metal stamping, rolling mills, benders, did bright metal plate, anodize, paint, injection molding, small assembly lines, die cast molding, and sewing soft trim. We made door hinges, moldings for inside and outside of the car, dash panels, glove boxes (compartments), seat adjustors, and zinc die cast fans for the air cooled Corvair engine. It was a great place to get your start in the business since you got a little of everything. I spent much of my time at Fort Street doing product costing and learned how all of the parts went together and how production line arrangement impacted cost. We did a complete set of financial statements for each plant in those days and did them by hand, the kind of experience for which there is no substitute. .

I remember that Ed Cole was President, Richard C. Gerstenberg was the Chairman of the Board, and Lou Millian was our Genl Manager.

I stayed at Fort Street until 1978 when I transferred to Grand Rapids Metal Fab and to many locations following, but none was more instructional than Detroit Fort Street.

I was there when we had the open house and I had the responsibility of showing the Mayor of Detroit around the plant. I still have the plated ashtrays with the Ternstedt Logo by which to remember it.

It was there that I began my MBA from Wayne State University after being encouraged by Don Neuss, who was our boss and prodded by my friend Paul Kornbacher to make use of my Veteran's Benefits. It took five or six years but I finally finished in 1981..

I drove to work in the monumental 23.4" snow of 1970 only to find that General Motors had closed operations. I ended my days there with an almost identical snowfall in 1977 when, while driving home from downtown Detroit, I could not see a single car ahead or behind me on the usually packed, Interstate 94.

I recently met with one of the fellows who was a good friend during those early days of employment in the difficult environment and we noted the strength of the relationships formed during those years. Many of the people became lifelong friends and remain so today.

The brown eyed girl and I will ever be grateful for the wonderful opportunity provided for us at Ternstedt and General Motors, and it is difficult to see the company fall on hard times. Having retired in 2001 after nearly 35 years, seldom does a day go by that I do not think of someone that I worked with and with whom I was friends at GM. In spite of its enormous size, it was a company of relationships and I was always impressed with the ability, knowledge, and dedication of the people, who were, for the most part, just good family people.

What comes clear is that shared hardships in a common endeavor create bonds that are not easily broken and that is true in churches and families as well. It is also clear that which is worth having is worth working for. While we mortals are never able to do enough work to earn our salvation, we are told that we "were created in Christ Jesus to do good works." God can run the universe without my help, He can provide for the church without my contributions, He can care for the widows and orphans and feed the poor without my works, yet, In His Grace, He has allowed for me to reach into the heavenly places and become united with the general effort by my Prayers, my Offerings, and my Good Works, which He has created for me to do. Grace once again.

Work does not, of course, merit our salvation, but it is certainly the appropriate and required response to salvation proffered. In those early days at General Motors, working in the ghetto plant, we endured danger, toil, and hardship, but as I sit retired and comfortable, "the toils of the road seem as nothing."

"But the toils of the road seem as nothing,
when we get to the end of the way."

I hope your day is blessed and you have been blessed by this reading.

⊸ **Epilogue** ⊶

Inching Toward the Hole-----

Well it seems I am spending more and more time visiting funeral parlors these days, and that the deceased whose family I visit have become more and more nearly my age. I remember the time when if a family member passed away, I would be standing somewhere on the far edges of the tent, so far away I could not hear what was going on as the graveside service progressed. These days, it seems that more likely than not, my chair is at graveside or, in many cases, it is I who am conducting the funeral service.

Not too long ago a relative passed away and the brown eyed girl and I were sitting on the front row with our feet touching the side of the dug grave, next to us sat my sister and her husband. When the service ended, I remember putting my arm around Donnieta's shoulder and whispering, "next stop hole for us girl" just to see her forced to laugh at an awkward moment.

It is how we handle death in our family, we laugh at it. We remember funny stories or awkward happenings, and replace tears with laughter. I suppose that others might think this is a crude response to death, but for all of our life we have been taught that each day of life is but one long march toward the grave, and that the substance of the days spent in the march is to be a preparation for the final destiny.

Today, I visited a funeral home for the second time in as many days and today the deceased was a much younger brother of a close friend. He was six years our junior and we treated him with all of the indignity due one who had the nerve and bad fortune to be born later than were we. If we went fishing, he tagged along. If we played catch, he wanted to be included. If we roved over the pasture, he followed.

Now it is he that has gone on ahead, and we who must follow – for follow we must. We visit with families, trying to not think that, "there but for the grace of God," stand I shaking the hands of those who have come, not because they could do something, for they knew they could not; rather they have come just to be there, and by their presence to say, "I care, I acknowledge your loss and your pain, you matter to me and the loss of this planet of the deceased matters to me."

I suppose it is this march toward the open grave that prompts me to write of these things I remember, for I fear that one day, in fact I am assured that one day, I will no longer be able to repeat the stories that I have spent a lifetime accumulating in my mind, that I will no longer be able to share with my children or grand children the peace and tranquility of a world quickly passing into antiquity.

And yet by these writings, I will be able to, years hence, tell these tales to great grandchildren yet unborn and somehow by that to be able to declare, "Remember me, I existed, I was, I loved, I lived, I cherished life in a world very different than your own, but in a way very much like you."

The old time preachers often used a phrase that started with, "If the Lord tarries...." which was their way of giving a nod to the scripture that warns, "Do not say, on the morrow I will do this....rather say, If the Lord wills, I will do such and such."

Well, "if the Lord tarries," I will one day — sooner — much sooner — than I would like to admit, pass from this earth, and I hope these stories will declare to those who have no opportunity to remember, "He was, and this is what he was like."

In the interim, I hope to continue the preparation for the far journey each of us finds himself upon, and invite you to join me.

Other Books by Robert Rogers Chaffin

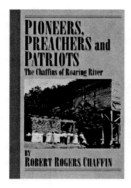

2005 Edition, 6.14x9.21, 276 pages
ISBN Complete: 0-9773179-3-5
$16.95

To Robert Chaffin, Roaring River will always remain the garden spot of the universe, the place that God had smiled on in a special way, the most desirable place to inhabit this side of the promised land. In telling the stories about this wonderful community, the author hopes that in some way it will bring to the reader's mind the sights, sounds and stories of your own past or will develop in you a greater appreciation of the courage and energy of your own ancestors. The story of the author's American ancestors is much like that of many American families who entered the colonies in the sixteen and seventeen hundreds, faced the hardships of settling a new land, the perils of numerous wars, political unrest and social upheaval but through it all placed their faith, family and fortune in the hands of an unchanging God, shepherding an ever changing land. These Chaffins of Roaring River, were but links in a long line of Pioneers, Patriots and Preachers.

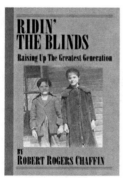

2008 Edition, Paperback, 6.14x9.21, 228 pages
ISBN: 978-0-9819172-0-7
$16.95

Like a great number of young people growing up in the years between World War I and World War II, Robert Rogers Chaffin's father-in-law, George Lafever, had a difficult life. He was orphaned at a young age and took to the rails when still barely a teenager. Through pictures, letters, a life sketch, and remembrances of his entertaining stories, his unique life has been memorialized in this book, which includes the great northern migration during the nineteen-twenties and thirties as well as the greater story of the whole Upper Cumberland Region. In the trying days and hardships of the Great Depression, George Lafever and his generation were put through a trial by fire which refined their character as the furnace refines gold. The pure toughness and resolve of their generation proved the salvation of freedom and democracy in the anxiety filled days of the Second World War.

http://www.publishedbywestview.com/ChaffinRR.html

Index

D

K

L

M

River Rats and Ridge Runners, 99, 127
Rochester, MI, 35, 209
Rocky Gap School, xi, 87, 91
Rome, TN, 21, 22, 65, 179
Ross, Bill, 19
Ross, Elaine, 19

S

School Snow Days in Carthage, xi, 105, 108
Scotch-Irish, xv
Sears Roebuck Catalogue, 71, 104, 279
Shamrock Café, 151, 152
Shooting Marbles, xi, 92, 93
Silver Point, TN, xiv, 308
skinny dipping, x, 46, 47
Smith County, 1, xi, 22, 99, 105, 107, 108, 109, 123, 138, 153, 161, 169, 190, 199, 228, 229, 230, 260, 263, 300, 301
Smith County High School, 169
Smith, Barney, 8, 93, 180, 192, 253
Smith, Perry and Ellie, 197
Smithville, TN, xiv
Southern, Dr. Paul, 35
Spring water, x, 21, 64
Stallings, Miss Inez, 20
Standing Stone State Park, 201, 202
Stanton, Fowler, 171, 213, 214, 217
Studebaker Automobiles, 12, 14, 134, 135, 188
Sunday Night Worship, 1, 26, 174, 305

T

Thanksgiving, 66, 68, 171, 202, 257, 259, 278, 280, 281, 290, 291, 293
The Inman Family, 83
The Ternstedt/Fisher Body Division GM, 311, 312, 314
Tinsley, Marie, 8
Turner, Judge Hubert, 69, 79, 118, 119, 135, 310

LaVergne, TN USA
15 September 2010
197229LV00002B/1/P